PENGUIN TRAVEL LIBRARY

South from Granada

Gerald Brenan was born in 1894 in Malta, and after spending some of his childhood in South Africa and India grew up in an isolated Cotswold village. At sixteen he ran away with the idea of reaching Central Asia but was foiled by the Balkan War and a lack of cash. He studied to enter the Indian Police but, on the outbreak of the First World War, joined up and spent over two years on the Western Front, winning an MC and a Croix de Guerre.

After the war he visited Spain and then decided to become a writer. For some years he lived in London and published his first novel at that time. A few years after his marriage to an American poetess he settled in a house near Málaga, but he and his wife returned to England during the Spanish Civil War. During the Second World War he was an Air Raid Warden and a Home Guard and used to write in his spare time. He returned to his Spanish home in 1952. He was awarded the CBE in 1982. His first major publication, *The Spanish Labyrinth* (1943), was immediately recognized as the most perceptive study of modern Spain to be published by a British writer. Other books include *The Face of Spain* (1950, which is also published in Penguin), *The Literature of the Spanish People* (1953), *A Holiday by the Sea* (1961), *The Lighthouse Always Says Yes* (1966), *St John of the Cross: His Life and Poetry* (1971), *Thoughts in a Dry Season* (1978) and two autobiographical works, *A Life of One's Own* (1962) and *Personal Record* (1974), which describes his consuming love affair with the painter Dora Carrington.

Gerald Brenan died in 1987. The obituary in *The Times* described him as 'a gifted writer whose best books arose from his lifelong concern with Spain and his understanding of its ways'.

GERALD BRENAN

SOUTH FROM GRANADA

*

Ille terrarum mihi praeter omnis
angulus ridet, ubi non Hymetto
mella decedunt viridique certat
baca Venafro,

ver ubi longum tepidasque praebet
Iuppiter brumas . . .
Horace, Odes II, 6

PENGUIN BOOKS
IN ASSOCIATION WITH
HAMISH HAMILTON

PENGUIN BOOKS

Published by the Penguin Group
Penguin Books Ltd, 80 Strand, London WC2R 0RL, England
Penguin Putnam Inc., 375 Hudson Street, New York, New York 10014, USA
Penguin Books Australia Ltd, Ringwood, Victoria, Australia
Penguin Books Canada Ltd, 10 Alcorn Avenue, Toronto, Ontario, Canada M4V 3B2
Penguin Books India (P) Ltd, 11 Community Centre, Panchsheel Park, New Delhi – 110 017, India
Penguin Books (NZ) Ltd, Cnr Rosedale and Airborne Roads, Albany, Auckland, New Zealand
Penguin Books (South Africa) (Pty) Ltd, 24 Sturdee Avenue, Rosebank 2196 South Africa

Penguin Books Ltd, Registered Offices: 80 Strand, London WC2R 0RL, England

www.penguin.com

First published by Hamish Hamilton 1957
Published in Penguin Books 1963

9

Printed in England by Clays Ltd, St Ives plc
Set in Monotype Garamond

CONTENTS

*

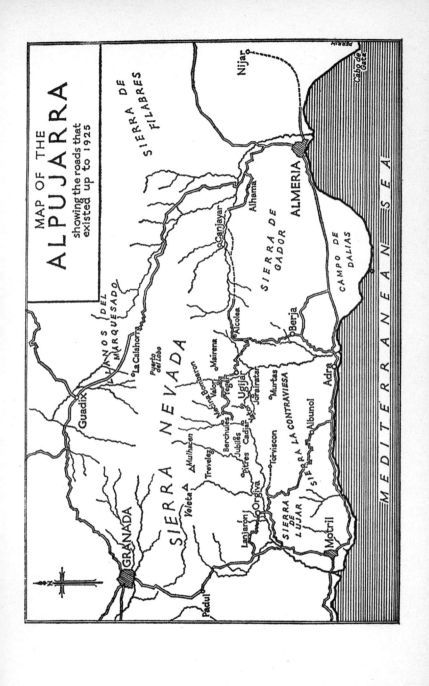

MAP OF THE
ALPUJARRA

showing the roads that
existed up to 1925

PERRIN

Níjar

Cabo de Gata

SIERRA DE FILABRES

ALMERIA

Canjayar

Alhama

SIERRA DE GADOR

Berja

CAMPO DE DALIAS

LLANOS DEL MARQUESADO

La Calahorra

Guadix

Puerto del Lobo

SIERRA NEVADA

Mairena

Bombaron

Mecina
Valor
Yegen
Ugijar
Alcolea

Jorairatar

Murtas

SIERRA DE LA CONTRAVIESA

Berchules

Jubilés
Mulhacen
Pitres Cadiar
Torviscon
Albuñol

Adra

Treveléz

Veleta

GRANADA

Lanjaron
Órgiva

SIERRA DE LUJAR

Padul

Motril

MEDITERRANEAN SEA

PREFACE

*

WHEN one looks south from Granada across the red towers of the Alhambra one sees a range of mountains known as the Sierra Nevada which have snow on them all the year round. This is the famous view, so endlessly reproduced on picture postcards, which brings the tourist to Andalusia in the spring. But forget the Alhambra, forget the nightingales, and consider only the mountains. They are high enough to boast of having small glaciers, and if you cross them you will come to a broad, hollow country, very broken and separated from the sea by a coastal range. It is this country, which till quite recently could only be explored on foot or mule-back, that is the subject of this book.

Or rather the subject is a village, by name Yegen, that lies within it. It is a poor village, one of the poorest of the eighty or so that stud the Alpujarra, as this fertile region is called, and it stands high above the sea. It is so remote that until the present road was built it took two days to reach it from Granada. But in its primitive way it is beautiful, and since I lived there for some six or seven years between 1920 and 1934 and took an interest in its affairs, I feel that I know enough to write at some length about it.

The principal part of this book then is devoted to an account of this village, with its customs, its folk-lore, its festivals, and a certain number of its more striking characters with their quarrels and love affairs. After this I have written of some of the other sites of the region, of the high mountains that bound it, and of Guadix with its cave quarter, which lies immediately beyond them. Then there is a chapter on archaeology and history, followed by four chapters on Almeria and Granada as they were in those days, especially in such matters as love, courtship, and marriage. Finally I have given a couple of chapters to an account of the visits to my mountain home of four well-known writers – Lytton Strachey, Virginia Woolf, David Garnett, and Roger Fry. Although these chapters inevitably make a break in the narrative and introduce an un-Spanish and so perhaps incongruous element, I felt that it would be a mistake to leave them out.

It will naturally be asked how I came to make my home in such a remote spot. The shortest explanation would be that I was rebelling against English middle-class life. Today in our formless society this seems to me an odd thing to do, but I can assure anyone who has grown up since 1920 that he can have no idea how stifling that life was or how very few outlets there were for a youth whose horizons had been changed by reading poetry and who could no longer be satisfied with the routine professions. The England I knew was petrified by class feeling and by rigid conventions, as well as in my case poisoned by memories of my public school, so that as soon as the war was over and I was out of uniform I set off to discover new and more breathable atmospheres. I took with me a good many books and a little money and the hope that I should be able to keep going for long enough to acquire something I badly needed – an education. After that, I would see.

Here I should like the lutes and violins to strike up and play a piece which might be called *Loores de España,* Praises of Spain. For I feel quite unequal to putting into a few words the peculiar feeling of acquiescence and delight which, almost from the first, this village and its way of life and, beyond it, the whole yellow, ox-hide land produced on me. I must make this quite clear, because the reader will not find much overt praise in this book. I have simply put down what I can remember having seen, and have taken it for granted that no one is going to find in Spain a model country like Sweden or Switzerland, conditioned by the rhythm of its machines, but on the contrary one which has up to now insisted on preserving a certain modicum of anarchy and non-compliance. How long this is going to continue I cannot say, but it is still true that south of the Pyrenees one finds a society which puts the deeper needs of human nature before the technical organization that is required to provide a higher standard of living. This is a land that nourishes at the same time the sense for poetry and the sense for reality, and neither of these accords with the utilitarian outlook.

There is only one other thing that I should like to put in this preface and that is an observation of a sociological kind. The village where I spent so many years was more fortunately placed than are many Andalusian pueblos, because it had plenty of water for irrigation and property was well divided. Almost everyone got enough to eat, yet the standard of food, dress, and comfort of all except two or three of the leading families was below that of the poorest English agricultural labourer or factory workman. Does that mean that they were miserable? On the contrary I would say that, though there is no way of measuring happiness, these peasants with the quickness of city dwellers got a good deal out of life. The narrow margin on which they had to manage caused them some anxiety in times of bad weather or of crop failure, and at certain seasons they had to work very long hours, yet no one ever left the village for the towns unless some trouble in the family had forced him to do so, and when, as happened from time to time, a man emigrated to America, it was nearly always with the intention of returning as soon as he had made enough money to live on. The principal reason for this was that by the fact of belonging to a closed community everyone felt assured of possessing a niche in society which was his by right, and which not even his own bad conduct could take away from him, and that was more than enough to counteract the lure of the large towns with their cinemas, taverns, and higher wages. In other words an increase in the standard of living is a poor substitute for the loss of the primitive community feeling, and Spanish villagers were wise enough to know this.

Do I need in a book of this sort to mention my sources? If so, let me say that the accounts I have given of local beliefs and customs are drawn from notes which I made at the time and which I have checked with my housekeeper, Rosario, who comes from my village and is a mine of information upon everything connected with it. In other places I have made use of fragments of diaries. Then, since my brief remarks on the foundation of Almeria are given differently in the guide books, I would like to state that I have drawn on the latest and best authority, E. Lévi-Provençal's *Histoire de l'Espagne Musulmane* (1942–50). For my pages on prehistory I have relied chiefly on the sections by leading Spanish archae-ologists contained in the early volumes of the great *Historia de España* directed by Don Ramón Menéndez Pidal, on various accounts of excavations, and on *The Prehistoric Foundations of Europe* by C. F. C. Hawkes, 1939. I have also consulted Don Julio Caro Baroja's admirable work *Los pueblos de España* (1946), and a number of books on Spanish folk-lore and kindred subjects. I give these names merely to show that when necessary I have gone to the proper trouble, for in fact by far the greater part of this book has been drawn from my own casual observations and experiences, sifted by a bad memory. All I have aimed at is to entertain a few armchair travellers, who may enjoy whiling away a rainy night in reading of how people live in remote mountain villages in the serene climate of the South Mediterranean. One flies over these villages in the air, one sees their strange names on the map, one may even, if one leaves the main road, bump past them in a car, but their life remains as mysterious as that of the girl with the unforgettable face one caught sight of for a moment through the window of a railway carriage. Here is a description of one of these villages.

I should like to thank my friends Don Modesto Laza Palacios for having answered the many questions on all sorts of subjects that I put to him, and Mr Robert Aitken for information on water-wheels and ploughs. I am also deeply indebted to my friend Mr Guy Murchie, author of that fascinating book on the air, *Song of the Sky*, for driving me in his car on a tour of the country described in this book. Some of the early chapters have appeared in *Der Monat*, published in Berlin, and in the *Anchor Review*, published by Doubleday in New York, both of them under the editorship of Melvin J. Lasky.

CHAPTER ONE

ARRIVAL AND DISCOVERY

*

IT was in September 1919 that I went to Spain for the first
time. I had just been demobilized and was looking for a house
where I could live for as long as possible on my officer's
bounty. I had had little education, for what one gets on the
modern side of a public school can scarcely be called that, and
the war had left me with a distaste for the usual careers.
Before making up my mind what I should do, I wanted to
spend a few years reading the books I had collected and soaking myself in the ways of Mediterranean life. However, my
choice of Spain rather than of Greece or Italy was not due to
any special feeling I had for it. Almost all I knew about that
country was that it had been neutral in the war and would
therefore, I imagined, be cheap to live in. This was essential,
for the longer I could make my money last, the longer I should
have in which to enjoy my leisure.

My first impressions after landing at Corunna were dis-
couraging. I spent a few days walking in Galicia, then travelled
across the tableland by a mixed goods-and-passenger train
that stopped for ten minutes at every station. As we crawled
over the endless yellow expanse, I was painfully struck by the
emptiness and monotony of the country. Not a bush, not a
tree, and the houses built of sun-dried bricks that were the
colour of the earth. If the whole of Spain were like this, I did
not see how I could settle down in it. Then, hardly had I got
to Madrid when it began to pour with rain, and I fell into the
clutches of two harpies who kept a boarding-house. They
demanded money in advance for every meal and then stood
over me while I ate it, snatching my plate away before I had
finished and gobbling down what was left in the kitchen.

Their eyes had the dry glint of people who have not eaten for a month. Then it began to rain again as soon as I reached Granada. I saw the Alhambra in a steady drizzle, and it seemed to me shoddy and bedraggled, like a gipsy girl sitting under a damp hedge. Could this be the fabulous Oriental palace of the picture postcards?

The people too disappointed me. I had expected to find men wrapped in long cloaks with daggers stuck in their belts and women in Goyaesque postures wearing high combs and mantillas. What I saw was a glum, short-legged race who hurried past under umbrellas or else talked in loud raucous voices till two in the morning. They did not even seem friendly. The only Spaniard I made contact with was the son of the owner of the *corralón* (the Andalusian version of an Arab fondak) where I put up near the station. He was a cripple, and since he could not work he spent his mornings teaching himself German, which he declared was the language of the future. I offered to give him a few lessons, in return for which he told me that the hope of Spain lay in farm machinery and industrialization and that before many years had passed these would be introduced by German technicians. It seemed that he was a socialist and believed in an approaching world revolution spreading from Berlin.

Those who have been to Granada will know that immediately to the south of it there is a high range of mountains, the Sierra Nevada, which has snow on it all the year round. On the other side of these mountains, between them and the sea, lies a stretch of country, well watered and planted with villages, which is known as the Alpujarra. I had picked it out on the map as being likely to provide a good site for a house, and so I prepared to go there. I bought one of those stiff, black-brimmed Sevillian hats, which I thought would make me less conspicuous, packed a few things in a rucksack, and, as soon as the rain stopped, set off.

My plan was to make a sweep westwards in the direction of Malaga and approach the Alpujarra from the farther side.

There too, in the Axarquia, I would find villages perched above the sea, and perhaps one of them would prove suitable for my purpose. But I had not taken in the problems offered by the map. The only one available was the *Mapa Provincial*, a small, luridly coloured sheet, about the size of a large handkerchief and intended chiefly as a reference chart for officials. It marked the villages, though not always in the right positions, but it left out the mountains and gave a purely schematic picture of the rivers and streams. I need not speak of the roads, because few of them had been built at this time, and most of my travelling would be done on mule tracks.

I set out after lunch and passed a couple of villages. After that it came on to rain. The road was a broad track, ankle deep in mud – at this time none of the Andalusian roads had been surfaced – and it stretched straight in front of me to a distant horizon of mountains. A ceiling of spongy clouds moved slowly by overhead, and on either side there was nothing to be seen but a rolling treeless plain, brick-red in colour but dusted with a thin sprinkling of stubble. I passed tilted wagons, drawn by teams of six or seven mules with a donkey to lead them, the men shouting and cracking their whips and the animals straining at their traces to draw the wheels through the mud. Then darkness fell and the stars unexpectedly came out. The crickets began to trill, and before long I saw the lights of Ventas de Huelma and heard the dogs barking.

The *parador* was a plain, whitewashed building with an enormous entrance door. Passing through it, I came into a vaulted hall, very white and cavernous, which began as a cobbled *descargado* or unloading place leading through to the stables and then, at right angles to the entrance, changed into a sort of tiled kitchen, hung round with mule-collars and other leather harness, and closed at the end by a hooded chimney. Here two women, wearing red shawls over their musty black dresses, were stirring a cooking-pot. At a short distance from them some muleteers were seated in glum silence along the walls and, pulling up an unoccupied chair, I joined them. We waited. At length, when I had almost given up hope of obtaining anything to eat, a low table was brought out, a dish of rice and *bacalao* – that is, salt cod – was placed on it, and we drew up our chairs. There were no plates. Each man, keeping his hat firmly on his head in the manner of a Spanish grandee asserting his equality to everyone present and to come, chose his section of the bowl, and after inviting myself and the others to do the same, dipped his spoon in it with great formality and began to eat. He continued eating till the partition that divided his section from his neighbour's had worn thin, when he laid down his spoon and, as soon as the others had done so too, got up and washed it at the pitcher and returned it to the *faja* or red-flannel waistband where he usually carried it. For the first time since I had landed, my heart warmed to the people of this country, who in such an admirable way combined simplicity with good manners.

As soon as supper was over, the men rolled and lit their cigarettes, and after a final glance at their animals stretched themselves out on the straw mattresses which were piled in a corner of the room, and pulled a rug over them. I did the same and found that the stamping and neighing of the mules and donkeys made a good soporific. Then at the first glimmer of dawn we all rose. The muleteers harnessed their mules, and after tossing down a glass of aniseed spirit set off along the straight treeless highroad, while I took a rough track that led off to the left. I had a long walk before me, for I proposed to cross the coastal range and sleep at a village on the farther side called Sedella, where I had heard that there was a good posada.

My road lay through a landscape devastated by the great earthquake of thirty years before. It was a broken, barren country, burned a pale gold by the sun and spotted with irregular patches of oak scrub and dry thistle stalks. I passed two villages – dreary, run-down, shoddily built settlements – but after the second met only a single person. This was a half-witted youth who was guarding a herd of black pigs, and when I spoke to him he waved his arms at me and made gibbering noises. By this time, through trying to follow the map, I had lost my way. The path I was on rose steadily through a jumble of bare rocks and slides of rubble, dotted with dwarfed ilexes. In the stony valley below, the leaves of the occasional poplar trees had turned yellow, and here and there in the distance I could see a lonely farm-house, drawn tight within its walls as a defence against brigands. It was very hot, and the mica schists on the rocks above glittered menacingly.

When at length, after much climbing, I reached the last crest, I found myself on the Sierra de Tejeda, a massif of strato-crystalline rocks that stands over seven thousand feet above the sea. The sun was already touching the horizon. I could pick out the villages of the Axarquia far below me, the smoke rising above them in short columns and then ending. From this height they looked like splashes of white paint dropped on to a surge of pale red hills that ran off the grey rock mountain like fingers and fell in successive cones and waves and rounded protuberances to the sea. Beyond that, very far off, floating on the haze, lay the coastline of Africa.

From immediately below me came the tinkle of goat-bells, and looking down I could discern, where the steep flank of the mountain splayed out, flocks of goats and sheep, with their shepherds, sharply defined in the oblique light, pacing beside them, their cloaks thrown over one shoulder. A more sensible person would have joined them and begged their hospitality for the night, but I was set on reaching the village. I began, therefore, to scramble down the sharp knife-edges and screes and then to leap and race over the slopes below. Soon complete darkness fell, and it was not till very late, scratched and torn and soaked in sweat, that I reached Sedella. Here I found that the good posada I had been recommended no longer existed. I was forced to take one where an old crone, awakened grumbling from her sleep, fried me a couple of

eggs in rancid oil and showed me to a bed where I was
devoured by an army of bugs till morning. So this was Spain!
I felt that I was at last coming to grips with the country.

The Axarquia is a region of high, rounded hills and intricate
valleys, planted with vineyards. It grows the muscatel grape
from which the famous sweet wine of Malaga is made. The
sea lies spread at its foot like a silk coverlet, but its only trees
are the fig tree and the almond, and I wanted a country that
should be better watered and more diversified. After waiting,
therefore, for my torn clothes to be mended I descended to the
coast road and turned eastwards along it to Motril. But before
reaching this place, which commands the entrance to the
Alpujarra from the south-west side, I was attacked by
dysentery.

It would be tedious to continue in detail this account of my
search for a house. Dysentery dulls the mind to every impression, besides which I have no wish to trespass on a ground
that, in his travel book on Mexico, has been so exhaustingly
explored by Mr Graham Greene. Let it suffice if I say that for
the next weeks I forced myself to keep going, driven by the
fear of using up too quickly my small bank balance if I stopped
to rest and get treatment. In this way I visited all the thirty or
so villages of the Western Alpujarra – those that lie between
Padul and Órgiva as well as the high, inaccessible ones between Cástaras and Trevélez – without finding a suitable
house to let. In very low spirits and with my complaint growing worse all the time, I found myself one evening in a village
of the coastal range called Murtas. Here in a posada that was
alive with bugs, where the only food consisted of an oily rice
cooked with the nastiest of dried cod, I reached my lowest
point. A halt was clearly necessary, and on the following day I
found a tolerable inn, almost free from insects, at Ugíjar. This
is a small town lying in a shallow valley bottom, which ranks
as the *cabeza de partido*, or administrative capital, of the Eastern
Alpujarra.

The country here pleased me better. Órgiva lies in a deep

mountain hollow, and its villages, half-hidden among orange groves and long-limbed olive trees, are airless and shut in. The Eastern Alpujarra, which inclines towards Almeria rather than towards Granada, is more open. Ugíjar in its red-cliffed, poplared valley seemed to me an enchanting place, and looking north from it I could see along the flank of the Sierra Nevada a row of villages, each surrounded by its olive groves and fruit trees, and evidently commanding a view to the south. After a day or two's rest I set out to explore these, and soon came on two that had houses to let. One was called Mairena and the other Yegen.

Mairena was a village chiefly inhabited by gipsies. In spite of my admiration for Borrow, I took only a moderate interest in these people, and wished to live among Spaniards. It was also an isolated village, at least an hour's walk from any road. Yegen, on the other hand, had a road, and this gave it a more habitable aspect. One can walk along a road by day or night without looking to see where one is going. Besides, there was something about the place that attracted me. It was a poor village, standing high above the sea, with an immense view in front of it. With its grey box-shaped houses of a battered Corbusier style, all running down the hill and fusing into one another, and its flat clay roofs and small smoking chimneys, it suggested something that had been made out of the earth by insects. It had too an abundance of water, flowing along the mountain-side in irrigation channels, descending at times through the streets, and turning two mills. But the house had to please as well, and fortunately it did so. It was an irregularly shaped, rambling affair, joined on to smaller houses on either side and comprising some nine living-rooms on the first floor as well as two large and habitable *azoteas* or attics. The ground floor, which the landlord reserved, was used for store-rooms and stables. But the rent asked for this – 200 pesetas a year – was more than I could afford. With the idea of making further inquiries at some of the villages I had passed – there was one called Niguëlas which had especially attracted me – as well as

in the hopes of beating this price down, I set off again on foot
for Granada, with my complaint heavily on me. When I got
back a fortnight later I found that the rent asked for the house
at Yegen had fallen to 120 pesetas, which at that time came to
£6 in English money. I took it.

The owner, Don Fadrique, was letting it under tragic circumstances. His only daughter had just died and he was going
to live with his wife's family near Granada. But he could not
give me possession till the New Year. I had thus almost two
months to wait till I could move in, and I decided to spend
them at Malaga, where by rest and careful dieting I hoped to
throw off my dysentery and with it the weakness and low
spirits that made travelling so irksome. I set out therefore on
foot by the still-unfinished coast road, buying as I went bread,
cheese, and oranges, and sleeping on the beaches. Since I was
in poor walking condition, I took five days to do the hundred
and thirty miles.

At Malaga I secured a clean bedroom, previously occupied
by a Norwegian sailor, near the bull-ring. After the rough life
of the villages, it was a pleasure to be in a large Mediterranean
city again. I found it a place of contrasts. Up on the crumbling
hill, devoured by the yellow light, the Moorish castle was
alive with beggars and gipsies: they dug their caves in its
walls and sat delousing one another in the sun among whiffs
of orange-flower and drying excrement. The children up to
the age of twelve ran naked. Then, if one dropped down a
stone's throw to the Park, one came on a complete change of
scene: here the victorias of the Madrid aristocracy rolled up
and down – Malaga was at this time at the height of its
repute as a winter resort – and sleek, jingling horses and
gleaming spokes flickered by under the lattice of the plane
trees. Or one could take one's seat on one of the stone benches
and watch the people on the sidewalks. With high combs
standing erect on their heads and black lace mantillas draped
over them, the young women of the middle classes paced
along in their mannequin step, collecting glances of admira-

tion from the men who passed them. The head-dress could be either uncouth or elegant, but all the eyes were bright with excitement and many of the faces were lovely.

For a day or two I steeped myself in the sights of the city, and then something disagreeable happened. I have always been careless in my money arrangements, and through some miscalculation the pesetas I had expected to receive did not arrive. For more than a week I was without any at all. My landlady provided me every morning with a roll of bread and a bowl of coffee, and on this and a few oranges, which I had bought with my last pennies, I kept myself going. To make my situation the more exasperating I found at the post office a letter from an old friend of my family. He was spending the winter in Malaga at the Regina Hotel and he invited me to stay there as his guest and, if the state of the roads permitted, to make some motor excursions to Seville and other places in the vicinity. But I was wearing an old corduroy suit, a pair of rope-soled shoes, and a Sevillian hat. He was a very correct man – dress had an almost religious significance in those days – and in such a garb I could not possibly appear before him. Indeed the fear of meeting him accidentally became such an obsession that I used to walk out every morning along the beach, past the fishermen's quarters and the industrial district of Huelin, and spend the days in a dull stupor by the sea. The waves made a melancholy sound on the grey sand, the factory smoke rose forlornly into the air, as they do for all those who have no food in their stomachs.

At length my money arrived. I was able to buy a good meal and, what was equally important, a couple of books. When I had finished these I decided that the time had come for me to leave Malaga. I chose a few things at an antique shop and took the train to Granada. Here, after getting some more pottery – the Fajalauza ware with its faded indigo designs of birds and flowers had only just taken to its present crude synthetic colours – I continued by bus and mule to Ugíjar.

Christmas had now arrived. The furniture I had ordered to

be made at the carpenter's was ready. I had fetched my suitcase from Granada and so had a few books to read. I spent the last days of waiting sitting under the orange trees with a copy of Spinoza's *Ethics* and, when that proved too exacting, with Bury's *History of Greece*. The years of boredom in base-camps and trenches had filled me with a hunger for knowledge, and the first tasks I had set myself when I was settled were to learn something about philosophy and to teach myself Greek. I felt ashamed of being twenty-five and of having read nothing but a few novels and some poetry.

CHAPTER TWO

THE ALPUJARRA

*

Iᴛ was one day early in January when I moved into my house.
I came up the steep, zigzagging track with two mule-loads of
furniture – a *catre* or folding trestle-bed, a table, two chairs, a
water pitcher, the china and pottery I had bought on my journeys, and some blankets and kitchen utensils. As I have said, I
was chronically short of money. I had at this time £130 in
War Certificates and £30 in the bank, and the only other sums
I could expect in the future were £15 every year at Christmas
and £10 on my birthday. What else I had saved on my captain's pay and gratuity had either been spent on books or been
lost in a bad investment. Then, though Spain was, as one
might put it, an intrinsically cheap country, it had prospered
during the war and the pound exchange was unfavourable. If,
therefore, I was to complete the furnishing of my house and to
enjoy a few years of peaceful living in it, I should have to
practise the strictest economy. As a start, I should have to do
my own cooking and housework.

I settled my things in the rooms and began to consider how
I should set about this. The first need was for water. Summon-
ing my courage, I seized the earthenware pitcher in my hand
and sallied out to fetch some from the fountain. A number of
women, with kerchiefs tied round their heads and full skirts
much gathered in at the waist, were standing there gossiping.
Their conversation ceased as I came up, and they stared at me
in silence. Then suddenly the whole flock of them rushed
towards me, seized the pitcher from my hand, filled it, and
carried it back in a body to the house. I realized that an un-
speakable breach of village law had been committed by my
even touching one of these women's objects, and that I should

probably give almost as serious offence if I ventured to cook
for myself.

That afternoon, as I moved about the house sweeping and
dusting, I became aware of female faces peeping at me from
windows across the street and vanishing as soon as I looked at
them. This was disconcerting. I closed the wooden shutters –
only two houses in the village had glass – and went on with my
work in semi-darkness. Then towards sunset I went up on to
the roof. As I have said, there was upstairs, covering part of
the house, a large attic known as the *azotea*, which was used
both for storing grain and for drying tomatoes and red pimen-
tos. It opened out on to the flat clay *terrado* or terrace roof.
From this a vast view of mountains, valleys, villages, and
distant sea lay spread out like an illustration of features of the
world in a child's geography book. Behind the house the
mountain rose gently in a succession of cultivated terraces,
while immediately at my feet lay the village, sliding down the
slope, an agglomeration of grey rectangular surfaces that from
where I stood looked like a Cubist picture by Braque. And
now the sun was setting. The goats and the cattle were being
driven home, the voices of the men and women calling to one
another lay like long streamers on the air, the white pigeons
were circling. As I stood absorbed in this spectacle, I became
aware of a sweet aromatic smell. Looking round me I saw that
every one of those flat grey roofs had a small chimney projecting from it and that from each of these chimneys there issued
a plume of blue smoke which, uniting with other plumes,
hung in a faint haze over the village. The women were cooking their suppers, and for fuel they used bushes of rosemary,
thyme, and lavender, which were brought in on donkeys'
backs from the hills close by.

I was still gazing at this view when from a small trap-door
in my roof there emerged a woman. She was dressed entirely
in a rusty black, with a black kerchief over her head, and her
age could not even be guessed at. Or rather, as I gradually
came to see, she had two ages – one belonging to her face,

which was as worn and channelled as that of a peasant woman
of fifty, and the other belonging to her lithe and nimble body
and to her sharp but dancing grey eyes, which were those of a
woman of under thirty. She came up to me with downcast
looks and explained that her name was Maria, that she was the
servant of the owner of the house, Don Fadrique, and that she
was ready, if I wished, to work for me. After a little pressing
she named a price – one peseta a day with her food – and I
took her.

I now settled down to live in my new house. My books – two
thousand of them – arrived on a wagon from Almeria, and
gradually I bought more chairs and tables of local workman-
ship and extended myself through the various rooms. My
habit was to work in the mornings, to take a walk in the after-
noons, and to spend the evenings either reading in my room or
talking to Maria and her friends in the kitchen. Sometimes too
I had formal visits from the gentry or from those who wished
to be considered as such, and invariably, though the paraffin
lamp gave little light to read by, I went to bed late.

One cannot live long in a Spanish village without being
drawn into its life. For the first week or two I was stared at
whenever I went out, then quite suddenly I was received with
smiles and words of welcome. In the pleasant Andalusian way,
presents of eggs and fruit and vegetables would be brought to
my house, and before long I was being invited to weddings
and baptisms and other family occasions. It surprised me to
see how easily they took for granted my presence among them.
In less isolated villages people had sometimes asked me if I
was prospecting for gold, but at Yegen they were not interested in my reasons for being there and asked no questions.
Was this due to a peasant's lack of curiosity? That is, I think,
too negative an explanation. Time was to show me that the
lives of these people were so entirely bound up with their
village that nothing that happened outside it or that could not
be interpreted in its terms had any meaning for them.

I have described how I came to settle in this remote place,

and must now give some account of the life of the villagers. I
propose to set down their occupations, their customs, their
folk-lore, their religious festivals, their love affairs and quarrels, their types and characters, and many other things. But
where shall I begin? I believe that the reader will most easily
form a picture in his mind if I start with a short description of
the country they lived in. Those who do not like geography
can skip a few pages.

The region known as the Alpujarra or Alpujarras – for
both the singular and plural forms are used – consists of a
long valley, running east and west, between the Sierra Nevada
and the coastal range. This valley falls into two main sections.
The western, which centres round Órgiva, is drained by a
river that flows into the sea at Motril, whereas the eastern,
whose chief town is Ugíjar, sends its waters to the sea at Adra.
These two sections are very different in character from one
another. The first is steep and narrow and is set round by the
highest crests of the snow mountains, while the second,
though backed by slopes that keep their snow till July, is
broad and open and in aspect altogether more southern. There
is also a third extension of the valley farther to the east, which
drains into the sea at Almeria by the river Andarax, but as this
lies outside the scope of this book I need not say anything
about it.

The mountains that enclose this valley require a word. The
Sierra Nevada, which is so abrupt and rocky on its northern
face, presents a smooth and gradual aspect to the south. For
this reason it has been possible to terrace and cultivate it up to
the height of 5,000 feet and more above sea-level. Its summits
reach to 11,600 feet, higher than the highest peaks of the Pyrenees, and its waters irrigate, in the literal sense of that word,
some seventy small towns and villages on its southern flank,
in addition to the large and populous plains of Granada and
Guadix that lie to the north. But viewed from the Alpujarra
the aspect of these mountains is not impressive. Owing to the
convexity of the slope their summits are invisible from below.

To see them one must climb the coastal range, and then what meets the eye will be a long, white, undulating line gradually descending to the east. There are no peaks, only slight swellings and dippings on the smooth hog's back, and the spurs are rounded and barrel-shaped.

To this gigantic mass of slovenly rock the coastal range presents a marked contrast. At its western end, above Órgiva, the Sierra de Lújar juts up in an imposing mass of triassic limestone. Adjoining this on the east is the Sierra la Contraviesa, a softly moulded range of red shaly formation, not much more than 4,000 feet in height but redeemed from mediocrity by the crumpled-curtain effect given by its spurs and ravines. Where it ends, due south from Yegen, the river of Ugíjar breaks through to the sea, and beyond that, extending as far as Almeria, lies the vast table mountain known as the Sierra de Gádor; waterless and uncultivated, it rises to nearly 8,000 feet above sea-level. It was these mountains that I saw when I looked out across the great space of air from my rooftop, and later on I shall give a fuller description of them.

Yegen lay on the slope of the Sierra Nevada, and a road connected it with Ugíjar. Standing on the hill above my house, one could see it come winding up in easy bends along the gradual flank of the mountain. It first passed Válor, a large white village where the sweet orange still ripened, and three miles farther on it reached my village. A green and pleasant walk even in the drought of summer, for the whole of these eight miles were terraced and planted with fruit trees and olive trees and trellised vines, and under them with wheat and maize and beans and other plants. Then after passing Yegen the road rounded a bluff. For a mile or two there was nothing to be seen but rocks and aromatic plants and the great gulf opening below. All at once one caught sight of Mecina Bombarón across a broad ravine. This was a large, partly whitewashed village with many substantial houses, spread out among woods of chestnut trees. It had a completely different character from Yegen, looked cold and northern, and was celebrated for its apples and potatoes. A few miles beyond it the road ended suddenly on the mountain-side. One day it would fork, the left branch running to the river at Cádiar nearly 3,000 feet below and on from there to Granada, and the other climbing yet higher to the chestnut woods and grassy streams of Bérchules. But this did not happen before 1931, and meanwhile we had a road free from wheeled traffic to walk on.

Compared to its neighbours, Válor and Mecina, the geographical characteristic of Yegen was its airy situation, jutting out a little from the mountain and lying – its height above the sea was 4,000 feet – between the orange and the chestnut zones. Economically it was its poverty. Although its land was good and well watered, and although almost every family had their plot or terrace, it lacked the usual nucleus of well-to-do people – the sort, that is, who shaved every Saturday night and on Sundays put on leather shoes and a tie. For the same reason it lacked the occasional big house with its tiled roof or walls of brick: all its architecture was primitive and Berber.

Suppose now that instead of following the road we climb the mule-track immediately above the village. The mountain slope here is not steep. Before long the olive trees end and a park-like disposition of large chestnut trees begins. There are streams everywhere. In the winter these flow down the ravines, but in summer they are led in artificial channels along the summits of the spurs. The characteristic tree is the poplar. They line the watercourses and they also grow in irrigated groves whose fine green grass invites one to lie down and act the part of a Giorgione shepherd, until one notices that they squelch with water. These poplars belong to a foreign species, native to Virginia, and introduced during the last century to provide poles for building: they have sticky, aromatic buds and a heart-shaped leaf and, though never allowed to grow large, they make a delicate pattern like perpendicular stitchwork on the huge, little-diversified mountain-side. In the evening light one saw their lines of thin spires rising one above the other to just below the horizon.

A thousand feet or so above the village one reached the main irrigation channel, which drew its water from a torrent far up in the mountains, and at once the trees ceased and a wilderness of grey rock and pincushion plants began. It was still some three hours' climb to the pass that gave on to the plateau on the other side. But if one looked behind one, what a view! The wrinkled waves of red and yellow and lilac mountains below had been spread out flat in a carpet that reached to the sea. The sound of running water could no longer be heard, the noises of the village had ceased. There was complete silence.

Instead, however, of climbing up the mountain, one could plunge down below the village. The paths here were steeper and overhung with long-branched olive trees. Soon they became almost precipitous. One left the irrigation channels, bordered in spring by purple irises and blue periwinkles, and entered a region of intense red cliffs dropping to ravines. Here stood the Piedra Fuerte, an isolated rock which had once held a Moorish castle and was now the home of a family of wild cats. In the cliffs, which were of soft sandstone, nested colonies of bee-eaters that darted through the air, making streaks of colour with their brilliant green and yellow plumage. Orange trees grew here with their yellow fruit, and there were prickly pears. When at length one reached the bottom one found oneself in a sandy river-bed overhung by tamarisks and oleanders.

The village which possessed this fertile tract of country, rich in almost every kind of crop and fruit tree, was itself a primitive place. Its population was a little over a thousand, and to lodge them it had some two hundred, or perhaps rather more, two-storeyed houses, built of uncut stones and earth and sometimes – especially in the case of the better houses – given a rough surfacing of mortar. The interior walls were plastered and white-washed, but, as in all the Alpujarran *pueblos* that kept to the old tradition, no whitewash was employed outside. The roofs were made of heavy stone slats, laid horizontally and covered with a thick coating of *launa* (a sort of schistous

clay formed from the decomposition of the grey magnesium
slate in the *barrancos*) and then trodden in. The weight of these
kept the walls firm during the tornados from which we
suffered during the cold months of the year. Some of these
slats, known in that case as *aleros*, were made to project about
a foot from the sides of the houses in order to protect the
walls, and the water was carried off from the roof by a spout.
One feature of this type of building was the flat *azoteas* or
attics, built up over a part of the *terrado* or roof terrace and
open in front. Here all through the autumn and winter months
one saw cobs of maize and strings of red peppers and of sliced
egg-plants and tomatoes hanging up to dry, and where no attic
existed there was generally a long open gallery on the first
floor that served the same purpose. As is usual in mountain
villages, the streets were crooked and narrow as well as steep
and, since the houses ran into one another and besides were
built upon a slope, the effect from a distance was of a confused
agglomeration of boxes, one box rising above another, and so
on to the top.

This style of architecture is found only in the Alpujarra and
in the Algerian and Moroccan Atlas, though the flat-roofed
house goes back in the dry south-eastern region of Spain to the
Early Bronze Age. Since the Alpujarra was colonized in the
Middle Ages by mountain Berbers, we may suppose that they
brought this type of building with them. In any case many of
the existing houses at Yegen are probably, though much
rebuilt, of Moorish construction.

Like most of the villages of the Sierra Nevada, Yegen was
composed of two *barrios* or quarters, built at a short distance
from one another. The *barrio de arriba* or upper quarter, which
was the one in which I lived, began just below the road and
ended at the church. Here there was a level space some two or
three acres in extent – a break in the endless slope – which was
given over to cultivation, and immediately below it the *barrio
de abajo*, or lower quarter, began. The extraordinarily strong
feelings of attachment which Spaniards have to their native

place showed themselves even in the case of these *barrios*, for, although there was no difference in their social composition, there was a decided feeling of rivalry between them. People made their friends chiefly in the one in which they lived, and if they had to move house avoided settling in the other. Both in politics and in private quarrels the two *barrios* tended to take different sides. But since there were no obstacles to inter-marriage, the feeling never went very deep and did not of course compare with the gulf which divided one pueblo or village from another.

Everyone who came within the jurisdiction of the village had his house in it, except for the four or five families who lived half an hour's walk away at Montenegro. In Moorish times this had been a single farm belonging to a wealthy Arab from Mecina Bombarón known as Aben Aboó, who in 1579 was one of the leaders of the rebellion against the Spaniards, but it was now divided into a number of small properties. It thus constituted what was known as a *caserío* or *cortijada* – something smaller, that is, than a *lugarcillo* (hamlet) or *barrio* (quarter) – and its independence from the village was shown by the fact that two families from the adjacent village of Yátor lived there. By ancient custom no 'foreigner' could hold or rent or be employed on land in an Alpujarran village, though if he were rich there would be no one to make objections. Another larger collection of houses – what would be called a *lugar* – had existed in Moorish times at Cuesta de Viñas on the eastern side of the village, but it had disappeared without leaving any trace. Close to its site stood a small *cortijo* or farm, which was managed from the village, and this was the only farm in permanent occupation within the boundaries of Yegen, with the exception of the cattle ranch owned by my landlord, Don Fadrique, a couple of hours' walk away in the mountains. Of this I shall speak later.

CHAPTER THREE

FRIENDS AND NEIGHBOURS

*

I⟁ was from Maria Andorra, as my servant was called, that I obtained my first introduction to Spanish life. Her mother had been a midwife and a wise-woman, and so I approached it from the direction of folk-lore, witchcraft, village customs, and such rapidly disappearing things. She knew all about the herbs used in dyeing and medicines, and she was also a great story-teller. Most of her tales were the familiar ones that one reads in Grimm or the *Arabian Nights*, but they generally had some spicy or bawdy point to them. Except in chaste, sexless Ireland, peasants have coarse minds, and I imagine that, till the folk-lore collector pulls out his notebook and pencil, they nearly always have this character.

Sometimes I would lead Maria on to talk of witchcraft. The *hechiceras*, or witches, she declared, had seen their best days. Since the building of the road a few years before there had been a marked decline in their activities. Their art demanded privacy, and for this reason they were greatly put out by engineering works. But had I, so she assured me, come to Yegen a few years earlier I should have seen them floating by moonlight through the air, perching like owls on the poplar trees, and flying off to the threshing-floors where they held their meetings. Her mother, though she did not tell me this, had been a notable *hechicera*, while the miller had been a warlock and she herself had several times seen him on his aerial peregrinations. This was remarkable, because he was a short, heavy man of past sixty, with none of the buoyancy one would have expected of a person who every Saturday night took off from his roof like a helicopter.

The symbol of a witch's power was a pestle and mortar,

which was handed down from mother to daughter. Since every family had one of these – they came second to the frying-pan in the list of household necessities, and some way before the kettle – it was not easy to tell which ones had magic properties and which had not. Perhaps it was only the old wooden mortars, recently supplanted by the brass kind, which possessed the necessary potency. They were still, in spite of the building of the road, very much in use for, although the art of flying had been lost, the concoction of love potions continued to be a flourishing business. In a changing world even the witches have to adapt themselves to new conditions, and with the increase of luxury and vice, which everyone agreed was a symptom of modern times, the art of making love philtres had acquired a new importance.

My servant, whether or not she had inherited her mother's arts, was an insinuating and dynamic character. Her surname of Andorra – she herself used her other surname of Moreno – signifies 'a woman who walks about all the time' and hence 'a street walker'. It had been her mother's name and also, I believe, her grandmother's, and it suited her so exactly that it clung to her. All her movements were quick and lithe, and under her dingy black clothes – in our village married women who were past twenty-five dressed in black – her body wriggled about like a snake's and sometimes in sheer exuberance seemed on the point of slipping out of them altogether. She danced well, with a sort of suppressed buoyancy, and after some exciting evening, when the gipsies had come in and, well plied with wine, she had joined in one or two *malagueñas*, she would collapse on a chair in a state of complete torpor. Her tragedy was her face. Although at this time she was scarcely past thirty, it was lined and worn like that of an elderly woman, and when I had been a year or two with her I discovered the reason. She never let water touch it, but every morning and evening washed it with a strong aniseed spirit which burned and shrivelled the skin till it looked like the side of a Spanish sierra.

It was not long before I got to know Maria's story. Her father had died young, and she had been brought up by her mother. Then at the age of eighteen or nineteen she had gone as a servant to my landlord's house. His wife, who had several delicate children, preferred to spend most of the year in her old home near Granada where the doctors were better, so that it was almost inevitable that Maria should become his mistress. For some time the affair was kept secret, but one day a child was born, a thin sickly girl called Angela, who at the time of my arrival in the village was about nine years old. On its birth my landlord made over to Maria a small house adjoining his own, while his wife, in an access of Christian forgiveness, carried the child to the font in her own arms.

Don Fadrique was a small, delicately-boned man with long sad moustaches and liquid eyes that projected a little from their sockets: one of the prawn-like race that flourish in the Mediterranean region and have the melancholy temperament of the physically under-equipped. He had reacted against his debility by developing a dry, cautious manner and an amused, sceptical attitude to people and life. Yet like all Alpujarreños he had a great love of the land. His heart as well as his purse lay in his high mountain farm and in his terraces of corn and vines, and the idle, towny existence he led in his mother-in-law's house near Granada bored him. His greatest pleasure was to sit in the kitchen, unshaved and collarless, in a worn coat and trousers, talking to the *gente del campo* and eating his favourite breakfast dish – a bowl of *migas* or maize polenta heaped with fried sardines with a sauce of hot chocolate poured over it.

Maria used to enjoy telling me how their intrigue had been conducted during the periods when his wife was living in the village. He would get up early to go to his farm, saddle his horse, and lead it out of the yard to a stable just up the street. Then he would slink back to her house and spend an hour in bed with her. From the way in which she told this I gathered that it was the cleverness of the deceit that appealed to her.

She had a true peasant's admiration for cunning, and besides was very envious.

But when I came to meet Don Fadrique's wife I was amazed. Doña Lucía was an exquisite creature, beautiful in a refined and almost Japanese style, passionate, romantic, and with a generosity and goodness of heart that I have rarely seen equalled in anyone. And she was tragic. She had seen four of her children die in early infancy, and now her one remaining daughter, a beautiful girl of seventeen, had died too, and only a son, a sickly and lymphatic youth, was left. Her mother, in whose house she spent so much of her time, was a blustering, domineering, noisy woman, and her marriage could scarcely be called a happy one. I shall have more to say of her later.

I used to see a good deal of Don Fadrique because, by a trick that he played on me, he had reserved a room in my house and came and stayed there whenever he wanted to. Although I resented his presence, I liked him personally. He was an educated and not unintelligent man, with a mild leaning to popular science and astronomy, yet he was never happy unless he was dressed in old clothes, palavering over crops and prices with his peasants. He had a quiet scorn for everything connected with city life, for all the superstructure of civilization including priests and religion, and liked to think of himself as a realist. I suspect that under this word there often lies as great a neurotic compulsion, as one-sided a perversion of normal experience, as under the word romantic. His passion for his cunning peasant mistress with her quick sexy body and her hen's face was a part of this attitude. His appetite for 'reality' was the craving of a weak but refined man who feels that he can strengthen himself by contact with what is earthy and low. There is such a thing as an Antaeus complex.

Maria had a sister called Pura, who often came and sat for hours in my kitchen without saying a word. She was a widow who owned a small plot of land which she worked alone with her son. One can hardly imagine a creature more bound to Nature: she looked like a radish which has been pulled out of the ground with the earth still clinging to its rootlets. She was uncouth in every possible way – her black hair wild and uncombed, her face and body as brown as old leather, and her breasts, which hung out when she sat down because her blouse had no buttons, as long as udders. She had a peculiar earthy smell, which she left behind her when she went out of the room, and her face, though in its general features handsome, was as empty and expressionless as an earthenware jug. In herself she was a harmless creature without an interest in life but her small plot of land. At whatever time of day one passed it one would see her bent double over it with a hand-hoe. She sometimes had epileptic fits, and her son, a swarthy silent youth, would beat her to make her give him money for cigarettes. When this happened, her loud, piercing cries would be heard all over the *barrio*.

Don Fadrique's craving to be united to the soil had once led him to assault her. He had gone one evening to her house, which had no furniture but two broken chairs and a table, and thrown her down on the straw mattress which was all she had for bed. She had not struggled, but she had kept up a prolonged monotonous screaming, like a pig that is being killed, as long as the business lasted. Then he buttoned up his trousers, shrugged his shoulders, and left.

'I always thought,' he remarked cryptically to Maria, 'that your sister was such a silent woman, but when you say two words to her in her house, she screams.'

However, he let her know that she could have some olive oil if she came for it to his bodega. As she was very avaricious, this satisfied her. She had done her duty by screaming, so honour had been saved.

There were three rather vaguely defined classes in the village – the gentry, the peasants, and the poor, meaning by the last those families who owned or rented only a strip or two of land and had to earn part of their living by working for others. The gentry – the 'people of category', as they liked to be called – were not as a rule interesting. Boredom had settled on their faces as dust settles in unoccupied rooms, for their social position shut them in and they were emotionally parasitic on their poorer neighbours, who did their living and had their pains and pleasures for them. I used to suffer from the visits of the schoolmistress's husband, who had once been a music master. He was an elderly man with grey bushy moustaches and round expressionless eyes marbled over with white, who came from the north of Spain. He felt deeply his fate in being exiled to a barbarous village where there was no café, no evening *paseo* or promenade, and few parties of cards, and to make up for this he would pay me interminable visits on the assumption that as an Englishman I must be suffering too. He was one of those people – there are many of them in Spain – who believe that every time a thing is said it becomes more certain, and so whenever he paid me a visit we had the same conversation. As soon as we had exhausted the subject of his wife's headaches and his lumbago, he would bring the subject on to England and its differences from Andalusia.

'You do not get much sun in England?'

'No, Don Eduardo, very little.'

'It rains all the time.'

'Yes, almost all the time.'

'And there is fog.'

'Yes, there is fog.'

'Still, you are able to grow oranges.'

'No, it is too cold for that. Our fruits are apples and plums.'

'And of course olives.'

'Unfortunately not. Olives need sunshine.'

'That is very strange. I have always understood that owing to the warm current that reaches you from the Gulf of Mexico you were able to grow plants from southern climates.'

'Not one.'

'But surely you have fig trees?'

'Yes, in a few places, but the fruit does not usually ripen.'

'Ah, so figs grow. I thought they did. And you have almond trees.'

'No, none at all.'

'How is that? I have never been in a country where there were no almond trees. Even in Burgos, where it is very cold, they grow.'

'But in Burgos there is sun.'

There was a silence while Don Eduardo thought out his next question. He was a man who liked certainty. His opinions hardened quickly into dogmas, because by force of repeating them emphatically he made them true. Thus all contradiction was disturbing to him and the smallest suspicion of doubt opened a gap in that phalanx of solid beliefs which he had assembled for his protection and reassurance. He was ready to fight, therefore, to the last ditch on the most insignificant matters, and when defeated would return to the attack a few minutes later from the same positions.

'Then how is it,' he said, fixing me with his glassy eyes, 'how is it that if you can't grow almond trees, you can grow sugar-cane? It is common knowledge that you English only use cane sugar.'

Yet Don Eduardo was in his own way an enlightened man. He was fond of censuring the idleness and lack of curiosity of his compatriots and of declaring that this was the reason for their backwardness. He was particularly proud of the fact that he was always occupied on something himself. Though he was almost blind from cataract, he repaired clocks and watches, and since there was a dearth of these in the village – to be precise there were only two – he would spend his days taking to pieces a broken clock that had belonged to his father and putting it together again. His daughter stuffed birds and did raffia work whenever she was not engaged on the housework, while his wife had an album of pressed flowers with their names written below them in a neat hand and the date on which they had been picked. Really one might almost call them a North European family.

Another characteristic figure was José Venegas, who kept the village store. He had emigrated as a young man to South

America, saved a little money, and come back to open his shop. He was a colourless, amiable man whose only ambitions in life were to sell every year a little more sugar, rice, and dried cod and to be addressed by the title of Don. This, however, the village refused him. Those three letters were the perquisite of those who could claim either gentle birth or a good schooling: mere money couldn't acquire them. For what was money? The wise men of the village – and almost every Spanish peasant becomes wise when he passes fifty – were agreed that money was the source of *vicio* or vice. Today the world was full of vice. They recalled those happy times when even the rich mixed rye or maize flour with their bread, when coffee and chocolate were taken by only a few elderly ladies, and no young man of under thirty would have dared to smoke in public. To spend money on show and ostentation was permissible, but to spend it on self-indulgence was vicious.

Federico, however, disagreed with this view of things. He was the son of a former alcalde who had sold the communal lands of the village – several thousand acres of mountain pasture and ilex forest – and put part of the proceeds in his pocket. As the phrase went, 'he had eaten them'. The money, however, had not lasted long. His son had emigrated to the Argentine, where he had spent a good many years as a waiter in an English club, and he had come back full of nostalgic recollections of those days.

'The women – whew! The luxury – whew! The vice – I tell you no one who has not seen it can imagine it. Armchairs like feather-beds! Stacks of illustrated papers! Hot running water in the pantries! The streets smelling like rivers of eau de Cologne! No, no, we Spaniards don't know the meaning of vice. We live like savages, like barbarians.'

To judge by the tone in which he spoke he had lived a roaring life across the seas – girls all the time, silk ties, whisky, hair shampoos. He held forth on the superiority of vice to virtue with the persuasiveness of a Chinese Epicurean philosopher. But his actions were different. He worked very hard, had not married, never came to dances, never paid visits. If one wished to see him, one had to go down to the strip of land that he cultivated himself with the aid of a boy. There he would be pruning his trellises of vines or else ploughing – a neatly built, dapper man with grey hair, gold-rimmed spectacles, and a very clean shirt. He would stop for a few moments to descant on his theme and then return furiously to his work. For this exponent of the unbridled life was always in a hurry: into our simple peasant world he had brought not only the bearing and refinement of a man of the cities, but also the waiter's scuttling habits.

CHAPTER FOUR

LYTTON STRACHEY'S VISIT

*

I HAD not long been settled in my house when I learned that I was to have visitors. My friend Ralph Partridge wrote that he proposed to arrive early in April and that he would bring with him a young woman known as Carrington and also a writer who had recently leaped into fame called Lytton Strachey. This was the best possible news, for it was six months since I had seen any of my friends, and I was beginning to feel my isolation. But perhaps, before describing their visit, I should explain how I had come to know them.

Ralph had been in my regiment during the war. We had been at Ypres and at Armentières together and after that on the Somme. Then, when the armistice came, he had returned to Oxford. He was at that time rather an indolent man given to sudden bursts of energy. He had a good mind, which he did not use, and a body that, if he had carried a club, would have allowed him to pass for Hercules. With his fine torso, his dancing blue eyes, and his rollicking high spirits he was almost irresistible to women, and this was fortunate because women, usually in the form of actresses and chorus girls, were the only things that much interested him. To men, on the other hand, he was inclined to be arrogant. Whether or not, as I liked to imagine, he had in previous incarnations been Agamemnon, Mark Antony, Gargantua, a nabob in the East India Company, and finally a young blood of the Regency, in this one he had succeeded in passing through the usual stages of an English education without acquiring the slightest tincture of Christian feeling. His career at school and in the army had given him a great contempt for both cowardice and conventionality, and one or other of these things was to be found in most people.

His behaviour at Oxford illustrates this. He did no work at all, but in a leisurely way took up rowing. Asked to row for the Varsity Eight, he refused to do so because that would interfere with his trip abroad, but later consented to row for his college and, when they did well, to compete for the Ladies' Plate at Henley, only making it a condition that he should not train. When Christ Church won in spite of his having spent the night before the race with a woman, he was asked to row for England in the Olympic Games. But this prospect did not attract him, and he refused.

It was soon after he first went to Oxford that he met Carrington – she was never known except by her surname – and fell deeply in love with her. She was a painter who had been one of the star pupils at the Slade, but in the last year of the war she had met Lytton Strachey during a week-end in Sussex and formed a sudden and violent attachment to him. He had not responded except in a vaguely benevolent way, but she had refused to be shaken off, and when, together with other Cambridge friends, among them Maynard Keynes and Sidney Saxon-Turner, he rented the Mill House at Tidmarsh, close to Pangbourne, she settled in as their housekeeper. Before long Ralph joined the party.

I cannot recollect now how I came to know Carrington, for we had other friends in common besides Ralph, but I remember very well going over to Tidmarsh for the first time and meeting Lytton Strachey. It was one of those heavily overcast English summer days. The trees and the grass were steeped in a vivid green, but the purplish clouds overhead shut out the light and made the interiors of the houses dark and gloomy. Carrington, with her restless blue eyes and her golden-brown hair cut in a straight page-boy bob, came to the door – she suggested to me one of the lute-playing angels, the fourth from the left, in Piero della Francesca's *Nativity* – and I was shown into the sitting-room. At the farther end of it there

was an extraordinary figure reclining in a deep armchair. At
the first glance, before I had accustomed my eyes to the lack of
light, I had the illusion – or rather, I should say, the image
came into my mind – of a darkly bearded he-goat glaring at me
from the bottom of a cave. Then I saw that it was a man and
took in gradually the long, relaxed figure, the Greco-ish face,
the brown sensitive eyes hidden behind thick glasses, the
large, coarse nose and ears, the fine, thin, blue-veined hands.
Most extraordinary was the voice, which was both very low
and in certain syllables very high-pitched, and which faded out
at the end of the sentence, sometimes even without finishing
it. I never attuned my ears to taking in everything that he said.

Tea was laid in the dining-room – farm butter, honey in the
comb, home-made cakes and jam, and currant loaf, served in
a pink lustre tea-service. Carrington was a devotee of Cobbett,
and her housekeeping and furnishing expressed not only the
comfort but the poetry of cottage and farmhouse life. Her
very English sensibility, in love with the country and with all
country things, gave everything she touched a special and
peculiar stamp. But what struck me more strongly about her
than anything else was the attention she paid to Lytton. Never
have I seen anyone who was so waited on hand and foot as he
was by her, or whose every word and gesture was received
with such reverence. In a young woman who in all other
respects was fiercely jealous of her independence, this was
extraordinary.

How is one to describe the first beginnings of a long friendship? Later impressions fuse with earlier ones and distort
them. Besides, I have to keep within the framework of this
book, which requires that I put down only what will be necessary to make Lytton Strachey's visit to my remote and primitive village come alive. Scouring my memory then, I seem to
remember that as I sat at the tea-table on that dark summer's
afternoon I was puzzled by the contrast presented by the three
people in front of me and wondered whether their peculiar
relation (adopted father and married children, as it came in

time to be) could last. They were in every way so extremely different from one another: Ralph with his look of an Oxford hearty – dirty white shorts, nondescript shirt, and then rather stylized way of speaking which contrasted with the Rabelaisian laugh, rolling blue eyes, and baritone voice in which he sang a jazz song or a ballad: Carrington with her simple, pre-Raphaelite clothes and her coaxing voice and smile that concealed so many intense and usually conflicting feelings: Lytton, elegant in his dark suit, gravely remote and fantastic, with something of the polished and dilettante air of a sixteenth-century cardinal. It was not any similarity of temperament or upbringing that had brought these three together, and Lytton's London friends, who resented their week-ends at Tidmarsh being diluted by people whom they looked on as outsiders, could not understand it. 'Bloomsbury' was still a small, closely guarded set, united both by old friendships and by a private philosophy, and it showed a strong resistance to accepting on an intimate footing people whom it did not regard as suitable.

It was February when I learned of my friends' expected visit, and this at once produced a crisis in my arrangements. Only two rooms of my house were as yet furnished, and I should need to buy more things of every sort and in particular more beds and bedding. Since my bank balance was down to ten pounds, I wrote to a relative and asked him if he would lend me a small sum for a few weeks. This was the time my bank needed to sell out some war loan and, feeling sure of his assent, I requested him to telegraph the money to Almeria. I give these personal details because, unless I describe the succession of trials and mishaps that preceded Lytton Strachey's journey to my house, I shall not have given the full story. His arrival there was a difficult consummation.

The distance from Yegen to Almeria is fifty-seven miles. I walked it in two days, chose the furniture I wanted, and then sat down to wait for the money to come. But the time passed and it did not do so. I had moved into a workmen's lodging-house off the market and sunk to my last peseta when a letter from my relative arrived containing a refusal. There was nothing to be done but to return to Yegen and wait there for the proceeds of the sale of my war loan to arrive. I spent my last pennies on some bread and oranges and set off, passing a cold night on the way under a rock.

I had scarcely got back when I went down with a severe attack of flu. My servant Maria nursed me through it, but it was a couple of weeks before I was fit to get about again. Then, for my bank had sent me some money, I set out once more for Almeria to fetch the furniture. This time I took the bus from Ugíjar, and after putting the things on the carrier's wagon, returned by the same route. But these delays had been fatal. The day after I reached Yegen a telegram was handed me which told me that my friends were already in Granada and would be leaving it in two days' time. They counted on my meeting them there and escorting them back to Yegen.

This was decidedly awkward. I had not expected them so soon, and owing to my chronic mismanagement I was again completely without money, though some was due to reach me within a few days. Nor had the wagon containing the furniture arrived. But delay was out of the question, and so I decided to set off at dawn on the following morning. I should have twenty-eight hours in which to cover seventy-one miles, and five pesetas, borrowed from Maria, to spend on the way.

The first hour took me two thousand feet down the mountainside to the village of Yátor. This is a small poverty-stricken place standing on the edge of a broad, gravelly river. Behind it rise fantastically fluted cliffs of soft red sandstone, and under these are poplar trees, olive trees, pomegranates, tamarisks, and a strip of irrigated land planted at this time of the year with broad beans. As I passed, women wearing scarlet underskirts and gaily coloured head-handkerchiefs were standing about under the olive trees or resting their pitchers by the crumbling walls, and I had the feeling of being in some Eastern country, perhaps in Persia. Actually Yátor is a village of miners who spend eleven months of the year in the lead mines of Linares, leaving their women and children behind them to cultivate their plots of land. These women have a reputation for beauty and also for looseness, and it was one of the jokes of the country round that the luckiest priest in the Alpujarra was the parish priest of Yátor, because he had so many attractive women at his beck and call.

From this place I ascended a *rambla* or dry river-bed and, crossing a low watershed, descended to Cádiar. This is a large and prosperous village standing on the river that runs westward to the sea at Motril and marking the central point or navel of the Alpujarra. After passing it, the tedious part of the journey began. For sixteen miles the track lay down the river valley, a narrow, monotonous trench lined with tamarisks and poplar trees. Two ventas provided sour wine and anis, but there were no villages, and the river had to be forded again and again. Then I came to the main road and to the ancient olive groves of Órgiva. A bus runs from here to Granada, but, as I had not the money for the fare, I kept on six miles to Lanjarón, which I reached at dusk.

Lanjarón is a long white village, almost a town, stretched like a balustrade along the steep mountain-side. It has hot springs and two hotels to accommodate the people who come to be cured of their kidney complaints and their rheumatism. It also has a Moorish castle, built on what would seem to be an inaccessible pinnacle below the town, but captured by Ferdinand of Aragon in 1500 with the aid of his artillery. The picked garrison who were defending it surrendered, with the exception of the Negro commander who preferred to leap to his death from a tower. While this was happening the mosque, in which the civilian population had taken refuge, was blown up and everyone in it killed.

I had supper at the posada and lay down on a straw mattress for a few hours. I still had thirty-two miles to make before I reached Granada, and I needed to be there by twelve o'clock if I was not to miss my friends. Starting off therefore before daylight, I got to the tram-lines on the outskirts of the city and boarded a tram. I was feeling weak, because I had not fully recovered from my attack of flu, and for the only time in my life I fainted. Then, recovering and hurrying to the hotel, I found that my friends had left half an hour before to take the bus to Órgiva. I caught them just as they were getting into it.

We were back at Lanjarón and installed in one of its hotels a couple of hours later. Extraordinary to see the waiters, the maids in caps, the bath lying white and empty like a hygienic coffin in its little room. Extraordinary too to sit in a cane arm-chair drinking cognac and talking to my friends. After the life I had been leading, the comfort and the friendly voices spread through my system like opium. But when we had exhausted the first burst of mutual communication, the problem of trans-porting Lytton Strachey to Yegen came up. He sat there silent and bearded, showing no signs of enthusiasm. In the end we decided to engage a carriage for the following morning to convey us as far as Órgiva and to send on two mules to meet us there and take us the rest of the journey.

We picked up the mules and then the question arose as to which route we should take. The shortest – it saved an hour – required us to ford the Río Grande instead of crossing the bridge. According to the muleteers this was feasible, but when we reached the ford and the mules went in almost to their girths in the racing water, Lytton drew back. There was nothing to be done but to eat our lunch under the olive trees and return to the hotel, arranging with the men to make a fresh start on the following day.

The evening passed in general low spirits. Everyone's nerves were on edge. Ralph and Carrington were having a lovers' quarrel, and Lytton was gloomy because, though he had been eager to see Spain, he had been most unwilling to come on this expedition. His stomach was delicate, Spanish food had disagreed with him, and he was not feeling in the mood for adventures. But Ralph, who was very loyal to his friends, was determined to visit me, and Lytton had refused to be left behind at Granada even if Carrington, in whose capacities he had little confidence, remained with him. This clinging to male protection was characteristic. Under his self-possessed manner he was a timid man who had arranged his life so that he should never be obliged to do anything that he found difficult. Now, one of the things that he could not do was to speak to people who were outside of his particular range of interests. Thus, though he had been toying for some time with a Spanish grammar, nothing would have induced him even to order a cup of coffee in that language. In France he refused to utter a word of French, although naturally he knew it well and read it aloud with a fair accent. He could not even give an order to an English servant. When, in his own house, he wanted some tea, he told Carrington and she told the maid, and if he was by himself he went without. To avoid the risk of being spoken to in trains he always, even when he was badly off, travelled first class. Such were the rules he had drawn up for himself. From an early age he had planned his life, his career, even his appearance, and this plan required that he should keep strictly within that small circle of people where he could fly under his own colours and make himself understood without effort. No doubt the peculiarities of his voice and intonation as well as his dislike of any sort of social pretence made communication with the world at large difficult for him.

That evening, then, at Lanjarón, was spoiled by recriminations. Did I really know the road? Ralph asked me. Were the muleteers to be trusted? Would there be beds and eatable food when we arrived? The conveyance of the great writer to my mountain village began to assume more and more the appearance of a difficult military operation. Carrington, caught between two fires, became clumsily appeasing and only Lytton said nothing. As for myself, I never doubted my powers to go anywhere or to do anything of a physical sort that I wished to, but under my friends' bombardment I felt my unfitness for assuming responsibility for other people.

It was in this harassed and ruffled frame of mind that we set off once more on the following morning. For the first hour or so everything went well. As the carriage rolled along, the sun lit up the silver leaves of the olive trees and the birds rose and sank like shuttles between them and the tall bean plants below. But no sooner had we left the carriage and descended into the river valley than our difficulties began. Lytton found that he could not ride on mule-back because he suffered from piles, so that every time the track crossed the river, which happened about every half a mile, he had laboriously to climb on to the animal and then dismount again. This delayed us. It was not till a little before sunset that we reached Cádiar, and he then felt so exhausted that he declared that he could not go any farther. We drew up at the posada and looked at its best bed, but one glance at it made him change his mind and decide to go on.

The day was coming to an end so rapidly that we did not dare to take the short and comparatively easy track through Yátor. There was nothing to be done but climb straight up the mountain-side to hit the end of the main road some two thousand five hundred feet above. It was a dramatic ascent by a steep path often bordered by precipices and no one could do it sitting side-saddle on a mule, as Lytton and Carrington had to, without an unpleasant feeling inside. Slowly, as we climbed, the light faded. A rosy band mounted in the sky behind us, and the chasms and pinnacles took on a shadowy depth and height. Then the stars came out just as we reached the road, and Carrington and I hurried on to give warning of our arrival and to get a meal prepared. The distance was still some six miles. When at length we reached the village and stood looking down in the starlight on its flat, greyish roofs, only the tiniest occasional glow from the smallest oil lamp in the glassless foot-square frame of a window showed that it was still awake.

I do not remember much about the next few days. Lytton was tired and therefore not in a mood for talking much. We went for a walk up the mountain-side and Carrington took some photographs. One of them, if I remember right, showed him sitting side-saddle on a mule, bearded, spectacled, very long and thin, with his coarse red nose, holding an open sunshade above him. Even in England he was a strange figure to meet on a country ramble: here he looked exotic, aristocratic, Oriental rather than English, and above all incongruous.

On his last evening, however, cheered by the thought that his visit was drawing to an end, he relaxed and became almost lively. When he was in the mood, his conversation had great charm. The delicacy and precision of his mind came out much better than they usually did in his books, because in these he subordinated sensitivity of language and spontaneity of phrase to a preconceived pattern. He was not, like Virginia Woolf, a natural writer, and even in his letters his pen never ran away with him. But in conversation he was himself. He needed more than most people an attuned and sympathetic audience, but, given this, he became the most easy of companions, listening as much as he talked, making whimsical or penetrating comments, and creating around him a feeling of naturalness and intimacy. One remembered afterwards his doubts and hesitations, his refusals to dogmatize, his flights of fantasy, his high, whispering voice fading out in the middle of a sentence, and forgot the very definite and well-ordered mind that lay underneath. But it is beyond my power to give any real account of so complex a character who, through some thickness in the needle, perhaps some deliberate plan of writing down to his readers, records himself with too poor fidelity in his literary works. One observed a number of discordant features – a feminine sensibility, a delight in the absurd, a taste for exaggeration and melodrama, a very mature judgement, and then some lack of human substance, some hereditary thinness in the blood that at times gave people who met him an odd feeling in the spine. He seemed almost indecently lacking in ordinariness.

However, what I remember best about Lytton Strachey – for though I was never on intimate or even on easy terms with him, I had opportunities for seeing him in his own house and elsewhere over many years – was the great gentleness of his tone and manner when he was with people whom he liked. As a young man he had, I understand, shown a bitter and satirical vein, and when, as often happened, he was unwell, he could be peevish and irritable. But friendship drew out his best qualities. There was a good deal in his cautiously hedonistic attitude to life that recalled the teachings of Epicurus. His world, like the Garden of that valetudinarian philosopher, consisted of a small, carefully chosen set of people whose society he enjoyed. Some of these were young men of good looks and intellectual promise whom he drew out and encouraged, for there was something of the teacher in him. Others were literary figures, such as Virginia Woolf, Maynard Keynes, Desmond and Molly MacCarthy, and E. M. Forster. Outside this he would make sallies into a wider field – luncheons with Lady Oxford or Lady Ottoline Morrell, dinner parties at Lady Colefax's and even at ducal houses – and return home full of mischievous and ironical comments. But within these limits he remained. Although, as a Strachey, he took a certain interest in public affairs and stood by his very moderate Liberal opinions, I got the impression that privately he thought of the world with its incomprehensible stupidity as something which it was best to keep at a distance. Unlike Voltaire, whom he admired so greatly, he regarded it as irreformable, and it was this attitude, I suspect, that angered Bertrand Russell and led him to speak harshly of him in a recent broadcast. The two men, who often met at Lady Ottoline's, were not made to like or understand one another, in spite of their sharing the same pacifist attitude to the war.

The day for my friends' departure came. A car arrived and took them to Almeria, where they caught the train for Madrid. The visit had been something of a strain for everyone. Much though I knew that I should miss Ralph and Carrington, whose presence in my house, in spite of all the difficulties, had given me the deepest pleasure, I breathed again at the thought that I should no longer be responsible for finding dishes that would suit Lytton's delicate digestion. The ruthless cuisine of Spanish villages, with its emphasis on potato omelettes, dried cod, and unrefined olive oil, had made my task a difficult one. And he must have been even more relieved at making his escape. When, three years later, Leonard and Virginia Woolf were preparing to come out and stay with me, he advised them strongly against attempting it, declaring in his high-pitched voice that it was 'death'.

CHAPTER FIVE

LOVE AFFAIRS AND POLITICS

*

As the months passed by and I came to be better acquainted with the villlage I had chosen for my home, I was surprised to discover what a very self-contained place it was. Even our gentry were not on visiting terms with those of the neighbouring villages, which we scarcely entered except on the occasion of their yearly festivals. Of the two nearest, Válor was disliked because its people were thought to put on airs, while Mecina was laughed at because of its old-fashioned dress and customs. The only ones that we were on good terms with were those that stood at some distance off, especially when they grew different crops and some trade was done with them.

There was naturally no courting between adjacent villages. It was unthinkable that a man or girl of Yegen should marry anyone from Válor or Mecina. They might, if the opportunity occurred, marry from a remoter town or locality, though even so there were, besides the schoolmistress, only two married women living among us who had been born in other places. One of these was my landlord's wife, Doña Lucía, while the other was the doctor's wife, and they had both met their husbands while these were studying at the University of Granada. What is more, there were only two men in the village besides myself who were not 'sons of the pueblo'. These were the priest and the officially appointed secretary to the municipal council, and both of them came from villages a few miles away. It will thus be easily understood that the sense these villagers had of belonging to a closed community – a Greek polis or a primitive tribe – was very strong. Everyone felt his life bound up with that of the pueblo he had been born into – a pueblo which, through its freely elected municipal officers, governed itself.

Politics were therefore – for Spain is a politically minded country – one of the favourite topics of conversation. Whenever one heard the words *granuja, bribón, sin vergüenza* – rogue, rascal, brazen-faced – one knew what the context was. But not national politics. Although the papers reported cabinet crises every few months and strikes and shooting affrays in Barcelona, no one in Yegen took the least interest in them. The only politics that interested the people of the Alpujarra were the politics of their own villages and, since these were not so simple as one might suppose, I will give a brief explanation of them.

At this time Spain was a parliamentary democracy in which two parties, the Liberal and the Conservative, competed for office. Both represented the interests of the middle classes, the only difference between them being that the Conservatives were for maintaining the position of the Church whereas the Liberals were mildly anti-clerical. Since the peasants and agricultural labourers took no interest in these matters, the two parties had organized their forces under local bosses, known as *caciques*, who were generally the largest landowners in each district. They used their influence, much as the English squires had once done, to bring the peasants to the polls and to persuade them to vote for their faction. In the mountain villages this was usually quite easy. People took sides as at a football match, for the satisfaction of seeing their own group win. Besides, the *cacique*, backed by his political machine, was a useful man to have as a friend, for he could help anyone who got into trouble, and even in some cases procure a more favourable assessment of his land tax.

The leading *cacique* of our region was the Conservative deputy to the Cortes, Don Natalio Rivas. He was a wealthy landowner who ruled the whole Alpujarra from Granada to Almeria like a king. He was also a cultured man who had written an excellent book on bull-fighting, and both locally and in

Madrid he had a great reputation. His deputy in the *partido*, or rural district of Ugíjar was a certain Don Paco Almendro, who lived in a large new house at Válor, and under him were the *caciques* of the separate villages. Originally most villages had had two, one a Conservative and the other a Liberal, who had taken turns in controlling the local municipal councils just as the two parties in Madrid had taken turns in forming the Government, but not long before my arrival this gentlemanly arrangement had broken down and genuine rivalry had set in. The result of this in our constituency was the complete submergence of the Liberals. Through Don Natalio's able persuasions, the old Liberal landlords were drawn over to the Conservative side, and the Liberal party ceased to be able to provide local *caciques* except in the few cases where one of its influential members had retained his allegiance. This was what had happened in our village, and thus we had real democratic politics instead of the usual paternal dictatorship by the richest man.

The cause of this peculiar state of affairs was that my landlord, Don Fadrique, who had inherited the Liberal *cacique*-ship from his father, had quarrelled violently with his brother-in-law, Don Manuel, the Conservative *cacique*. They were the two richest men in the village and lived one in the upper and the other in the lower *barrio*. Don Fadrique had now retired to Granada, leaving the affairs of his faction in confusion, but there was a sufficient number of his supporters left to produce a real contest at elections. Nothing, of course, could prevent Don Natalio's being elected by a huge majority to the Cortes, but it was the seats on the municipal council that interested the people of Yegen, and some Liberals were always returned for them. Not that this word 'Liberal' was ever used or even understood. The two parties were known simply as 'we' and 'they', or after the names of the *caciques*. That was because no one thought in terms of national parties, but solely in those of local ones.

A few weeks before my arrival at Yegen a quarrel that was

partly concerned with politics had led to a great tragedy. There was a man in the upper *barrio* whose name was Don Aquilino. He was ambitious and had set his mind on succeeding Don Fadrique as the Liberal *cacique*, but land was necessary to any-one who aspired to such a position, and he had very little. This lack of acres rankled all the more because his grandparents had been, by the standards of the village, considerable landowners. He should have inherited half of what they left, but after their death there had been a lawsuit in which political influence – or so he believed – had played a part, and most of the property had gone to his cousin Don Manuel. He therefore felt a pas-sionate hatred for his cousin, and to pay him out began to bring one lawsuit after another against him. He always lost – that was a foregone conclusion – but Don Manuel had to pay his legal expenses, and his cousin was ready to ruin himself in order to injure his enemy. Besides, his Liberal lawyer, moved by political rancour, charged him half fees.

In Don Manuel's house the hatred against his cousin soon reached fever pitch. With every new lawsuit he saw his corn and his vines and his olives melting away. He stormed and raved, exclaiming as Henry II had done of Becket: 'Is there no one who will rid me of this pestilential man?' And his *encargado* or bailiff, who was also both his foster-brother and his half-brother, took his words to heart. One evening he set out with his knife and lay in wait for his employer's enemy on a solitary path that came down the mountain-side in a ravine.

Before long Don Aquilino came along, holding his son, a boy of nine, by the hand. In his other hand he carried an axe. He was in high spirits, and when he saw Don Manuel's man waiting for him he began to taunt him. 'I've just come,' he said, 'from looking at that fine vineyard you have up there. Get ready to lose it, for in a few weeks' time it will be mine.' And he called him by his nickname, Faldones or Long Skirts – a thing which in Spain is very insulting, for nicknames should never be used to a person's face.

The other's reply was to snatch his axe from his hand and give him a blow which almost cut through his neck. The boy, going down on his hands and knees in the brushwood, crept off and gave the alarm. The *juez* set out with a party and arrested the murderer.

Half an hour later Don Manuel, apparently unaware of what had happened, went into the post office, which was kept by Don Aquilino's niece, to buy some stamps. 'They say that Faldones has killed my uncle,' said the woman. 'And about time too,' the *cacique* replied. 'The man was asking for it.' She repeated what he had said to the Liberals' lawyer who came out to make an investigation, and both Don Manuel and his bailiff were thrown into prison.

However, one is not a *cacique* for nothing. The case against the one fell through for lack of evidence, and Faldones, though given a long sentence, was released after three years. But the affair cost a good deal of money as well as remorse and anxiety, and Don Manuel returned to the village a broken man. His enemy's family suffered even more. Don Aquilino's widow sold what was left of her husband's property and moved with her four children to Granada, where she set up a small pension for students. But the pension failed. She and one of her daughters died, while the others – who were too pretty for their situation in life – took up with men and sank by slow degrees to a life of destitution. The son became a chauffeur, but with almost his first fare had the bad luck to run over and kill a day labourer, was put in prison for this, and then, as he had not been insured, left the country to avoid having to support the man's family. By an irony of the law, the motorist is financially responsible for the injury he accidentally causes, but not the deliberate murderer.

The rule of the *caciques* came to an end in 1922 when General Primo de Rivera made himself dictator. Since then they have found few defenders in Spain, though perhaps a system that gave the country peace for fifty years under a parliamentary régime might claim to have some merits. Yet the rapid pardoning of the killer, though due to political influence, was surely not unreasonable. Neither he nor his instigator was a bad or violent man, and both certainly regretted what had happened. They had acted under great provocation and in a passion. In fact, almost all serious crimes in Spain have been of this sort: the premeditated murder, the stealthy poisoning of wife or husband or rich but too-healthy aunt, is not a thing that accords with the Spanish temperament. When in the late twenties Barcelona produced a trunk murder, it was felt that at last the Catalans had justified their claim to be, in the full sense of that word, Europeans.

This tragic story shows how in the Spain of those days politics and litigation were intertwined, each one leading inevitably to the other, with the lawyers in the nearest town abetting both. They were the vices of a frugal peasant society with an obsessionary greed for land, and took the place of the gambling and drinking of the Andalusian cities. Another and more ordinary example of this mania is provided by Cecilio. He was a well-to-do peasant farmer with a lean body, glittering eyes, and a large hooked nose. By a mixture of hard work, parsimony, and political intrigue he and his family were slowly rising in the social scale. Two more generations and they might hope to send a son to the university who would come back, set up as a lawyer and be addressed by the title of Don. His wife Asunción was a fit partner in these schemes. She had married off her two skinny daughters to peasant farmers who were a shade better off than themselves, and with her long yellow face and black head-handkerchief and mincing conversation she was always the acme of decorum. As is common in Spain, where a feudal feeling has lingered on from remote times – for feudality is the natural response to social insecurity – she had a patron in a certain Doña Matilde, an old maid who had once been a nun. From this she drew, or thought she drew, prestige: one of her daughters slept in the old lady's house, and her husband gave advice in the management of her land. There was between them that continual exchange of presents – eggs, fruit, chickens, vegetables – which makes such a pleasant feature of life in Spanish villages.

But it was Cecilio who was the acknowledged genius of the family. Hawk-beaked like an Armenian or a Kurd, with crafty, feverish eyes, he was a sort of malign Micawber, restlessly optimistic and engrossed in perpetual plots and plans for making money. Alternately in the municipal council or conspiring against it, he had a reputation for undermining the side he was on and selling himself to the other one. How many illustrious Yegenese governments he had toppled down in the course of the past twenty years I cannot say, but no one trusted him. Besides, he had a rancorous disposition. Although as a rule he kept clear of the law himself, he was very fond of working up grievances among simple-minded villagers against people who had offended him, and then urging them to bring lawsuits. The case lost, he would persuade them to appeal, till both sides were ruined. The lawyers of Ugíjar, our nearest town, therefore made much of him: he brought them business, while their flatteries bolstered up his self-esteem and encouraged him in his intrigues. However, he had one grave weakness: he was a drunkard. When he rode down to town on his mule, the odds were that he would come reeling back late at night without that little wad of notes that he had carried down in his belt. Things at length reached such a point that in spite of all his cunning plans he was beginning to lose money, and then a lucky thing happened. He caught a chill and died. His family put on the deepest mourning, Asunción's nose turned a point sharper and thinner than before, but they were all secretly relieved.

My close acquaintance with this family was due to my friendship with their eldest son, Paco. He was a thin, bony youth, not very robust in health and in appearance much like his father. In character, however, he was different, for he was pleasant to deal with and had his mother's prudence. His intimacy with the odd Englishman who lived in Don Fadrique's house gave him the same prestige that she derived from her friendship with the old nun. But perhaps prestige is not entirely the word. Spaniards are serviceable people who like to be mixed up in their neighbours' affairs: any enlargement of their field of activity that combines pleasure with a little self-interest is welcome to them. At all events, he became for many years my friend and counseller and, when the occasion demanded, boon companion. Together we visited the fairs of the neighbouring villages, made journeys to the Marquesado, which lies north across the cordillera, to buy oats, or went partridge shooting. He fell into the habit of calling in for a few minutes every day, and I got pleasure in his quiet wit and Andalusian *discreción*.

One of my principal amusements lay in giving dances. There are no sleepy little villages in Andalusia and, except in August when the men were out threshing all night, there were dances in one house or another every week. Those I gave were popular, because my house was a large one. All I had to do was to buy a bottle of anis and a packet of tobacco and arrange for a lutist and a couple of guitarists to come in. Invitations would go out to a few families, and then, as the music struck up and those inviting, reiterating chords floated through the air, the girls, accompanied by their mothers or married sisters, would begin to arrive. No one could be excluded, the front door had to stand ajar, so that before long perhaps a hundred people would have pushed their way in. In the granary, which I had converted into a sitting-room, there was scarcely room to move. Round and round shuffled the stiff couples, their faces set and expressionless, as wooden and solemn as if they had been in church, while the lutes and the guitars, their players leaning caressingly over them, wove their spells in the air – music that was always saying the same thing, music that was always beginning with fresh insistence again. In between the dances there were songs. A *zagal* or shepherd-boy would sit on a low chair and lean his forehead on his hands. The guitars would strike up and suddenly a high piercing voice would shoot out like a jet of water, like a cry of astonishment or despair, would maintain itself floating in a succession of burbles and trills to fade out gradually in a low wail. Such is the famous *cante jondo* or *cante andaluz*, so much more moving when sung by illiterate country people than by music-hall professionals.

But where were the old Andalusian dances, the *fandangos* and *sevillanas* and *malagueñas*? Within the last dozen years they had become disreputable. Every woman who had reached the age of thirty-five could dance them, but none would do so in front of others. Historians, if such backwaters interest them, will note that the second decade of the twentieth century marked a wholesale destruction of peasant arts and customs in Southern Europe. German dyes replaced mineral ones in pottery; local costumes, folk customs, country dances vanished. Uniformity came in. The roads built for the motorists put an end to the autochthonous life of the villages, and with that to the remnants of a culture that went back to classical times. Only the church with its pagan ritual remained.

No; for there were still, for a few years longer, the gipsies. In Spain they were the true conservatives. Their dress was the dress of fifty years before, their music and dances – with one or two exceptions – were those that had once been played and danced by every Spaniard. What distinguishes their arts from those of *gachés* or non-gipsies is their sense of humour, often their sheer silliness, which except in moments of great grief or passion turns everything into a joke. Thus, though they keep the old tunes, the only words they can fit into them are a patter of obscenities. We had two families of gipsies settled in our village: one a basket-maker and his wife – quiet people – and the other an oldish man, Federo, who sported fierce black moustaches and kept a forge. His son, Ramón, a very ugly fellow, helped him, and with him lived Ramón's wife, Matilde, two grown-up daughters, and a boy. Like most gipsies, they appeared to live in abject poverty. Their only household possessions were a large frying-pan, an iron tripod, and a couple of stones for chairs, and at night they all dossed down together on a heap of straw. But their poverty was deceptive: they did not really do so badly, and when they had a little extra money they spent it on a *juerga* – that is, on a binge.

There was an amusing story told about Federo. He had been several times married and had always been noted for his jealousy of his wives. On the occasion of his last marriage there had been a young priest in the village who, being fresh from the seminary and on that account full of missionary zeal, had set his heart on persuading the young gipsy woman to come to church. Federo, for whom such motives were un-intelligible, got it into his head that he was trying to seduce her. He therefore went to confession and with many wild mouthings and groans, such as gipsies can always put on, poured out a story of how some years before he had murdered a priest who had made advances to one of his wives. The padre absolved him, but was so intimidated by what he had heard that he never spoke to a female member of his family again. When Federo was drunk he used to tell, or rather act, this story with great gusto.

His daughter-in-law Matilde often came round and sat in my kitchen. She was a gentle but lively young woman, flimsily pretty in the delicate-boned *gitana* way, whose tragedy was that she had no children. She talked freely about herself and her family, yet under her screen of words one felt the gipsy reserve and concealment. Cold as ice where anyone but her ugly husband was concerned, her common coin of conversation was a flow of obscenities uttered with a bright engaging smile. Sometimes in the evening she would bring her whole family. I would produce drinks and they would dance and sing. Her husband's performance was ghoulishly comic and macabre, and as he leaped about with wild capers and crack-ings of the fingers he would turn his eyeballs so that only the whites showed. The women danced *sevillanas*, while Federo, after putting down three or four *copillas*, would sing a *soleá* about death and its sorrows in the most melancholy tone.

On almost every fine night of the year, if one went up on to the roof to look at the weather, one would hear the notes of a guitar. This came either from a dance in the lower *barrio* or from the young men making their *rondas* or rounds. They would get together in twos or threes, stop opposite the houses of the girls they fancied, and play a tune. The one whose girl was being serenaded would then sing a *copla* or four-lined verse in her honour, and if she was pleased by his attention she would get up and show herself at the window. But if the girl had jilted him he would sing a verse full of insults. Something of the same sort happened on Midsummer's Eve. The young men would decorate their girls' houses during the night with branches, flowers, and bunches of cherries, but if they quarrelled with them they would put up thorns and nettles.

Love affairs were of course, when work was over, the principal occupation. Every young man wanted or professed to want to sleep with his *novia*, but none of them could, because the girls knew that if they consented to do this their chance of marriage would be done for. They therefore played with the men a teasing angler's game, and only those who had money behind them could be sure of a catch. As it happened, nearly all the pretty girls in our village were poor, so that the state of love was usually long drawn out and tense. The young men whose families had land would take up with one of them, but as soon as the time came for settling down their parents would fix up a match with one of the rich ugly ones. The other girls had therefore to work hard if they were to overrule the parents and secure their men, while the heiresses – those, that is, who could expect a hundred pounds' worth of land for their dowry – could afford to sit back and wait, though consumed with envy at the temporary success of their rivals.

If one kept one's eyes open one could learn a great deal at a dance. For all its formality and sobriety it was as full of hidden drama as a Chelsea party. There was the tension given by jealousy, the hostility, felt in the air, of those girls and young men who had not come because the pressure of other girls and men kept them away. New quarrels were started, new

c

friendships begun, and there was always a row of sharp eyes to scrutinize each glance and movement. The following day would be spent in comparing notes and reckoning up the changes that had taken place.

During the latter period of my life at Yegen I used to see a good deal of a family known as the Rats. They were rather a special lot. Father Rat was a shepherd – a simple man with a noble head and dignified manner. Dressed in less ragged clothes, one would have taken him for a grandee, but in his own family he counted for little because he had no talent. Mother Rat, who looked like a toad, was a witch, and therefore extremely knowing, while her two sons were notable guitar players. I was more attracted by the girls. The elder of these, Isabel – pronounced 'Saber' – was a quick-witted young woman with a lively style of singing, while the younger, Ana, had a snaky, contortionist's body which went into perpendicular ripples when she danced. She was half a gipsy, for Mother Rat had generously seen to it that all her children should have different fathers. It is the usual fate of shepherds – those sailors of the wavy sierras, condemned to long absences from their families – that their wives should be unfaithful to them.

I do not remember how my interest in the Rats began, but one day Paco and I decided to take up with the two girls. He chose Isabel and I Ana, and our joint courtship began. From the first it was a harassing business, full of false gleams of hope and sudden disappointments, for though the girls – who drew prestige from our attentions – responded in public, the moment we were alone with them they turned a cold shoulder. We soon realized that they were using us to raise their stock and create jealousy among youths of their own kind, but we also discovered that by courting them we too were creating useful flutters among other young women. I find it strange that Stendhal, who had so much to say on the strategy of love, should never have described the sham courtship, carried on by two people to create an amorous publicity around them. In general there is no better way of making a group of girls interested in one than to make love openly to the most forward and dashing among them.

Paco at first seemed to have a certain success with Isabel. She was *muy salada*, noted for her wit, and he was quick in reply. His courtship therefore took the form of long duels of repartee, so full of obscure metaphors, cappings of proverbs, and local references that I could scarcely follow it. But Ana had a mulish mind, and her only public response to me would be a few rippling movements such as a cobra might make to an incompetent flute player. I soon therefore got tired of her.

Before this happened, however, I was put through a test which I will describe. High up on the mountain Mother Rat spent the spring months in a little stone hut that stood beside a stream of water and a solitary poplar tree. Here she made sheep's-milk cheeses and lived on these and on the luscious black cherries which grew wild above the chestnut zone, with for more solid fare loaves of yellow maize bread, which one of her daughters baked and took up to her twice a week. I used sometimes to pass this way on my daily walks, and when I did she would offer me a refreshment of new curds spread out on a mulberry leaf and a handful of cherries. I ate them, but on my telling my servant Maria what I had done she fell into a great fright. The old Rat, she said, was a dangerous witch, and the mildest thing she would give me would be a love potion which would deliver me over body and soul to her daughter. When I laughed at this she called in Paco and Asunción, who both assured me that I was in grave danger. Since the men of the village invariably scoffed at stories of witchcraft as old women's nonsense, I was a good deal surprised at Paco's remonstrances till I realized that this scepticism was merely a manly pretence and that they believed everything that the women did.

For the old Mother Rat, it seemed, was the principal witch in the village, the one most deeply versed in the necromantic arts. It was she who had been the chief partner of the miller as he flew so lightly through the air above the house-tops. More-over she was the guardian of a treasure of silver and gold left behind by the Moors and buried near her cot on the mountain-side. Who knows what use she might not make of a person who came under her enchantments?

'But was she,' I inquired of Maria, 'a *hechicera*, white witch, or a *bruja*, black one?'

Before replying Maria drew me away from the chimney, and looking at me very steadily as though to impress me with the importance of what she was going to say:

'She is one of those you last mentioned,' she answered.

However, it would appear that I am not susceptible to Mediterranean spells and enchantments, for nothing unusual happened to me. Mother Rat's love potions produced no more effect than Maria's had done.

One after another the days, the weeks, the months passed. What with reading, walking, and mixing in village life I was never at a loose end. I attribute this in great part to the gaiety and vitality of the peasant community among whom I had made my home. This small self-sufficing world had something of the zest for life and also of the sense of measure and balance of the ancient Greeks. When I read in Plato how they had regarded their cities and political constitutions as works of art and had attributed to them not so much moral qualities as aesthetic ones, I thought I understood why this village, which was no smaller than many of the self-governing republics of the Aegean, proved so satisfying. It was just the right size, had just the right amount of irrigated land distributed in the most suitable way, just the proper degree of isolation and strength of tradition to draw out the lively and human quali-ties of its inhabitants as far as they could go. A larger or a less isolated community would have left the peasant orbit, which allowed it to be self-sufficing, and become merged in the life of the modern nation. Yegen kept its idiosyncrasy.

Its physical situation, too, stimulated the imagination. Four thousand feet above the sea, on a gradual mountain slope running with water, ribbed with grey rock, green with poplars and corn and every sort of fruit tree, it stood bunched together like a colony of swallows' nests above the vacancy. Looking down from one of its flat roof-tops, one saw far below the slope steepening into precipitous red gorges that fell to a maze of sandy watercourses or *ramblas*. It was not a valley that the eye plunged into, though it was bounded by mountains: it was a basin scoured out and riddled with valleys.

The general impression that the place gave was of being at a great elevation above the rest of the world. There was an isolation, a silence, broken only by the noises of the village and by the burble of running water – a feeling of air surrounding one, of fields of air washing one that I have never come across anywhere else. Mountains and clouds were the chief constituents. Twenty miles away, across the great gulf of space, rose a flat-topped mountain, the Sierra de Gádor, bare, blue or yellow ochre, treeless, waterless, and covering some four hundred square miles of ground. In winter a few shepherds fed their flocks on it and on All Souls' Eve burned bonfires to keep away the evil spirits. Many years before the miners had come, sour-faced lonely men, burrowing for lead and copper in the shale face. Then a family of gipsies had taken up their abode there, stolen children from the neighbouring villages, bled them and drunk their blood. Since those days the mountain had been haunted. To the right of it there lay a gap through which one caught a brief view of the sea, and after that, still farther to the right, came the coast range, the Sierra la Contraviesa, ribbed and smooth and folded as though it were a heap of crumpled velvet. It ended in another great rock mountain, the Sierra de Lújar, which stands above Órgiva.

The clouds were curious. All through the rainless summer months a pile of white cumulus – flat-bottomed, snowy-domed, with curving baroque flanges – stood over the Sierra de Gádor. It threw a dark patch, like the shadow of an immense hat, over the grey triassic rocks, but no rain ever came

from it. Then in winter there were the clouds that I called por-
poises or whales. They stood quite still all day in ones or twos
above the village and when evening came turned to gold or
blood red. They were, it would seem, high clouds fixed and
held there by waves of moist sea air rising to surmount the
great sierra. English clouds form seascapes or castlescapes and
change continually. The clouds of the Alpujarra had individual
existences and lived in the same place for weeks at a time.

But the strangest and most delectable quality of the climate
of Yegen was its windlessness. The air was almost all the year
round quite still. Even in summer, when a strong sea wind
blows day and night at lower elevations, it was only between
midnight and dawn that the smallest ripple stirred the poplar
trees. The harvesters had to do their winnowing by night with
the aid of lanterns. There was a single exception to this. Once
a year, usually in January or February, a long flat line of grey
cloud would appear above the cordillera. This was the signal
for everyone in the fields to hurry home. Very soon, in gusts
at first, then in one prolonged tremendous thrust as though a
dam of air had broken above the mountain tops, the north
wind would pour down. With hurricane force it rushed along
the mountain-side, carrying away branches as it went, causing
the houses to shake and tremble and making such a roaring in
the chimney that one could scarcely hear oneself speak. It was
impossible to light a fire, although the air had turned an icy
cold. One could not go out in the streets, because of the danger from falling slats. Once, breaking into the stable below, it
lifted up the floor of the granary where I sat and sent a whirl of
air coursing round the room. But it was beautiful to look at.
From the windows – for except on hands and knees it was not
advisable to go on to the roof – one saw against the thin blue
sky light flakes of snow blown in long horizontal lines from
the reservoirs on the mountain summits and frenzied olive
trees, their grey underleaf showing, tugging and straining to
escape. Then one went to bed. There was nothing else to be
done when the tiger wind blew, and there was anyhow the

assurance that within twenty-four hours it would have ceased as suddenly as it began.

Other vivid occasions were the days of rain. We lay close to what may be called a rainshed. In Almeria, which has a semi-desert climate, it only rains with an east wind. In Granada, where the annual fall is heavy, the water comes from the west. We lay near the end of the Granada region. In huge spongy masses, above us and below us, the purple clouds would be driven along from the west. For days the rain would fall, the roads be washed away, the bridges slide and break, and then the mists would clear and we would see below us at various altitudes a congeries of clouds of different shapes and formations, some dense and heavy, some mere whisps of mist, like fish and water-weed seen as the mud clears in a pond. But the first rains after a dry period were an anxiety. Wherever the pigeons had scratched on the roof, the water would pour through, and I would have to go up in the middle of the night with a torch of esparto grass and stamp clay into the holes. Then, as I looked round me through the black downpour, I would see other torches on other roofs, and by their light other figures stamping.

CHAPTER SIX

THE VILLAGE CALENDAR

*

THE calendar of a South European village is made up by the seasonal work on the land and by the rites and festivals that correspond to it. In my village this calendar was a particularly full one because, since the winters were relatively mild and water for irrigation abundant, a great variety of crops was grown. The year began with olive picking and, as this was mainly a woman's task, the olive groves were invaded by gay parties of matrons and girls, wearing white head-handkerchiefs and brightly coloured dresses and accompanied by younger children. The girls climbed the trees, and if any man approached too close there would be screams and a scuttle to descend, because none of them wore drawers. The olives were collected in striped rugs laid out on the ground, then tipped into panniers and carried off to an oil mill. Here a donkey, revolving in semi-darkness in the low confined space, pulled a cone-shaped stone that crushed the olives and released a stream of oil into the vats.

While the women were busy in this way the men were pruning the vines and fruit trees, after which came the planting of the onions and garlic (the two principal cash crops) and the hoeing of the corn. Then early in May the cutting of the barley and soon after the wheat began on the coast. Gradually it spread up the mountain-side, reaching our village in July (every three hundred feet of altitude makes a difference of four days), but on the high mountain farms not starting before September. The crop was cut with a short curved sickle. The reaper seized in his left hand a bunch of stalks and severed them with his right a little below the ear. They were then collected in panniers and carried off on donkey-back to the threshing-floor. If there was a moon the barley would be reaped and collected by night, since, if it gets too dry, the grain falls out.

In August, when all the corn has been cut, came the *parva*, as it was called here, or threshing. This was the culminating moment of the year, the true harvest. The unthreshed corn, or *mies*, was spread out on the circular paved threshing-floors that were dotted about on the mountain-side, generally on some rocky bluff which would catch the wind. Two mules were harnessed to the *tabla*, a small plank of wood armed with iron or quartzite teeth, and a man balancing on it held the reins. Another man stood by and brandished a long whip, and the mules cantered round and round. As soon as they were tired another pair took their place. All day long these circuses revolved on the mountain-side, the drivers leaning back mutely on their reins like charioteers, the mules' coats glistening with sweat and the man with the whip breaking into an occasional shout. Then, as darkness fell, preparations for the winnowing would begin. A group of men and women would assemble on the threshing-floor, a lantern would be lit, someone would strum on a guitar. Unexpectedly a voice would rise into the night, would hang for a few seconds in the air, and then fade back into the silence again. From the poplar trees close by the trill of a nightingale answered it.

And now the wind had begun to blow. At first it came in little puffs, then it died down, then it came on again. Whenever it seemed strong enough, one or two men would take their long wooden forks of ash or *almez* (the lotus or nettle tree) and begin tossing up the ears. This went on at intervals all night. The wind blew most steadily towards sunrise, and often I would come out of my room, where I had sat up reading, and climb the slope to watch the work going on. The great trough of mountains below would fill, as from a tank of water, with rippling light, the shadows would turn violet, then lavender, would become thin and float away, while, as I

approached the threshing-floor, I would see the chaff stream-
ing out like a white cloak in the breeze and the heavy grain
falling, as the gold coins fell on Danaë, on to the heap below.
Then without clouds or veils the sun's disc appeared above
the Sierra de Gádor and began to mount rapidly. The sleeping
figures rose and stretched themselves: the men took a pull at
their wine-skins, the women packed their baskets of provisions and returned home. Within half an hour they would be
out again at the streamside washing clothes.

Late spring and early summer were the busiest seasons. The
beans, whose flowers scented the air at Easter, had to be
picked and the potatoes planted. At the same time, tomatoes,
pimentoes, egg-plants, french beans, melons, watermelons
had to be sown. Then came the cutting of the wheat and a
quick ploughing and replanting with Indian corn, the collection of lentils, chick peas, and vetches, followed by the great
celebration of the *parva*. Almost at once the grapes, which
were grown on trellises and irrigated, were picked and trodden in the wine vats, and all the other fruits of the autumn
garnered. Tomatoes, pimentoes, and figs were spread out on
mats on the rooftops and dried, chestnuts were brought in,
onions, garlic, and potatoes dug up and either sold or stored.
The husking of the maize or Indian corn had a ritual. A group
of young men and girls would sit in a circle in the *azotea*, or
open attic, with a jug of wine and a plate of cakes or roasted
chestnuts beside them, and whenever a girl turned up a cob
that had red grains she would strike all the young men lightly
on the forehead with her knife: when it was a young man who
turned one up, he would embrace in turn all the girls. By
'embracing' was meant putting one's arm round someone's
shoulder and patting them. It never meant kissing. This was
such a serious operation that some very proper girls would not
allow their young men to kiss them before they were married.

My village was almost self-supporting. The poorer families
ate nothing that was not grown in the parish, except fresh fish
(which was brought up on mule-back from the coast in a

night's journey) and dried cod. Cotton materials, earthenware, ironmongery, and cheap trinkets reached us from the towns, but the villagers wove and dyed their own woollen fabrics, their blankets of cotton-rag, and their silk handkerchiefs and bedcovers. In other words, the economy of an Alpujarran village had scarcely changed since medieval times. And the instruments of husbandry were of an even greater antiquity. Our plough was closely modelled on the Roman plough, while a slightly different form with an upright handle, which was in use on the coast and through the greater part of Andalusia, was the same as that shown on Greek vases. No doubt this was the primitive plough of the whole Mediterranean region. Equally ancient was the threshing board or sled – both Amos and Isaiah allude to it – and as for our sickle, it was identical in form with those found in Bronze Age tombs near Almeria. Yet our system of agriculture must not be written off as backward. Towards 1930 a few petrol-driven winnowing machines were introduced and found useful, but so perfectly suited were the other implements to the local conditions that I doubt whether it would be possible to improve on them. Since at this time I was reading Virgil and working my way through the twelve volumes of Frazer's *Golden Bough* and the Old Testament, I got a special pleasure from these archaic survivals.

Spring was, as in most countries, the best season. It began on the coast in February or March, and then spread like a stain of green up the mountain-side, reaching the village in April. The fig leaves and the mulberry leaves opened, the wheat and the barley shot up a little more every night, the sticky poplar buds unwrapped and displayed their thin, silky sails. The swallows arrived and began to build their nests, and before long one heard the cuckoo and the nightingale. Above the village the whole mountain was breaking into life. Those families who had plots of land there moved up to their *cortijos* – rough stone-built cabins built under the chestnut trees – and the making of cheeses began. Shouts, songs, brays of asses,

cockcrows, bleating of sheep and goats resounded everywhere.

Far up the Mecina valley, two or three hours' walk away,
there was a scattered ilex wood – all that remained of the *monte*
or oak forest that had once covered the slope above the chestnut zone. A little beyond this Don Fadrique had his farm, with
about seventy head of cattle, a flock of goats, and a few sheep.
I used sometimes to go there on the excuse of botanizing;
columbines, gentians, saxifrages, scillas lined the stream, and
one could bathe in the icy snow water. Here lived Juan el
Mudo, so called because his father had been dumb, a tall
athletic man who was married to the buxom Araceli, Doña
Lucía's last maid, running the farm on a sharecropper's lease
and maintaining through his wife's influence an intimate feudal relationship with his master. Most of the land was pasture,
but they sowed some rye and reaped it at the end of August.
Don Fadrique kept a room here for himself, and when I
wished for a change from village life I used to go and stay in it.
I then discovered that there is nothing like a spell of monotony and deprivation from books for renewing the faculties.
By day the solitude and emptiness of the mountain valley ate
into my mind: I searched for flowers, I found a dipper's nest
under a waterfall, I watched the falcons and eagles that circled
overhead, and then I came back in the evening to sit by the
log fire with the silent Juan, the gentle, bearded Felipe, clad in
rags, and a couple of wild, speechless shepherd boys. When
after a few days of this I returned to the village, I felt that I was
entering a metropolis.

These shepherd boys, or rather goat-herds, deserve some
description. They were often strikingly good-looking, with
long snaky locks of hair falling over their necks, and olive
complexions, but they had grown up in the isolation of the
mountain farms or watching their flocks of goats in the *secanos*,
and so had almost lost the power of speech. When spoken to
they answered in a sing-song voice that was difficult to understand and loud enough to carry from one hill-top to another.

Listening to them, it seemed to me as though in all Mediterranean lands there was one common speech for goat-herds and that a youth from the Spanish sierras would be able to make himself understood in the mountains of Sicily or Albania. On the rare occasions when they came down to the village they were shy and hid themselves away, but sooner or later, since their beauty made them attractive to the girls, they would find themselves married. Then their purgatory began, for their wives were invariably unfaithful to them. If they were tough, they beat them, but more often they were gentle, defenceless creatures, and then, as if in self-excuse, they developed their powers of speech and became good conversationalists. Such was Felipe, whose wife Victoriana had a dozen lovers, among them her employer. He had a face like Christ, a character as weak as water, and was the only person in that remote *cortijo* one could converse with.

Some of his stories were about wolves. He maintained that if one met a single wolf and looked it steadily in the face it would run away, but that if there were two of them there was nothing for it but to wave a stick and shout and hope for the best. To shoot at them with a sling provoked them. However, he had not been brave enough to test his theory, for on the only occasion when he had seen a wolf he had scrambled up a live-oak, in case, as he remarked, there might be another in the offing. The wolf had then slunk away. Lately, however, there had not been any wolves. The cutting of the *monte* had discouraged them, and none had been seen for some years. The last one had jumped over the wall of the corral in the middle of the night and eaten the sheep-dog but left the flock alone. Today, however, they are back again. The police regulation forbidding anyone to carry firearms has given them a free ticket, and last year (1953) two of them came down to the very edge of the village and broke into a sheepfold, killing every one of the sheep.

The agricultural events of the year were celebrated, as I have said, with appropriate rituals. The first of these was the

carnival. The young people dressed up, put on masks, and
organized a procession. Among the various Moors, giants,
and other figures of fancy who walked or were carried past,
there was always a litter in which two young men, one of
them dressed as a girl, pretended to make love to one another
with obscene words and gestures. This seemed to me to bear
out Frazer's view that the carnival is derived from the Roman
Saturnalia. Afterwards people lit small fires on their rooftops
and toasted popcorn, and in the evening there were dances.
The last day was celebrated by a torchlight procession in which
a stuffed fox-skin (or failing this a rabbit-skin) was carried in
triumph round the village and buried in front of the church,
with mock religious ceremonies and a sermon. This rite presumably represented the burial of the old year.

The Easter ceremonies had a peculiar vividness. From the
morning of Palm Sunday a silence fell on the village and lasted
till the end of the week. During this time no one shouted or
sang, and the sound of the pestle and mortar, that gay prelude
to every Andalusian meal, ceased to be heard. Then on the
night of Holy Thursday the figure of the Crucified Christ was
borne in slow procession with torches and candles as far as the
stone calvary that stands among the olive trees a little below
the village. At every halt a low, sad *copla* was sung. On the
following evening there was a yet more lugubrious procession, when his dead body was carried in silence in a glass
coffin to the same place and then brought back to the church
to be interred. That night a group of old women bearing
esparto torches would walk, as in a *via crucis*, round the outside of the church, moaning and singing *saetas* (not in that
flamenco or debased gipsy style that is the fashion for *saetas*
today, but in the purer *cante andaluz* of Granada), while
within the building the candles of the *capilla ardiente* burned
round the tomb. Then at ten o'clock on Saturday morning, as
the priest was saying mass, the Gloria bell was rung as a sign
that the Resurrection had taken place, and the holy water for
the year was blessed. People carried back glasses of it from

the church to sprinkle on their houses to keep away the evil spirits.

The fast was now ended, but the final scene of the drama had yet to be played. At daybreak on Easter Sunday the young men got the church key from the sacristan, took out the figure of the Risen Christ, and carried it to the square at the lower end of the village. He was represented as a young man in a green dress and, as if to associate him with Adonis and Osiris and all the other man-gods who had died in order that the corn might spring again and the sap rise yet once more in the stems, he was crowned with leaves; a bunch of flowers was placed in his right hand and a sheaf of barley in his left. He was set up on a platform in the humble square with its low unplastered houses, and the villagers – especially the poorer families – collected round with cries of *Viva, viva el Señor*. Then at nine o'clock the priest opened the doors of the church. The alcalde and all the principal persons of the village were waiting and when the Virgin was carried out in her green, star-spangled dress they fell into line behind her and formed a procession. This was the dramatic moment of the Easter ceremonies, which even the simplest of the shepherd boys understood, for the Virgin had found the grave open and missed her son, and was sallying out to seek for him. With slow steps, in complete silence, the procession moved down the uneven street, the stiff green-robed figure swaying from side to side till it came to the entrance to the square. The little enclosure was filled with people. Every window was crammed with women's faces, and the low roof-tops were lined by men who made a long ragged fringe as of cranes or storks against the sky. As soon as the figure of the Virgin arrived in front of that of Christ, she curtsied to him three times: the priest stepped forward to sprinkle him with holy water and incense him, and she was brought up tottering to the edge of the platform on which he stood. Then, when she was only a couple of feet away, his arms, which moved on strings, were raised in a jerky movement to touch her shoulders. This was the signal for the silence to break. The drummer, a tall, lank youth who stood in a corner of the square, raised his hands above his head, and with contorted face brought them down on his drum. Every voice shouted *Viva la Purísima, Viva el Señor*, trumpets blew, boys beat on sheets of tin, and the men on the rooftops let off rockets and fired their shot-guns. To reload them through the muzzle took much waving of arms and ramrods, and their sudden, nervous gestures carried one out of Europe into Africa.

And now the procession, bearing both the reeling Mother and her Son, had re-formed and was returning at the same snail's pace to the church. The drum beat, the trumpets blew, the women broke out into singing. It was not a litany they sang but one of those four-lined verses known as *coplas*, of which everyone knew by heart a large number. The boys' voices, high and piercing, rose above all the others. More rockets hissed into the sky, more guns were let off, till at length among loud huzzas the procession, bearing the two solemn marionette-like figures, re-entered the church.

That afternoon the youth of the village collected round the swings. The young men had spent the previous night erecting them in the streets in front of their girls' houses. They were different from English children's swings, for, instead of a seat, a plank was suspended lengthwise from two ropes and a man and a girl took their places at each end of it. Every evening for a fortnight or more, the swinging went on to the accompaniment of a special swinging song and only people of marriageable age were allowed to take part, because this was a rite to make the crops, which had just been renewed by the death and resurrection of the God, put on strength and grow.

The next festival came on St Mark's day, which falls on the twenty-fifth of April. For the Spanish peasant St Mark is not the author of the Synoptic Gospels, fountain-head with Q of the narratives of St Matthew and St Luke and the subject of many learned works by Tübingen professors, but the patron saint of bulls and of all grazing animals. It is on his day, therefore, that they are brought to be blessed. A procession was formed behind his wooden image, everyone leading his cow or goat or mule or donkey, each with a bunch of flowers tied to its horn or ear, and the shepherds and goat-herds driving their herds in front of them. In this manner the whole animal population was brought through the narrow streets to the church square, where the priest, turning round, blessed and incensed them. As soon as this had been done, small bracelet-shaped rolls of bread known as *roscos* were distributed, one for each person and animal. They were the gift of a confraternity whose members drew lots each year as to which of them was to provide the flour and make them. After being blessed by the priest, they were hung on the horns of the cows and goats and over the ears of the donkeys and the procession resumed its march through the lower *barrio*. Other *roscos* were handed round to friends and relatives, to whom they were believed to bring luck, and at the end of the day each of the animals was given a piece. In our village, with its steep, crooked streets, no sight was more picturesque or pagan-seeming than this procession of many sorts of animals, decorated with flowers and led by their owners – old men, women, and children.

May Day had no place in our calendar, but on the third of May fell the day of the Cross – *la Cruz de Mayo*. This is a great occasion in many parts of Spain, when the children set up little crosses in the streets, decorate them with flowers, and waylay passers-by for pennies, but in our village we spent it in killing the Devil. Parties of young people set off for the fields, ate and drank under the olive trees, and thus fortified went in search of the Universal Enemy. They found him in the form of a tall plant of wood spurge, which has the reputation of being poisonous to animals, and having selected their specimen they tore it up by the roots, tied a rope to it, and dragged it round the country and through the streets with shouts of triumph. When they had grown tired of this, they attached it firmly to a tree and left it. Meanwhile the houses would be decorated with branches and flowers, homespun silk hangings would be taken out of the chests in which they were stored, and an altar set up in the principal room with a wooden cross on it. In the evening there would be dancing and drinking in front of it. The Day of the Cross was, of course, a substitute devised by the Church to take the place of May Day, with its pagan associations. Originally the ceremony celebrated the death and resurrection of the tree spirit, just as Easter celebrated that of the corn.

The next occasion observed by the village was Midsummer Day. On the evening before it, the young men decorated the doorways of their girls with branches and sang serenades, and early on the following morning the girls would go to the spring, dip their faces and hands in the water, and sing songs. In the afternoon they put on their gayest kerchiefs and went in a body with the young men to eat the wild cherries that grew high up on the mountain-side. Then came the feast of the Assumption, in August, when they made up parties to eat figs in the *secanos*, and in September the birthday of the Virgin sent them again to the fields to eat melons.

All these festivals that I have described were associated with the growth of plants and trees, the collection of fruits, and the fertility of cattle. A Christian veneer had been given them, but they were much older than Christianity. Easter alone super-imposed on the vegetation ritual a deeper significance, for the drama that was played out then was a sign that not only the corn but man too would rise again. On that week Christ and the Virgin transcended Adonis and Demeter. But our other rites were pagan and, since the essence of paganism is gaiety, they mostly ended in eating and drinking and in excursions to the fields which were in fact courting parties. So little tolerance did the village show for sad things that, while All Saints was made the occasion for a dance with much drinking of wine and toasting of chestnuts, All Souls, the feast of the dead, was passed over, except that a *candil* or oil-lamp was kept lit all night for every deceased member of the family. No visits were made to the cemetery, as in other parts of Spain, no wreaths deposited on the tombs. The living village alone was real, and the dead were not long remembered.

The last festival of the year was Christmas. Everyone went to the *misa del gallo*, or midnight mass, and then stayed quietly at home. It was the solstice. The only special feature was the appearance of that disagreeable noise-making instrument, the *zambomba*. This consists of a piece of rabbit-skin or goat-skin drawn tightly across the mouth of a broken flowerpot or drainpipe: a stick is inserted through the skin and, after the hand has been wetted, is pushed up and down, so that it gives out a half-squeaking, half-moaning sound. The sexual significance is obvious, and no doubt it was originally intended as a magical rite to give strength to the declining sun. In Yegen it was chiefly the young men who performed upon it and, when girls were present, they did so with a conscious gusto, and among much tittering and laughter. In the towns it has now sunk to being a children's toy.

In Cádiar and in some villages, however, Christmas was celebrated in the old style, by dances that took place after dark on the roofs of the houses. Fires were lit, parties of young men and girls toasted chestnuts and played on the *zambomba* and then danced holding hands in a circle and singing. These dances were known as the *remelinos* or *remolinos* – that is, whirling dances. On the Feast of the Purification of the Virgin on 2 February, they held them again and ate *rosetas* or popcorn, and this continued every fine night till Carnival. Once upon a time these dances had been held at Yegen too, but they had been given up because it was said that they damaged the roofs.

The weeks around Christmas were always fine and sunny. The violets were in flower on the banks, and a little white plant like candytuft. The usual windless calm prevailed. Then the women went out to the olive groves to pick the last crop of the year, and before long the cold winds and rain that marked our two months' winter began. In the streets below my house the ivy came into flower, and every time I went out in the sunshine I smelt it.

CHAPTER SEVEN

SCHOOL AND CHURCH

*

MY village had little use for the benefits provided by science. It could have had electric lighting, like both Válor and Mecina, but through its indifference and apathy it failed to secure the services of the electricity company. It could also have had the telephone, but when the wires were brought along the road it turned down the offer of a call-box. What, it not unreasonably asked, was the point of wasting good money on a thing which no one would use?

Schooling, however, was a different matter. The state insisted that there must be a school, and so a school there was and even a schoolmistress to teach in it. Here those children who did not have to help their parents by herding goats assembled each morning to imbibe the rudiments of a modern education. They learned by heart a number of hymns and prayers, picked up some acquaintance with the Bible stories, and by way of arithmetic mastered the cardinal numbers up to twenty, or if they were clever up to a hundred. They also acquired the names of the four major continents and twelve principal nations, and learned to recognize the most important animals, beginning with the domestic cow and dog and ending with the camel, the elephant, and the lion. A coloured oleograph that hung on the wall facilitated this by showing a cow being milked into a pail, a hunter attended by his dog, a camel posing against a palm tree, and a lion devouring an antelope.

But what of reading and writing? In theory these formed part of the curriculum, but only, I think, as ideals to which the serious and talented child should be encouraged to aspire. In practice they were out of reach. It was rare for any boy or girl in these schools to get beyond a recognition of a few of the letters. Indeed, among the older generation in the village there were scarcely more than three or four, other than those who carried Don or Doña before their names, who could read a line. The young men learned because when they went on military service the sergeants put them through a course of reading and writing. Yet what did this 'analphabetism', so much decried by journalists and politicians, matter? In our village there was nothing to read, so that even those who had learned soon forgot again, because there were so few occasions for putting their knowledge into practice.

But were there, it will be asked, no newspapers? Yes, indeed, for the doctor and the shopkeeper subscribed to one. It was a Granada sheet that they took, giving the local news but rarely mentioning anything that happened outside Spain, unless it was the state of the Pope's health or the celebration of a religious service at the Vatican. I found therefore that when I first arrived in the village and spoke of the war in which I had been taking part, many people supposed I had been fighting the Moors. Were not all wars against the Moors? Was not that false and treacherous race the universal enemy? As for England and France, they were just vague terms expressing the remote, indeterminate countries from which those more or less familiar figures, the wandering Englishman and Frenchman, had come. The Englishman had the reputation of being interested in mines and of having remarkable sexual powers. The Frenchman was a person who in a fight could always be defeated hands down by a Spaniard. But nothing was known of their countries. When after some years in the village I returned to England on a short visit, my servant Maria lamented with a vague wave of the arm that I should have to travel through all that *Europa de Francia*, 'all that Europe of France'. The phrase expressed for her a wilderness of uncertainty and sadness.

But what did this ignorance matter? The people of Yegen knew everything that was needed for their prosperity and happiness, and would have gained nothing but a few pedantic phrases from knowing more. Within the limits prescribed by their way of living, they were sensible and civilized and managed their affairs better than do many larger communities. As Spanish peasants and Catholics they had behind them an old tradition, and it often happened that the less school education they had had, the more vivid their conversation was. For then they had to speak of what they really knew.

Sometimes, however, when they thought they knew something they could be very tiresome. Thus I now and then came across elderly people who had got it into their heads that the Spaniard speaks Spanish, the Englishman English, and the Frenchman French in the same way in which each kind of bird has its own call-note or song. So when they were told that I was English they assumed that I could speak only my own language, and even when they heard me speak Spanish they would shut their ears and declare: 'I can't understand what that man is saying.' Since there is no obstinacy so great as Spanish obstinacy, they would persist in their attitude although, when I kept within the limits of a peasant's vocabulary, I spoke fluently and with a fair accent. Like Don Eduardo, they would fight to the last rather than give up one of their cherished opinions.

Of the hundred or so hamlets and villages that stud the fertile Alpujarra – counting from Padul and Motril on the west to Ohanes and Dalías on the east – Yegen was, to employ the expressive Spanish phrase, one of the most abandoned. This was not due to its size – for its population ranged round a thousand – nor to its poverty – for nearly everyone had some land – but to the fact that it contained so few people of means. In this it contrasted with both Válor and Mecina Bombarón, two aristocratic villages, which had possessed this character even in Moorish times. Although they were not so large or important as were several other places in the region, they had each of them in turn, during the rising of 1568, provided the insurgents with a king.

Yegen, I imagine, had always been a village where humble

families predominated. Its Berber settlers had built it in four distinct *barrios*, two of them at some distance from the others, with the mosque standing, where the church does today, on the only available piece of flat ground. When the Christians arrived they abandoned the outlying *barrios* and took up their residence in the two that still exist just above and below the church. They moved in with twenty-one families, or say a hundred people. The descendants of these multiplied till the 1880s, when the phylloxera plague destroyed the vines and started an emigration to South America which halved the population. Since then it had risen again, and in 1920 was probably as high as the land would support.

The abandoned character of our village showed itself among other things in its attitude to religion. No Liberal doctrines of anti-clericalism had reached it, much less the anarchist ideas that prevailed in Almeria or the socialist ones of Granada, but it took its religious life with a certain carelessness and insouciance. A considerable number of the villagers never confessed or went to mass, yet everyone joined enthusiastically in the various services and processions that were held in honour of the Virgin. On most Sunday evenings of the year there would be a procession of the rosary through the streets after dark. The major-domos would carry a banner, a string of men and boys would follow with candles, and the people whose houses lay on the route would put lights in their windows. If anyone cared to contribute a few pesetas, the procession would stop opposite his house and sing a *copla*, or verse, to the Virgin. The *novenas* too in the church were well attended. They took place after dark. The musicians – a guitar player and a lutist – sat with the choir of boys in the wooden gallery and, in addition to the litanies and hymns, *coplas* were sung in the traditional *cante jondo*. The more pious families, including some who rarely went to mass, would also set up altars in their houses and invite their friends in to eat sweet cakes and join them in reciting the rosary. After funerals a *novena* would be said every night for nine nights in succession in the house of the deceased, and all the friends and relations would attend.

Where one noticed the laxity was at Sunday-morning mass. The women, wearing either black mantillas or head-handkerchiefs, would fill up the front of the church, while at the back stood a group of men who talked and chatted and occasionally even smoked during the service. Other men stood in the square outside and considered that they had heard mass if they merely looked through the door and crossed themselves when they heard the bell for the elevation. Dogs ran in and out, children played, and there was a general atmosphere of indifference. When later I did some research into the religious history of Spain during the sixteenth century, I came across many contemporary complaints of the same sort of behaviour. Indeed in this age of faith customs were by modern standards extremely irreverent, for people danced in the church, ate and drank in it, laughed and talked and took snuff during the services, and met in the chapels to flirt and carry on their love affairs. This suggested that Yegen had not, in the religious indifference of the nineteenth century, reverted to laxity but on the contrary had preserved the careless manners, founded on familiarity and confidence, of an earlier period. In this respect also it was medieval.

When I first arrived in the village the priest was a certain Don Horacio. He was a very ugly man, but with the sort of ugliness that puts one at ease because it seems natural and human. He wore a large gold plate in his mouth that flashed and glittered when he smiled, and he was so genial and sympathetic that all the women loved him. People said that this was because he had spent many years in Cuba, where the priests mix more with the people than they do in Spain and stand less on their dignity. In any case he was most obliging to me, and when I told him that I was a Protestant he brushed this aside as a matter of small importance and, patting me on the back, said: 'Never mind that, man. You come to mass and you'll find it will do you no harm. But a word in your ear.

Don't tell people that you are a Protestant. The country people are very ignorant and won't understand.' On inquiring, I found that some of them thought that Protestants were people with tails.

After this Don Horacio used to send the sacristan for me as soon as the bell had ceased tolling. When I arrived at the church he would conduct me himself to the bishop's throne that stood beside the altar. It was an embarrassing situation. Below me was a sea of women's faces, women's eyes, women's hands, the latter busy with all those complicated crossings – *santiguadas* and *persignadas* – that are peculiar to Andalusia. Their owners sat cross-legged on separate mats on the ground, their faces framed in black lace mantillas and head-handkerchiefs and all their pairs of dark, expressionless eyes directed on me. At the back of the building stood the men, not more than a dozen or so, and looking as unconcerned as possible.

'Don't trouble to kneel or cross yourself,' said Don Horacio, stepping across to me in the middle of the service when he noticed my embarrassment. 'Just sit and make yourself at ease.'

After mass came the sermon. The priest mounted the pulpit and gave out the text. The subject he preached on was the abnegation of Joseph and the loving care he took of his wife and small child. Immediately all the women's faces switched from myself to him and, as they bent their necks back and looked up at him with wide-open mouths and eyes, I was reminded of a nest of young birds waiting for their parents to feed them. But most of the men at the back, who might well have profited by the sermon, had walked out.

After the service was over Don Horacio took my arm and asked me how I had liked it. I muttered an appreciation. 'That's right, man. That's right. I see you're half a Catholic already. Our religion is a very good one and in any case the only one suited to Spaniards.'

Although all the women adored Don Horacio, there was never a breath of scandal about him until he fell in love with

the doctor's sister-in-law. He used to go to the doctor's house
every evening to play snap. This doctor was a short, disagreeable man who talked so thickly that he could hardly be
understood, was extremely near-sighted, and looked like a
boar. Although he had never been in the army, he was known
as *el Capitán* out of compliment to his father, who had been a
comandante or major. He was married to a woman so gigantic-
ally fat – *como un colchón de grande*, as big round as a mattress, as
my Maria put it – that she never went out of doors because her
feet would not support her on the cobbles. Like most fat
women she was amiable, and she had an unmarried sister,
Cándida, who was almost as fat as herself and, though not very
young, just as placid and good-natured.

Boredom and propinquity, as the proverb says, make bad
counsellors. Before long Don Horacio was falling hopelessly
in love and finding his love returned. The two agreed to run
away together. A car had been ordered and was waiting on the
road, and a note was sent to tell her it was there – but it was
the doctor who opened it. Don Horacio left the village a few
weeks later and never returned.

Some years after this I met him in a café at Granada. With his
charming gold-flash smile, he put his arm round my shoulder
and sat down beside me and then, without waiting a moment,
began to ask me how Doña Cándida was. When I answered
'fairly well', he launched out into praise of her beauty, her
sweetness, her angelic grace and goodness of heart, as though
she were the prize of all the rich and many-villaged Alpujarra.

'What a waste!' he exclaimed. 'What a waste! There she is
pining away with no one to appreciate her!'

For some time after Don Horacio's disgrace we were without a priest. A coarse, bull-faced man, who lived in something
worse than sin with the fat, greasy woman who kept the
posada at Mecina, came over every Sunday on a mule and said
mass. These remote villages were the dumping grounds for
bad specimens. Then the bishop tried sending an incumbent,
but the women, who wanted Don Horacio back, collected on

the road and drove him away with stones. Years passed before
Don Indalecio arrived. He was an old man of great girth and
height, but such a martyr to gout that he rarely got out of bed.
People said, I do not know with what truth, that he drank. He
brought with him his housekeeper, who was familiarly known
as Pan Blanco or White Bread. The story that lay behind this
nickname was that many years before, when Pan Blanco was
a girl in a village close by, she had been engaged to be married.
A few days before the ceremony she had gone to Don Indalecio, who was then young too, for confession. He fell in love
with her and set his heart on getting her at any price. Going to
his mother, therefore, he told her that he would kill himself if
he could not have her, so she agreed to speak to the girl.

'Maria,' she said, 'I have a question to ask you. Would you
rather eat black bread all your life or white bread?'

'White bread,' said the girl.

'I'm glad to see you so sensible,' the priest's mother replied.
'All you have to do now is to give up this marriage, which is
quite beneath you anyway, and to take service as housekeeper
with my son.'

She did so. The enraged lover drew his revolver and shot at
the priest, missing his large black body but hitting his little
finger. As a proof of the truth of the story it was pointed out
that the finger was gone.

The last time I saw this priest was in January 1933. After
being bed-ridden for months, he had dragged himself up for
the village festival. The rockets were going off, the guns being
fired, the cheering growing louder. Heaving from side to side
on its gilded platform, the Infant Jesus, who was our patron,
approached. And there came Don Indalecio, stumbling along
between the rows of candles, his huge black frame towering
above the crowd, with one hand resting heavily on Pan
Blanco's shoulder.

I must not however give the impression that all the priests
of the Alpujarra were inclined to women. Don Prudencio of
Válor and Don Domingo of Ugíjar were both model priests,

and so no doubt were many others. Yet, in justification of those who were not, it must be explained that there is a reason why sacerdotal celibacy has not always been so strictly observed in Spain as in northern countries. Originally, if Marcel Bloch is right, this rule came in because of the popular belief that a mass celebrated by a priest whose body had been soiled by sexual intercourse lacked efficacy; but the Spaniards did not accept this, because they had been influenced by the Moslem view that sex was not spiritually polluting. Thus their priests resisted the injunctions of the Lateran Council, and down to the first half of the sixteenth century it was almost the rule for them to keep a *barragana* or concubine, with whom they went through a civil marriage and who had to wear a special dress. Although there was a tightening up of discipline after the Council of Trent, popular rhymes show that down to the beginning of the nineteenth century the priest who kept a concubine was not uncommon. For who cared? The Spanish villager admires a priest who is chaste if in other ways he seems to him a good man, but he does not think the worse of one who shows that he has natural instincts. Under the taunts of the Protestants, fear of scandal has today become a mania in the Catholic Church, but in fact in any unhypocritical country such as Spain the priest's influence depends not upon his being free from this or that sin, but on his general character. Thus if in the days I am speaking of Andalusian village priests sometimes kept a 'housekeeper', they did not necessarily lose caste by doing so. On the contrary, there were many people who felt easier in their minds when their daughters went to confession.

More shocking to my mind than the private failings of our priests was the condition of the cemetery. When the wall round it fell down, no money could be found for repairing it, and for years the dogs used to climb in, dig up the recently interred bodies (the soil was too shallow to allow of deep burial), and eat them. Cemeteries are usually well looked after in Spain, and this Oriental disregard is something I have never heard of anywhere else.

We had no priest, we had no doctor – for Don José had given up his practice – and our yearly festival was the poorest in the neighbourhood. Yegen was a village without prestige. From Laujar and Berja to Padul and Órgiva, people used to ask me why I had gone to live in such an outlandish place when I could have chosen the civilized delights and amenities of the larger pueblos. But there was one thing that they could not deny us: we possessed the finest spring of water in the country. It was also the best to taste. Spaniards, as has often been remarked, prize water not only for its abundance but for its flavour. Their palate, which is often so crude in its appreciation of wine, is of an exquisite sensibility when it is confronted with the natural liquid. The taste of ours, coming straight as it did from deep underground fissures and caverns in the strato-crystalline rocks where it had lain maturing after trickling down from the snow, was particularly satisfying, and muleteers from Almeria, where the water is either saline or else tasteless and flat, used to become eloquent when they discoursed on the pleasure of drinking a glass of it.

It welled up from under a rock at the top of the village into a deep pool. When one stood by the edge of this and looked down, one saw the pebbles gleaming on the bottom among fragments of coloured pottery and the long green water-weeds waving gently and ceaselessly to and fro as if in a trance. Tufts of maidenhair fern, rooted in the rock wall, hung over it, and so much calmness and stillness seemed extraordinary when contrasted with the powerful stream that overflowed from it and fell directly through the flat roof of a mill on to the wheel below.

These water-mills of the Andalusian mountain villages are of a peculiar and very primitive sort, for their wheels are set horizontally instead of vertically and are turned by the oblique percussion of the water against a number of upright vanes, arranged like spokes. The grindstone runs on the same axis in a lower chamber, which greatly simplifies the mechanism and makes them economical both of space and cost. The entire mill is contained in a small two-storeyed building, set up against the steep hillside and not more than twelve feet in height. They are thought to have made their first appearance in Spain in Visigothic or Byzantine times (between A.D. 550 and 620 most of Andalusia was ruled by a Greek exarch), for though the Romans had heard of the water-mill – there is a description of one in Vitruvius – their innate conservatism and the abundant supplies of slave-labour available to them made them prefer the old method of grinding in local querns. From Galicia this type of mill was carried to Ireland, where the Vikings found it and spread it to Norway and the islands off Scotland, while in Spain the industrious Arabs and Berbers took it up and extended its use.

The water of our *nacimiento* or spring worked two mills, while another outlet fed the *fuente* or drinking fountain and was piped to my house. Then, below the upper mill and issuing from it, ran the stream in which the women washed clothes. Laundering was the great occupation of the female half of the population, and many married women practised it on every fine day in the year. They enjoyed the vigorous exercise, the splash of the water, the open air, and above all the gossip which made the *lavadero* in a special way their club. Any man who ventured to linger by it would be subjected to the fire of their critical remarks and driven off. They also liked to get their sons' and husbands' shirts spotlessly clean and white, even if they wore them out in the process. Since hot water was never used, this meant that they had to be washed and rinsed on several days in succession and in the intervals put out to steep in shallow basins in the sunlight. When clothes got very dirty, a lye was made of wood ash and they were rubbed and scrubbed and left to soak in that. A paste was also made of this, though without olive oil or caustic soda, and taken down in a basin to the *lavadero*. The poor used this instead of soap, which was still thought of as a luxury. Indeed, until some twenty years before, even the rich had used it only for their personal toilet.

The Spanish villager's notion of cleanliness was to change

his underclothes frequently. He washed his body at the most twice a year. Occasionally, in the heat of summer, boys or young men would bathe in one of the two large *balsas* or irrigation ponds dug on the mountain-side some way above the village, but the water was cold and therefore thought to be dangerous. It was regarded as extraordinary that I liked to bathe in them, and the women of the *cortijos*, when they saw me about to undress, would be put to a great struggle between their curiosity and their modesty. However, at some distance below the village, on the mule path to Yátor, there was a spring which fed a tiny pool of lukewarm water known as the women's bath. Tradition said that it had been used for that purpose in Moorish times. Now and then a party of girls, bursting with a sense of their immense daring, would visit it, and one by one, with many shrieks and giggles, take off their top garments and sit in the water. A goat-herd, spying from behind a bush at the top of the crest, would see a figure, clad in a long thick coarse slip, and get a thrill from the knowledge that she had nothing on underneath it. If the girls noticed him, they would set up a loud chattering and shrieking like a chapel of starlings, and the youth would creep shamefacedly away. For in those days every woman, however poor, wore cotton stockings, and a chance glimpse of a naked foot or ankle would be enough to make the male heart beat faster. Then suddenly towards 1927 the fashion for very short skirts came in, and it became common, when a girl stooped or knelt to wash a floor, to see exposed to view a piece of white thigh. No one commented or criticized.

The prostitute was, of course, an institution: every village had two or three. A very plain one who lived a few doors from my house was called Máxima. When I first remember her she was an unmarried woman in her early thirties who was already weighed down, as the Spaniards put it, with five or six children. It was the need of providing for these that led her to adopt a mercenary attitude to love-making. She was a good-natured creature who never used bad language or displayed *mala doctrina*, as Don Eduardo called it, and for that reason she was treated with kindness by the most respectable families, to whose houses she would go to scrub floors and, when short of food, to beg for bread or olive oil. Such alms were given to those who needed them. Another woman who followed this trade was la Prisca, or the Peach. She was a clever, well-spoken woman who knew how to read and write and was therefore much in demand for inditing love letters, into which she generally slipped something bawdy or suggestive. She had a professional manner, a quick on-the-spot air, as of a hospital nurse who is conscious of her own proficiency and usefulness, and this and her complete lack of humility caused her to be kept at a distance by the respectable women who dealt so freely with Máxima. She had two children, both daughters, who grew up to be beauties: when their father, who had been her first lover, tried to put them in an orphanage, she carried them off to Granada, where in time they became the mistresses of two well-to-do shopkeepers. Máxima's daughters, on the other hand, went into service and married day-labourers.

It was a mark of the humble style in which our village lived that the charge la Prisca made to the muleteers who came up from the coast and were her best customers was one peseta, rising, with a present of food, to two for the whole night. Máxima, whose customers were the young men of the village, was even more moderate in her terms. Since these lads rarely had any ready money, they paid in kind, and the usual fee would be two eggs, or when the hens were not laying, one egg. I set down these particulars of village economy in the hopes that one day some learned historian, turning up this book on the shelves of a library in New Zealand or Tierra del Fuego, may find them helpful in filling the gaps of his knowledge on the change of price levels during the last decades of a vanished civilization. Perhaps, if he stops to think, he will come to the conclusion that the cobalt bombs destroyed a pattern of living which, though rude and primitive, was worth preserving.

CHAPTER EIGHT

THE FAIR AT UGÍJAR

*

OUR nearest town was Ugíjar – a difficult name to pronounce till one got accustomed to it. It could be reached in about two and a half hours by following the road, but it was quicker as well as pleasanter to take the short cut. One began by dropping steeply down below the village till one came to the Puente, a natural bridge that took one from the green-terraced, olive-shady mountain slope to the bare, rolling *secanos* on the other side. It was a dramatic place, this bridge or neck of land, for it was less than six feet in width and on either side of it the red sandstone cliffs fell sheer for perhaps three hundred feet to one or other of the ravine-beds below.

These *secanos* – the word means dry, that is, unirrigated land – require a few words of explanation. It would seem that in Quaternary times the great hollow between the Sierra Nevada and the coastal range was filled by a lake. The rains washed down the triassic limestone and the red marls that covered the lower slopes of these mountains and deposited them on the lake bottom to the depth of several hundred feet. Then the lake drained away to the sea, and the force of the torrents cut deep channels in its dry bed. But the soil of this bed – a fine argillaceous sand – had the peculiarity that, though readily broken up by water, its grains were so cohesive that they could permit the formation of perpendicular and even overhanging cliffs many hundreds of feet in height. Thus the ravines that were cut out in what was now a rolling, down-like country had steep and precipitous sides which were often fretted and channelled by the water into curious shapes. At the eastern extremity of the Alpujarra, as one climbs up from Almeria to the plateau of Guadix, there are cliffs of this

formation that rise sheer for a thousand feet and the view
looking northwards from Alhama of their intricate red and
ochre and lavender faces, carved into cones and ravines and
completely devoid of vegetation, is one of the most fantastic
and nightmarish in Europe.

Landscapes such as these are indistinguishable except to the
geologist's eye from those given by thick strata of loess. This
is the term applied to deposits of wind-blown sand that have
been laid down on the edge of deserts, but early geologists
extended it to cover alluvial deposits of the sort I have been
describing as well. Now loess is one of the history-making
formations. In some countries, where the rainfall is insuffi-
cient, it creates bad lands, but it is also responsible for the
fertility of the Mississippi valley and for the strange, lunar
landscapes of Honan, where Chinese civilization first developed. According to Marcel Granet, the natural bridges which
this formation leaves between two heads of ravines (caused by
their having eaten their way back between cliffs until they
almost join) played an important part in delimiting the feudal
kingdoms that preceded the Empire and in furnishing them
with ready-made defences. The nature of the soil also stimulated the civilizing practice of irrigation because, while loess
in its natural state is barren, when broken up and watered it is
particularly fertile. This is equally true of the alluvial soil of the
rolling country below Yegen. Here it is barren because there
is no water available for it, but farther to the east it is terraced
and irrigated and planted with trellises of vines. These give the
hard-skinned Almeria grape which is exported to England.

The track to Ugíjar lies along one of the spurs of this down-
like country. When the sun was shining the walk was airy and
gay. The soil was bare except for scattered plants of lavender
or genista and wiry tufts of esparto grass, but occasionally one
came on a caper plant hanging over a bank or dangling down
the precipitous side of a gully. Its huge pink-and-white
flowers, bristling with stamens and anthers, and its tough
thorny leaves were nourished by roots that burrowed for

moisture more than a hundred feet into the parched earth. These hills had once been planted with vines (not the kind grown on trellises, which require irrigation, but those which produce wine grapes), but the phylloxera plague had killed them, and now they grew nothing. A small wood of umbrella pines showed that they had once been forested.

One descended all the time and finally crossed two broad *ramblas* or water-courses. These *ramblas* were the natural routes for pack animals, and until the present network of motor roads was built, the line of mules or donkeys moving slowly up a sandy river-bed was one of the characteristic sights of the country and a symbol of its timeless Oriental mode of life. Ugíjar lay just beyond the second *rambla* – as it often had water in it, they called it *río*, or river – a small, neat, compact place, surrounded by orange groves. It had tiled roofs, half a dozen shops, and a market square as well as a *parador* or coaching-inn from which at daybreak every morning a motor-bus left for Almeria, nearly sixty miles away. In October it held a *feria* or cattle market in its river-bed. The town interested me for another reason. It is almost certainly the Odysseia, later latinized to Ulyssea, which is mentioned by Strabo as having had a temple to Athene, in which Ulysses on one of his voyages had nailed up his shields and ships' beaks. Although it lies some twenty miles from the sea across rough country, there was an excellent reason for his having left his memorial here (supposing, that is, that he had included Spain in his travels), for the sand in the river-bed is rich in gold. In 1929 a French company was so impressed by the quantity they found that they proposed to set up an artificial lake close by and pan it out. Perhaps some trace of this legend is to be found in the fact that the Virgin of Ugíjar, la Virgen de los Martirios, is a cult figure for the fishermen of the coast. In storms they invoke her almost as frequently as they do the Virgen del Mar of Almeria and Adra.

When I sat reading in my library I could hear the cries of the hawkers and *arrieros* in the steep, narrow street outside, and I used to try and guess what they sold. One of them was an old man who carried roughly printed broadsheets in ballad verse relating to famous crimes that had been committed – how a father had stabbed his daughter to the heart because he believed that she had a lover, but discovered too late that the person he had seen was her brother just returned from America; how a man had killed his brother-in-law with an axe for seducing his wife; and so forth. There were also pietistic ballads which described remarkable miracles: a brigand was converted by a wooden cross that shed tears and spoke to him; a dead man was restored to life after being sprinkled with holy water, confessed where he had hidden the goods he had stolen, and then sank back into the grave again. They were the last relics of the legends that had been taken up with such success by the dramatists of the seventeenth century. On one occasion two men came round with a full-grown wolf which they had cribbed up in a wooden cage, strapped to the back of a mule. It seems that in the Sierra Morena there were men who gained a living by capturing wolf cubs and rearing them. When fully grown they carried them about from village to village, collecting pennies from the people who crowded to see them, and more substantial sums from the shepherds and owners of flocks, to whom they pretended that they had trapped their animal in the vicinity. It was extraordinary to see the beast's indomitableness in captivity: it could scarcely move in its narrow cage, yet when people teased it with straws it drew back its lip and snarled with a frightening ferocity.

One winter's evening Maria came into my room in a state of great excitement. The *títeres*, that is the puppet show, had arrived and was to give a performance. I went out and found that what she called a puppet show was really a troupe of strolling actors. In our village the words 'theatre' and 'actors' were not understood, and so all dramatic representations were known as puppet shows. The play was to be given in a stable. Here I should explain that in Alpujarran villages the ground floors are always used as stables or store-rooms, and the living-

rooms are on the first floor. The stable that had been selected
by the actors was large enough to seat perhaps a hundred
people, and at one end of it a small rickety stage had been
rigged up with boards and trestles. The lighting was provided
by four paraffin lamps, and there was also a curtain. But what
a curtain! Made of some thin cotton material, it dangled help-
lessly from a string and, every time it was to be pulled, a ladder
had to be erected, a small boy had to ascend the ladder and
several knots and fastenings be undone. However, this was a
trifle. By seven o'clock the auditorium was full, and after the
usual long wait that is customary in Spanish theatres, as soon
as the stage manager, who in this case was the leading actor,
had judged by various pokings of his head round the corner of
the curtain that the impatience of the audience had reached its
highest point, the performance began.

There were only three actors – a man, a woman, and a boy.
They did not, to my disappointment, put on a play, but instead
gave a series of short sketches, illustrative of life in the
Asturias or among the middle classes in the capital – feeble
imitations of the feeble *fin de fiestas* of the Madrid stage which
passed completely over the heads of the audience. They were,
of course, in verse, and sandwiched between them were recita-
tions of an elaborately rhetorical kind which few present could
follow. To my surprise one of these was addressed to me – 'the
famous and world-renowned *inglés*, patron of all the arts and
especially of the most noble, the most refined, the most cultured of all, commonly known as the Thespian'. As the performance went on, the shouting and banging on the doors set
up by the youths and small boys outside, who thought they
ought to be admitted without payment, became deafening.
The actors broke off several times in the middle of their dia-
logue to protest at these interruptions and to appeal to the
honour and *caballerosidad* and finally to the shame or *vergüenza*
of the village. 'Is it to be said that this is the sole spot in the
whole of our sacred fatherland where the arts are not
honoured?' But all in vain, since the only people who could

hear them were the audience, sitting there with looks of stoical incomprehension on their faces as though they were in church, till at last, to the regret of nobody, I think, the show came to an end.

That evening I sent an invitation to the actors, requesting the honour of their company at lunch next day. They came. In addition to the three performers of the night before there was a gloomy, cadaverous man with a sallow complexion and a faded black scarf tied in a bow round his collarless neck – the tragedian. He had had an epileptic fit the previous day, and this had prevented the company from putting on the piece they usually gave and obliged them to fall back upon some lighter sketches. The leading lady was also absent: she had been left behind at a village inn a day's journey off in the throes of child-birth. All the actors complained bitterly of the barbarity of our village and of its indifference to the arts. Not only had the shouting and banging on the door made it impossible for them to carry on, but they had had to put up with a donkey in their dressing-room. A donkey! Never, not even among the Hurdes, had such an insult been offered them before. The cultural level to which this village had sunk was really a disgrace to the nation.

After lunch they asked if they might be allowed to give me some better idea of their art. The tragedian took off. Striking an attitude, he recited in a ranting style several almost incomprehensibly bombastic passages. Hamlet's advice to the actors came irresistibly to the mind. The comedian followed, but nothing could have been less comic than his artificial patter, stuffed with recondite allusions. Then the boy took a turn. He really had some talent, but his elders would not let him alone, interrupting him and correcting him at every instant; very soon, one saw, his natural vivacity and imitativeness would be frozen into the others' stilted jargon, so important to acquire because it was the hallmark of 'art'.

As we sat drinking cognac, I asked the tragedian how he had come to take up this profession. He had been a carpenter at Algeciras, he told me, earning a good wage – far better than that which he earned now – but had thrown it up for being an actor. However, in spite of the hardships and ignominies of the player's life, he did not regret the choice he had made. 'A carpenter', he declared, 'may be more highly valued by the populace, but when all is said and done there is a nobility about the arts that compensates for everything.' When they took their leave I accompanied them as far as the road to show them my respect for their profession. Then after some further speech-making they set off, the new leading lady wearing the stage curtain wrapped round her body as a shawl and the tragedian carrying the rest of the properties in a black bundle.

A fortnight later I got an invitation to come and see them act some two leagues away at Cádiar. Seats in the front row had been reserved for me and my party – I need scarcely say that I was not allowed to pay for the tickets – and when we entered the auditorium, which was this time a wine-cellar, the four actors came down with great pomp to receive us. Were we not the people who, more than anyone else in the country round, honoured the arts? But then we were English. It was well known that in the whole world there was no country where the arts were so greatly honoured as in England. I came back feeling that I had made a journey into the *siglo de oro*, for this was very much how the travelling companies of players had lived and behaved in the time of Lope de Vega.

The principal excitements of the year were the village fiestas. Ours, which took place in January, was a poor one, though I did not find it the worse for that. Its cheap little images, its band that played out of tune, its rockets that fizzled and shot up but rarely burst into light, gave it an attractive pathos. But both Mecina and Válor had splendid fiestas with *columpios* or swing-boats, stalls that sold ribbons and headkerchiefs and brooches as well as nougat and caramels, and whole constellations of soaring, golden-tailed rockets. Válor also put on a battle of Christians and Moors, in which a great many guns went off and a great deal of noise was made and usually several people were injured.

The most important occasion in the Alpujarra, however, was the *feria* or cattle-fair of Ugíjar. This came early in October, and was held just outside the town on the dry, stony river-bed. Horses and mules were brought together from all the district round, stalls and drinking booths were built out of green branches, and moustached and whiskered gipsies, wearing stiff Sevillian hats and red-flannel waist-bands, walked about or showed the paces of their animals. The scene was soberly gay: while the horses and mules were trotted up and down, the hoarse voices of the ambulant vendors cried their wares and parties of men and women sat picnicking under the orange trees with a reserved and solemn look on their faces. Below them the pebble river, whose sand held gold, ran smoothly between its poplars and rose-flowered oleanders, while in the background, half-hidden by the shimmering leaves, rose a curtain of smooth red cliffs in which one could see, thirty feet above the ground, a row of square-cut cave dwellings. They were of unknown age, and who knows, I said, if Ulysses had not slept in one of them.

The last day of the *feria* was the feast of the Virgen de los Martirios, the Patroness of Ugíjar. She was a small, squat Virgin with a dark almost black face and a gold-spangled scarlet dress. Her colour made people think that she was a gipsy, and so, as was natural, the gipsies as well as the fishermen of the coast had a special cult for her. There were many of the *gitano* race in these parts. Mairena, just above Ugíjar, was a great centre for them, and so was the neighbouring village of Laroles. These places commanded the entrance to the high pass of La Ragua, which led over the Sierra Nevada to the Marquesado, a region much given to horse-coping. The Alpujarra provided a steady market for mules and donkeys, and the gipsies would bring them across the pass from the fairs of Guadix and Fiñana and sell them. The great fair of Ronda was also important and, when it came on, the roads westwards would be thronged with dark, copper-coloured men wearing stiff-brimmed black hats and coloured handkerchiefs round their necks and driving animals in front of them. They did not stop at the inns. In every village there was a family of their own race, and there they put up.

The procession of the Virgen de los Martirios was an impressive affair. She was brought out of the church among a furious ringing of bells and firing of rockets and shotguns. Thirty men bore her gaily decorated float and her long gold-spangled train, and all the priests of the neighbourhood were in attendance. By ancient custom, every village of the *partido* or administrative district of Ugíjar had the right to carry her for part of the way. The route was marked off into sections, the bearers were marshalled and stood ready, and, as the Virgin arrived at each waiting group, the major-domo who led with his silver-headed staff would call out 'Yegen' or 'Mairena', and the men of that village would take over. Sometimes, however, those who were carrying the Virgin refused to give her up, and then there would be an uproar, and insults and even blows would be exchanged until the major-domo succeeded in imposing his authority. The cortège was a long one: immediately behind the image came the priests, their naturally portly figures swollen out by their full canonicals, then followed the Civil Guard with their leathery faces and creaking uniforms, and finally the municipal authorities of Ugíjar and its subject villages, laughing and chatting, each village with its banner. The tail was made up by the people who had made a vow to walk in it, the women as a rule going shoeless but, to save their modesty, in stockings. When, as the first stars appeared, the procession completed its circle and the Virgin re-entered her sanctuary, all the bells would be set jangling and ringing, rockets would soar up into the sky and salvoes of shots be fired. Then quiet descended. In a moment everybody was in a hurry to get off. The streets would be thronged with red-caparisoned mules, each carrying two or even three people, bent on getting back to their villages as quickly as possible. Some had a three hours' journey or even longer before they could reach their beds.

CHAPTER NINE

MASONS AND ANIMALS

*

In my garden the apricots and the persimmons ripened and there was an orange tree that bore fruit every spring. Yet that did not mean that the winters were mild. Although I only once knew it to snow and cannot remember seeing ice, there was a sharp touch in the air like an underlying shadow, and it turned suddenly cold after sunset. By night the stars sparkled with unnatural brilliance and the distant mountains rose clear above the surrounding dimness. Our village might be on the latitude of Tunis, but it stood at a height of four thousand feet above the sea.

The question of heating the house thus became important. In the kitchen there was an open fireplace, but in my sitting-room, which was also the library, there was only the *mesa camilla*. This classic piece of furniture and the domestic rites accompanying it demand some explanation. Imagine then a circular deal table with a brazier of wood ash or charcoal set under it. Drape over it a red-flannel tablecloth that reaches on every side to the ground, and let three, four, or six persons sit around it with the skirts of this tablecloth, which are split into sections, tucked about them. Let them have short coats or shawls thrown lightly over their backs and let their faces be leaning towards one another – either deep in a game of cards or sewing, or else perfectly still and motionless, merely rippling the silence from time to time by some placid observation. Then you will have a picture of what family life is like during one-half of the year in every town and village of this country.

It has sometimes occurred to me that one of the causes of the decline of Spain in the seventeenth century may have lain in this circular table. The forests were cut down, firewood became scarce, the domestic idea spread, the men's habit of buttoning themselves up in cosy confabulation with their womenfolk – the wife's aunt, her mother, the elder children – instead of stretching their legs by the fire and leaving them to sit cross-legged on cushions in their *estrada*. Round the *mesa camilla* family life grew denser, thicker, more Orientally bourgeois: reading ceased in the prim harem atmosphere and the clubs or cafés – which till recent times were sordid, badly lit places – offered the only outlet and escape. Spain became the classic land of stagnation, the self-immersed Ottoman Empire of the West – a condition from which it did not finally emerge until the present century. The only people to gain were the engaged couples, who, once the young man had been accepted and admitted to the house, could hold hands blissfully for hours at a time under the flannel tablecloth.

A few months' experience of this piece of furniture, which every half-hour had to be stirred and patted, and whatever was done to it gave off toxic fumes, determined me to find some better method of keeping warm. I therefore obtained Don Fadrique's permission to take over for my own use the granary in which he stored his dried peas and grain. This was a long, irregularly shaped room that rose twenty feet above the garden and orchard on thick walls of pisé and looked out over the open country. The mason cut windows to make the most of this view, and built a hooded fireplace that filled the whole of one end. Outside this fireplace I hung a heavy red curtain from wall to wall in order to keep off draughts. In this way I had a room within a room where on the coldest nights four people could sit and have their meal by a good fire.

There was a peculiar beauty about the making of fire in this part of the country. The solid fuel consisted of small oak logs brought down from the mountains, but there was a lighter fuel or kindling of *bolinas* and *piornos*, which were thick matted cushions of dry genista or gorse, as well as of smaller bushes of rosemary, lavender, and cistus. When one put a *piorno* on the fire and held a match to it, a growing, living plant of flame leapt up the chimney and threw its light and heat over the ceiling and walls. The other bushes gave out an aromatic smell, and all of them left a fine white ash on the table and on one's hair and eyelashes as they died down. This was a nuisance, but I could never resist the pleasure of seeing them burn.

This chimney-corner is associated with some of my happiest memories of these years at Yegen. I would come back tired and stiff from a long expedition and, while I washed and changed my clothes, the fire would be lit and a meal brought in. My post would be waiting for me and a copy of the *Nation* – that ancestor of the *New Statesman* – and over my coffee I would read my letters and begin to answer them. The chair I sat in was an old barber's chair which I had bought at Almeria: not elegant, but comfortable, and so perfectly adapted both for reading and for writing that I ended by feeling a genuine affection for it. The fire blazed up as I threw on a *piorno*, and in its flames I saw the faces of my distant friends. In most kinds of happiness there is an element of *añoranza*, or longing for what is absent, because the mind focuses best on those things of which it is deprived.

The chimney in the granary was not the only improvement I made. Some years later I put in a second fireplace at the opposite end of the house. Here there was a small room, known for its triangular shape as the *pañoleta* or kerchief room, which overlooked the village. The windows caught the evening sun, and the view of the grey roofs with all their chimneys smoking and the women standing on them and the white circling pigeons and the drooping olive trees and the scarlet fish-shaped cloud floating motionless above struck a pensive *quattrocentista* note. But quite apart from these alterations, I had to have in a mason for a few days every year. These houses built on the mountain-side were always slipping, and the cracks that were then formed needed to be stopped with plaster. The Spanish word for house repairs or for building of any kind is *obra*, which means simply 'work'. One has an *obra*, one is *de obra*, and this is such a frequent and common and, I may add, inexpensive procedure that the word 'work' is considered sufficient to express it.

The village mason was called José Agustín. He was an elderly man much given to the bottle. Because his wife had left him to work in the cotton mills at Malaga and he had quarrelled with his family, he lived alone with his grown-up son and had his meals in the posada. He was a glum, unsociable person with a raucous voice and very thick eyebrows, and as a mason he suffered from the defect that he could not be depended on. He would promise to start work on a certain day, all the furniture would be moved to the far end of the house, and then he would not turn up. A week later he would appear at six o'clock in the morning with his buckets and ladders and, since he could not be kept waiting a moment, there would be a rush to clear the rooms again before he began knocking the walls about and filling the air with plaster dust. But he was good at his work, and if one was careful always to address him as *Maestro*, or Master, and to ply him with *aguardiente*, or aniseed spirit, he did his job well. Where anything of an artistic sort was needed, such as the building of a chimney-piece with its plaster mouldings or of a decorated bracket in a wall, he shone particularly, for he came of a long line of masons and was proud of his skill.

As he grew older the *maestro* got queer in the head and began to have delusions of grandeur. He would tell me that he had been specially sent for to build the National Palace at the Seville Exhibition, but that he had refused. He wasn't going to put himself out for anyone, not he. Or else that he had been chosen by a committee of architects to add new rooms to the Alhambra in *estilo moro*, Moorish style, but that No, he wasn't having any. 'They can go down on their knees and beg me, but No, I say, *no me da la gana*. I won't, because I don't choose to.' And I really believe that, even had he been offered some important job, he would have refused it, just to show his superiority.

In the end he gave up working and would spend his days drinking in his house or taking long solitary walks by himself. Once I ran into him high up on the mountain, above the tree level, pacing slowly across the stony waste behind a little donkey. His head was sunk on his chest and he was muttering incoherently. He passed me without speaking, sunk in his thoughts of the great architectural schemes which the rulers of the land had entrusted to him but which, No, he would have nothing to do with. His son, who succeeded him as mason, was also a curious-tempered man, much given to the bottle and apt to play unpleasant practical jokes on his clients. He took offence very easily, and when he did so would down tools and go off in the middle of his job, leaving the house in a state of confusion and disorder.

Before José Agustín there had been another mason called Frascillo. He was still alive, an old man with delicate features and a white beard, but now he worked on his own plot of land or as a day-labourer. I had him in sometimes to look after my garden, which he did very badly, because I enjoyed his conversation. He was a clever man who could read and write fluently, and he talked with a particular elegance, enunciating his words very clearly and using a larger vocabulary than was usual in the village. Some of his phrases were both apt and flowery. But there was something strange about him – what the village called *misterioso*. He lived alone with his daughter and never let anyone cross the threshold of his house. Perhaps, since he was a man of refined feelings, he was ashamed of its poverty.

This daughter Paquita was a tall, remarkably pretty girl, but she was subject to fits of madness. When this happened, she became a nymphomaniac. She would leave her house at night and go up to the threshing-floor where the harvesters from the coast were sleeping, and would lie down with them. She also slept with her father. He told people that he had agreed to do this in the hopes that it might cure her of her madness: somewhere he had heard that an incestuous relation acted like a purge and freed the mind from its obsessions. But it did not cure her. What was worse, she had a child that was completely insane and had to be sent to a mental home. Then, after her father's death, she drifted to Granada where she took up with one man after another, entering the asylum during her mad fits and, when they ceased, coming out again. In all Andalusian towns there is a floating population of women of this sort whose only hope for their old age is that they may have a son who will support them. Paquita is still living in Granada – I came across her the other day selling newspapers – but she has no son.

The only other member of her family was a brother called José who was generally known by the family nickname of Pocas Chichas, Little Wits. Here let me say, for the sake of anyone who is interested in these matters, that nearly all Spanish villagers have nicknames that are handed down from father to son. They take the place of surnames, which (except in the case of the gentry) are not generally known and figure only on legal documents and identity cards. The only thing that differentiates them from surnames is that they cannot be used to anyone's face or in his presence. To do this would be to commit an unpardonable breach of manners. It would have been particularly regrettable to have slipped into this mistake with José Pocas Chichas because his nickname was a sore point with him. He was both clever and good-looking yet, as he must have been aware, he was touched with the family complaint of oddity. This came out, among other ways, in a fondness for poetry. One day he returned home from Barcelona, where he had been working in a factory, with a copy of Góngora in his pocket. He brought it to show me, together with some booklets on vegetarianism, for which there was a cult on the Mediterranean seaboard, but I could not make out how much he had got from it. However, it soon turned out that he had literary aspirations. These cases are not uncommon among the working classes in the south of Spain. Andalusians are a people with a natural feeling for art and beauty, and though singing and guitar playing provide an outlet for some, there are others whose inclinations lie towards verse, and they cannot forget that literature and its handmaiden journalism offer great prizes. All provincial journalists in Spain begin as poets. Thus it happened that poor José got it into his head that his escape from the low esteem in which he was held in the village lay in writing articles. He never wrote any, but his belief that he could prevented him from working his little strip of land effectively and condemned him and his wife and children – for in spite of his being looked down upon by the girls, he eventually married – to hopeless poverty. It is still his dream that I can help him to place his unwritten essays.

In addition to the human population of our village, there were the animals. At whatever hour of the day one walked down one of its rough, stony streets, one would hear a shrill voice calling out *Miso, Miso, Misi-ico*. This would come from a woman standing in the doorway of her house and calling her cat. Many of the women devoted a good deal of time every day to this occupation, though the cats never came. They knew well at what hour the fish vendor was likely to pass by with his loaded *capachos*, and then they did not need calling.

It is one of the Englishman's most cherished beliefs that whereas he is devoted to animals and will risk his life any day to save a dog or a cat, or to give a fox a little healthy exercise, the foreigner, and particularly the Spaniard and the Italian, does not like them and often treats them with cruelty. I can only say that it would be easy to make out a case for the exact opposite. Watch a Spanish shepherd with his flock of goats or sheep. They all know his voice, respond to his shouts, and follow him. And he has a name for every one of them. Then contrast this with the way in which these animals are driven along the road in England or with the roughness and clumsiness with which cattle are often handled. Their shepherds and drovers know them, if at all, by their marketable points and not by their individual characters. But the Spaniard respects his animals and shows great patience with them. He is not in a hurry to get back to his tea, so he has plenty of time to give to them.

It is the same thing with poultry. In our utilitarian country they are regarded either as machines for laying eggs or as slabs of immature meat which must be confined in cages so that they can fatten. This idea is distasteful to the Spanish mind, because it is derogatory to the creature's dignity. You may kill an animal or make it work for you, but you cannot deprive it of its dignity as a living creature without losing some of your own. I remember an old and very poor woman who kept a pet hen and who to excuse herself for not putting it in the pot when it ceased to lay eggs used to declare that it was 'very noble'. No one thought this an absurd statement because 'nobility' is the quality in a man that makes him respected, and animals and birds may well have this quality too.

The dog, however, is not the noble animal in Spain that it is in England. The reason for this is that in Spanish villages and working-class streets it gets so much tormented by little boys that it grows up to be cowardly. Then it forfeits respect. Yet the men, in their undemonstrative way, are often as attached to their dogs as the women are to their cats. They do not make a fuss of them, but they admit them as companions. If one sees so many half-starved dogs and cats in Spain, that is simply because the poor do not have enough food to give them. Real love of animals is a feeling that can only develop when a certain standard of living has been attained. But frequent the small shopkeepers in the towns, and one will come across as passionate a devotion to them as can be found anywhere, especially among the old maids and childless couples. Any lukewarmness towards the keeping of pets that one may observe in larger families is due to the fact that Spanish home life is centred on the children, who draw to themselves most of the love and attention that are available. This suggests that the worship of animals on which we English pride ourselves may not be so flattering to our finer feelings as we like to imagine. Of all the European peoples we are the one that cares least about children. Such has been our reputation since Chaucer's time, and such it still is today. We are selfish and like our enjoyments, and we find that pets give less trouble.

There is, however, another side to this question, and I will illustrate it by telling a story. Plácido and Isabel were a young couple with four or five children who lived in great poverty. They owned a few strips of land and a small donkey, with the aid of which Plácido used to supplement his peasant's earnings by collecting and selling brushwood. Then one day the donkey fell and broke its leg. This was a calamity, since they could not afford to buy another, and I went to see if I could help them over it.

I found Isabel, nursing a baby and surrounded by several grubby infants, on the verge of tears.

'There's nothing to be done,' she said. 'Nothing. We'll have to throw the donkey away. It goes to my heart, as it's been brought up with the children and is almost one of the family. Such a good little beast too – it has never been known to show the least malice. The tiniest of our children can play with it. I really think I mind it more on the *animalico*'s account than on ours.'

I asked her what she meant by saying that she would throw it away. 'Oh, just that,' she answered, and on being pressed explained that they would push it down a precipitous slope into the ravine where dead and dying animals were thrown. There it would lie with two or three legs broken till it died or the vultures finished it off.

'But how can you even think of such a thing?' I exclaimed. 'Just imagine what it will suffer. You must kill it first.'

'Oh, we could never do that,' she replied. 'Haven't I said that it has been brought up in our house among the family? Poor little animal, we could never treat it in that way.'

And it turned out that no one in the village ever killed mules or donkeys or cows. Pigs were slaughtered and also kids and lambs, but other animals were either thrown down the ravine or tied to a post till they starved to death. Such was the custom, which was defended on the grounds that no one could kill animals that had been brought up in the house. In this predicament, for I am very fond of donkeys, I approached Federico the smith, and offered him a sum of money to kill it. As a rule gipsies are not squeamish about slaughtering animals and they willingly eat donkey's flesh, which after all is the chief constituent of Spanish sausages; but he felt that the opinion of the village would be against him if he accepted, and therefore refused. All I could do was to make Plácido promise to push the donkey over a real precipice where it would be instantaneously killed, though whether he carried this out I doubt. Village customs had a way of imposing themselves.

The same repugnance to doing the disagreeable but, as we think, humane thing is responsible for the large number of stray cats and dogs in Spanish towns. When people move house and cannot take their pets with them, they let them go in the street to take their chance. Many persons are averse to killing even kittens and puppies, and when our present gardener, a gruff but extremely tender-hearted man, has to dispose of a litter of kittens he cannot eat his dinner afterwards and lies awake half the night. Only the other day a stray cat planted itself on us and, as we did not like it and already had more animals than we could stand, I suggested that the vet should kill it. This led to a protest from our Spanish servants. 'Why not take it into Malaga,' they said, 'and let it loose there? The poor animal may find a home with someone.' My English susceptibilities rose against this, yet after all that is much how, till pensions came in, we treated our old and unwanted people. It is only animals that we do not allow to suffer.

One does, however, come across cases of real brutality. One day while I was at Yegen a dog fell off a roof and lay in the street with its legs broken. The small boys tied a cord to it and dragged it round the village yelping piteously. Their elders watched in silence and did nothing. Now this was not an exceptional event, but a characteristic one. A mysterious change comes over some Spaniards in the presence of death and suffering. These things seem to draw out of them some deep approval, as if their own death-instincts had been unloosed and given vicarious satisfaction. It is not sadism or love of cruelty, but a sort of fascinated absorption in what they regarded as the culminating moment of existence. They unite themselves to it, as the voyeur may do to the spectacle of another person's orgasm. I have seen this attitude displayed on many different occasions in Spanish life, including some of the most important and sacred, and have noted that the prelude to it is often a numbing of the ordinary responses. When, for example, they are put in the position of witnessing some act of which they would normally disapprove, both the wish and the power to intervene are atrophied. This is a feature which struck me very strongly during the early days of the Spanish Civil War. On both sides the murdering was done without official sanction by a very small number of persons, most of whom were under twenty-four, and the majority in whose name it was done maintained a passive attitude. It was very rare for anyone to protest openly. Was this because Spaniards are lacking in moral courage, or because there was all the time some part of their nature, a part to which they could not even privately admit, that took sides with the killing and drew a lugubrious satisfaction from it? Anyhow, as one walked about the streets, one saw the mask of passivity clamped on their faces and numbing them. Napier in his *History of the Peninsular War* observed that though Spaniards have more virtues than other people and fewer vices, it so happens that their virtues are passive and their vices active. This is a view that is worth considering.

Andalusians do not eat cats and dogs even when they are very hungry, but in Estremadura they are regarded as delicacies. A woman from Alcántara who is fond of cats and would never kill one herself, tells me that she had eaten cat stew and that it is tastier than either rabbit or hare. The Estremadurans also eat martens and weasels and foxes, and declare, though I do not believe it, that a fried leg of fox is the best thing imaginable. But then they are a race of cattlemen and hunters, ancestors of the Argentine *gauchos*, and put in the pot whatever the gun brings down. The only animal they bar is the wolf. Gipsies eat frogs, snakes, and lizards, as well as farmyard animals that have died a natural death, while there is a whole village near Jerez which till a few years ago spent its nights hunting the camels that ran wild in the marshes at the mouth of the Guadalquivir. As for birds, they are all eaten in the south of Spain, and the list includes eagles, owls, and hawks. The only ones rejected are sea-gulls, crows, and vultures and the sacred swallow and stork. The saying that runs *Pájaro que vuela, para la cazuela*, 'Bird that flies, for the pot serves', is pretty thoroughly carried out. However, at Yegen, perhaps because there was little real hunger, the small birds were not interfered with. The sportsman was satisfied if he could bag a rabbit or partridge, and perhaps one of those fat thrushes or blackbirds that assembled in late autumn to feed on the olives. The pigeons, which were the property of my landlord and nested in the dovecot on the roof of my house, were rarely touched. Their flesh was little liked, and they were kept solely for their guano.

I have said something about the birds and animals at Yegen, so I will end this chapter with a few words on the silkworms. They were kept on cane trays suspended from the ceiling of clean, well-ventilated rooms or attics, and fed with freshly picked mulberry leaves. They ate so greedily that one could hear the sound of their jaws munching from all over the house. When they were ready to spin, they were given bushes of *bolina*, a cushion-shaped genista much sought after for bakers' ovens, to attach their cocoons to, and after that were covered over with cloths so as to be in the dark. Silkworms are not easy to breed, on account of their extraordinary sensitivity. A slight but sudden change of temperature will make them swell up and sweat a milky substance which after a little kills them, and they cannot endure a bad stench. So great, for example, is their antipathy to the smell of frying fish that a few whiffs of it seeping in from next door will make them turn yellow and die, while they are only a shade less outraged by the smell of pig manure or of human excreta. Loud noises too can be harmful if they occur during the period of spinning, because when they are startled the insects turn their heads sharply and so cut the thread. If, therefore, by any chance a thunderstorm came up in June, a continuous noise had to be maintained by beating rhythmically on a tin tray so that the thunderclaps should pass unnoticed.

Silkworms do well in the Alpujarra, because the light, airy climate suits both them and the mulberry tree off which they feed. Unless the leaf has the exact properties and degree of moisture required, the insects develop an intestinal fungus that kills them. For this reason the villages of the Sierra Nevada have been noted since the eleventh century for their silk production. The custom has been for a certain amount of silk to be spun locally into kerchiefs and bedcovers, but for the best cocoons to be sent on muleback to the factories in Almeria and Granada to be reeled. When, early in the nineteenth century, the last of these factories was closed, the export of silk was interrupted for a time, but in 1869 a French industrialist from Lyon set up a new factory at Ugíjar, which gave employment to a hundred or so people till the invention of artificial silk in the 1920s obliged it to shut down. Quite recently, with the revival of the market for real silk, it has been opened again.

CHAPTER TEN

BELIEFS AND RITUALS

*

I USED to amuse myself by collecting *coplas* or popular songs and by recording in a notebook beliefs and customs of a folklorish kind. Since no picture of Spanish village life can be complete unless it contains some account of these things, I will set down a few of the more striking of them here.

I will begin by saying a little more than I have already done about the *hechiceras* or witches. They were regarded as having a different nature from other human beings, which was passed on, whether they wished it or not, from parents to children. Another name for them was *los lanudos*, or 'the hairy people', and unlike the *brujas* they were classed as Christians, though of a rather dubious and half-hearted kind. Evidently there had at some time been a general whitewashing of the arts of witchcraft, for the *hechiceras* had taken over the flying powers of the *brujas*, or black witches, who no longer existed in our district, without acquiring their malice and venom. No doubt one must give credit for this to the enlightened attitude of the Spanish Inquisition, which treated witches as hysterics and refused to persecute them.

Until the building of the road put an end to their activities, these *hechiceras* and *hechiceros* used to fly about on dark nights and thick misty days, and as they passed one heard the sound of sweet music. Opinions differed as to whether they anointed themselves with fat prepared according to a secret formula, and took off naked from the rooftops, or whether they launched themselves without pharmaceutical aids in short white nightdresses, but it was generally agreed that as they left the earth they pronounced a magical formula. This was the time-honoured one of *Guía, guía, sin Dios y Santa María*, 'Lead,

lead, without God or Holy Mary.' It was also said that they liked to carry babies with them. Indeed, it would appear that they never took part in the gatherings on the threshing-floors unless they were either pregnant or weaning a child, because it was only then that *hechiceros* or male witches were attracted to them. Out on these floors, of course, they danced and made love, and it was said that there was a young man of Trevélez who as a child had been carried off by a witch on one of her flights and who remembered everything that had gone on there. Once when I was staying in that village I tried to look him up, but could find no one who knew anything about him or indeed who had ever heard of witches. This was probably because they were on the defensive. Trevélez, which stands at a height of more than 5,000 feet above the sea and is, I believe, the highest village in Europe, has a great reputation for witchcraft (there is a mathematical relation connecting the number of witches in Spain with the height above sea-level), and it is even said that the famous hams that come from there and which used to be sold at Fortnum and Mason's owe their particular flavour to the spells said over them.

Another opinion on witches' flying came from a very old one-eyed woman called Encarnación, whom many years later my wife employed in dyeing wool for her. A particularly beautiful saffron tint was obtained from a plant known as *torvisco* – its botanical name is *Daphne gnidium* – by boiling it with pomegranate rind and barley straw. But the custom of using home-made dyes had gone out, and there were few people left who knew the secret. This old crone declared that although the pestle and mortar, handed down from generation to generation, was the hallmark of the *hechicera*, it was the reel used in winding wool that they employed in flying. Putting it on their heads, they drew up their skirts over it and then took to the air. In her mother's time it had also been common for a girl who had been initiated into the *hechicera*'s arts to give her young man a drink which turned him into a donkey, after which she mounted him naked, or rather with her skirts

bundled round her head, and so rode about very pleasantly
through the air all night. But these things belonged to the past,
to those happy days when every poplar tree had its vine coiling
round it, when the poor never lacked for oil or bread, because
the wagons did not take the food away to the towns, and if
nowadays one wanted such a drink one would have to get a
doctor's prescription for it.

I was anxious to find out whether the people who were said
to be *hechiceras* believed themselves that they were. One could
not ask them directly, for that would have been impolite. One
had to fish about. The conclusion I came to after a good deal
of roundabout conversation was that none of the women who
were pointed out as being witches had any awareness of possessing occult powers, much less of having at some time been
able to fly. They all thought that the witch was someone else.
This conflicts with Miss Margaret Murray's theory that witchcraft is a deliberate cult, a lineal descendant of the worship of
the pagan gods and a conscious rival to Christianity. But does
this theory have any foundation in fact? Belief in witchcraft
was never stronger than when the pagan gods were openly
worshipped, as anyone may see who reads Apuleius' *Golden Ass*.

We had other superstitions of a more or less interesting
kind. For example, there was the belief, which is common to
the whole of Andalusia, that when a woman has nine male
children in succession, the ninth child has a special grace. This
begins to show itself from the age of about six, and when the
child grows up he will not only be a person of great gifts, but
a lucky one as well. Such people have remarkable powers of
healing. Thus Maria told me that when she was weaning her
daughter she developed a swelling in the breast which stopped
the flow of the milk. She called in one of these ninth sons – he
was then a boy of twelve – and he stroked her breasts three
times a day for three days with his hands. This cured her.

People who are named Maria are also lucky, and are called
in in sickness, and more especially for removing the evil eye.
This is a hazard to which beautiful children are especially

liable. When one of these is 'looked at', the crown of its head falls in and it begins to wither away. The remedy is for the father to go out before sunrise and gather an armful of *torvisco*, which like the wood spurge has the reputation of belonging to the devil. The *torvisco* is wrapped in a cloth, so that the sun shall not shine on it, and a girl, who must be a virgin and have the name Maria, 'weighs' the child in it. That is, she lays the plant in an open basket of esparto, sets the child upon it, and lifts the basket into the air. After this, three women who are called Maria – this time they need not be virgins – come into the room where the child is lying alone, without anyone seeing them. They take it between them in their arms and place it on the floor upon the *torvisco*. This done, the priest is sent for to say a prayer. The rite is concluded by spreading the plant out under the bed: if it dries up, the child will recover, but should it remain moist the child will weaken and die. Belief in the evil eye and in this remedy for it were so universal in Yegen, and indeed in all Andalusia, that my servant told me that she had taken part at least fifty times in these ceremonies during the past fifteen years. The people who cast the spell are old and ill-favoured persons, generally gipsies. .

Men and women who for one reason or another had *gracia*, or grace, were in demand in many sorts of situations. For example, when something was missing and was thought to have been stolen, a form of table-turning was resorted to. Three women, each of whom possessed grace, would take a sieve and hold it horizontally between them by three pairs of fire tongs. The sieve would then turn and as it did so they would ask it questions. 'Did so-and-so take it?' When the name of the thief was mentioned the sieve stopped. This method of divination, or coscinomancy as it is sometimes called, is referred to by the Greek writer Lucian in his essay on a charlatan called Alexander. It was apparently much in favour among the Paphlagonians.

In *The Golden Bough* Frazer speaks of certain charms intended to promote the growth of the vegetation which was known as Gardens of Adonis. In Yegen we had something of the same sort, but diverted (as had also been the case in pagan times) to the purposes of courtship. The plant used in these rites was the sweet basil, whose botanical name is *Ocymum basilium* and whose Spanish is *albahaca*. It is a bushy annual herb with a pale green leaf, an inconspicuous white flower, and a strong and penetrating smell. The Arabs introduced it from India, where it is sacred to Krishna, and it soon became a common pot-herb, symbolizing love and in particular a young woman. Originally, I think, it had a purely sexual meaning attached to it. When Parkinson tells us in his *Paradisus in Sole* that 'gently handled it gives a pleasant smell, but being hardly wrung and bruised it will breed scorpions' he was translating into literal terms a statement that was intended to be metaphorical.

In my village it was the custom for girls to grow this plant in pots, and on Midsummer Day to present one of them to their young man or *novio*. They kept the pots on their balconies, and if a girl had no *novio* the youths who wished to court her would climb up at night, pick a piece of it, and place it behind their ear. On the following day they would walk past her house wearing it in this manner so that she could see them. This was also done with *claveles* or carnations (a plant introduced from Italy in the seventeenth century) and if no one stole a girl's pot-plants she would feel neglected. Another thing that a young man could do was to beg from a girl the white carnation she wore in her hair: if she gave it to him, he offered her a red carnation instead, and they became *novios*. Or else he would ask her to wash for him a clean handkerchief that had a flower stamped or embroidered on it, and if she agreed to do this it was a sign that she accepted him. Thus when in Spanish and Italian Renaissance poetry one finds these and other flowers mentioned – the rose, the mint, the balsam, and (a later arrival) the *alhelí* or stock – one has to bear in mind that they may be there not simply because they are types of beauty, but because they have a place and meaning in the rite of love. One of the things that we have lost today – perhaps we never had it in England – is the sense that all the most important acts in life, and particularly courtship, have their ritual.

We had no *xanas*, or water nymphs, at Yegen as in the north of Spain, but we had the *duende*. This is a domestic elf or sprite who concerns himself with the things of the house, either helping or obstructing, mislaying or finding. At the worst he is a poltergeist and causes people to move to other quarters. But whether anyone in our village really believed in him, I doubt. He has today become too much a figure of speech to have any objective existence, especially as he cannot be seen. However, the word can also be used in a different sense. In Andalusia people say of a person or thing that has some mysterious power attached to it, or rather that can for a brief space of time call on such a power, that it 'has *duende*'. This can be said, for example, of a bullfighter who has just roused a storm of applause by a succession of miraculous passes with the cape. It can also be said of a *flamenco* singer who at a *juerga*, or drinking party, goes so far beyond his ordinary powers that his listeners are transported. The *duende*, that is, is the personification of the dionysiac spirit breaking through into action, and since the country is Spain, in a sombre manner. Thus García Lorca reports a famous gipsy singer, Manuel Torres, as saying that all music and singing that 'has black sounds in it' has *duende*. Another phrase of the same sort is *tiene ángel*, 'has angel', which is an idiomatic way of saying 'has charm or grace'. A person can have *mal ángel* as well as *buen ángel* – that is, be a sinister sort of person – and he can even be *desangelado* 'unangeled' or colourless. In addition to this he can have *buena* (or *mala*) *sombra*, that is, can 'cast a good (or a bad) shadow'. All these expressions, which are only partly translatable, imply a belief in a supernatural power or mana (the Moors call it *baraka*) which dwells in people and affects their character and capabilities, except that the phrase *tiene duende* suggests a merely temporary and occasional possession, because the *duende* only manifests himself in moments of great emotion. In Yegen, however, we did not use this phrase: we said instead *tiene solitaria*. The *solitaria* is the tapeworm, and is here conceived of as a sort of indwelling sprite, something like a leprechaun, which enables the singer to give that extra something which makes his song so deeply disturbing and poignant. This expression is also used at Malaga.

Some folk beliefs are so jealously guarded that one may live for years in a place without having any inkling of them. I can give an example of this in a discovery I made only a short time before I left the village. I had gone for a walk to a remote valley above the cultivation level and had lain down to drink at a stream, when I became aware of something moving close to me. Lifting my head I saw a large grey dog, which for a moment I took to be a wolf, standing only a few yards away and looking fixedly at me. On returning home I reported this little adventure to my servant, and she, with a very serious air, said: 'Why didn't you ask it what it wanted?' It turned out that she believed that the souls of the dead who cannot find rest – *las almas en pena*, as they are called – are turned into dogs or other animals, who wander about till they can reveal to someone what it is that is troubling them. It might be, for example, that during their lives they had robbed someone and hidden the money away, and that until it is restored they cannot be at peace.

One evening as I was sitting on the roof of my house I heard a deep muffled hooting like that of a railway shunter's horn, only much louder; it was gradually taken up by other horns in other parts of the village and from the hills round, till I felt besieged by an army of eerie and lugubrious sounds. On inquiring I was told that this was the *cencerrada* or charivari. When either a widow or a widower announced their intention of getting married, the village lads went out with cows' horns and conches and blew on them. This was repeated every day with gradually increasing intensity for several weeks, till the marriage took place. The unfortunate couple had also to suffer from *pregones*, a word which the dictionary translates as 'public announcements'. Young men and children would collect outde their houses and sirepeat verses, most of which would be obscene and scurrilous, warning them not to marry the other party. Here is an example of one of the more innocent:

> Don't you marry José
> for he is the father of misery.
> I spent a year with him
> and I passed that year in pain.
> All he ever gave me to eat
> was a dish of lentil pottage,
> a stale barley cake
> and a mess of hasty pudding.
> Then when we went hungry to bed
> he turned over and fell asleep.
> That's the sort of man he is –
> snores all night and wets the bed.
> Let the *cencerrada* go on.

Anthropologists tell us that the horns and conches either represent the spirit of the dead husband or wife who objects to their spouse marrying again, or else that they are intended to keep him off. However that may be, the *cencerrada* was a real ordeal. The continual horn-blowing wore down the nerves of the engaged persons, and the *pregones* finished them off. On at least two occasions while I was in the village, a couple who had had their banns announced in church broke down and decided that they could not go through with it. Widows in particular so dreaded the publicity that they rarely remarried; instead, if they came from poor families and had no position to keep up, they simply went to live with their man. They were then spared not only the horn-blowing and the *pregones* but also the dreadful noise and tumult that greeted these couples when they came out of church and which went on round their house and bedroom window all night.

The *cencerrada* is still kept up vigorously in most parts of Spain, and not only in isolated villages. I have come across it recently in small towns as well. It has survived the fate of most other folk customs, because it expresses popular opinion upon second marriages as well as the need that small communities feel every now and then for breaking out. It is this that accounts for the indecency and scurrility of the *pregones*, which offer such a contrast to the usual gravity and reserve of Spanish villagers. The *cencerrada* is a licensed occasion, like the Carnival and the Roman Saturnalia: inhibitions can be relaxed, because personal responsibility is not felt for what is said and done. It is the village as a whole that is speaking, and therefore no offence is given and no grudge will be felt afterwards. And indeed the *pregones* lack a personal sting: rude though they are, their insults follow a general and traditional pattern.

In every Spanish village the greatest concentration of old customs and superstitions occurs on Midsummer Day. As midnight strikes, St John, whose feast it is, blesses everything on the earth – the fields, the crops, the trees, the wild plants, and the rivers and springs. He especially blesses the water, and his blessing gives miraculous properties to *la flor del agua*, the flower of the water. In some parts of Spain this is a water-weed whose possession gives happiness, but in Yegen it was the water itself and particularly the surface of the water, in which, as I have already said, the village girls bathed their hands and faces before sunrise. Properly speaking it should, I think, be the dew, which in early times was regarded as dropping from the stars. There are villages in the province of Soria and in Navarre where the girls roll naked in it.

Preparations for this great moment began on the evening before. The young men spent the first hours of the night 'making their rounds' – that is, serenading – but as soon as the position of Antares above the Cerrajón de Murtas showed that midnight had come and the magical influence fallen, they set off for the fields to gather branches and flowers and especially boughs of almond and cherry to decorate their girls' windows and balconies. A verse explains the reason for this:

> *El día de San Juan, madre,*
> *cuaja la almendra y la nuez.*
> *También cuajan los amores*
> *de los que se quieren bien.*

On St John's day, mother,
set the almond and the nut.
Those who love one another well –
their love sets too.

While this was going on, the girls were sitting indoors and
trying to foretell who their future husbands would be. One
way of doing this was to break raw eggs into water and look
through a silk handkerchief at the shape they formed. The
young man's face would then appear. Another way was by
peeling wild artichokes and throwing their scales in the fire.
Or, if you had counted ten stars on ten successive nights be-
before Midsummer Day, the stars would make you dream of
your husband. The first words overheard in the street after
sunrise would also reveal the secret. Meanwhile the older
women were out picking simples. Between midnight and sunrise the evil powers that afflict the earth lose their strength,
and the medicinal plants which no illness can resist, as well as
the magic herbs which give eternal life and happiness and
reveal hidden treasure, can be gathered. Chief among these
was the *hierba del sillero*, a small rock-rose whose botanical
name is *Fumana glutinosa*. Its round, yellow face, like the disc
of the sun, makes it the sacred plant of the day of Helios. In
other parts of Spain the St John's wort and the mugwort are
preferred.

If the first hours of Midsummer Day were thought of as a
stationary period, when everything on the earth held its breath
and blessings descended from above, the rising of the sun was
a triumph. It came up, as is said all over Spain, dancing. But in
our village there was a more curious and primitive view. It
was believed that a young woman who put a silk handkerchief
over her eyes and looked at the sunrise would for a moment
see the sun and the moon on top of one another. They were
luchando, fighting, which was a euphemistic way of saying that
they were copulating. This is presumably what is referred to in
the Psalms when the sun is spoken of as coming like a bridegroom out of his chamber, and there is a famous stanza in the

Faerie Queene (Book 1, Canto v) which echoes the same idea in the language of Pagan mythology. By the union of the sun and moon on Midsummer Day all nature renewed itself.

Such were the midsummer rites at Yegen and in most parts of Spain, but in a few districts entirely different ones were observed. This was the case in the neighbouring province of Malaga. Here the chief ceremony consisted – and still consists – in putting outside the doors of the houses at sunrise *peleles* or dummies that had been stuffed with straw and which often had a sexual or bacchic significance. Phalluses made of sausages would be placed in appropriate positions, female bodies would be bellied out with pumpkins and calabashes and decorated with strings of figs, and jars of wine would be placed beside them. Other dummies would be hung on ropes stretched across the street, and in the evening they would all be set on fire and burned with a great crackling of home-made fireworks and loudly shouted insults and obscenities. Bundles of old clothes were burned at the same time, and the whole operation was known as 'burning Judas'. Earlier in the afternoon the young people had gone off to the fields, taking with them baskets of *roscos*, or ring-shaped rolls of bread, specially made for the occasion, and white cheeses.

One may ask what is the reason for the difference of ritual. My friend, Don Julio Caro Baroja, tells me that the custom of 'burning Judas' is observed all over Northern Spain on the Saturday of Holy Week. In some districts of Navarre and Old Castile it is also usual to hang up an unnamed dummy, representing the old spirit of vegetation, on the sacred tree on Midsummer Eve, and afterwards to burn it. It would seem that at Malaga, which was repopulated from Old Castile, the two customs became confused, while the other rites were forgotten. I think it likely that it was the Moorish influence which decided this. On Midsummer Day it was the custom for the Spanish Moslems to put on new clothes and then go off to the fields, where they lit bonfires and danced. They also ate special dishes of vegetables and hung the male figs, wrapped in straw, on the female trees in order to fertilize them. Possibly they burned dummies as well. From this we may conclude that the expulsion of the Morisco population was not as complete as the documents suggest.

I will end these notes on magic rituals with one which took place in our village on Holy Saturday. As soon as the Gloria bell, marking the moment of the Resurrection, had rung, women of a pious turn of mind would go out and collect pebbles in the streams and irrigation channels. They took them home, recited a Padre Nuestro to each of them, and put them carefully away in a paper. When later in the year a storm came up and threatened to pass over the village, they would go up on to the roof and throw one stone in the direction of the storm and one to either side of it, thus making the figure of a cross. The storm would then go away. If the notions of certain villages near Soria are taken into account, their fear of storms came originally from the belief that a strong wind could make them pregnant. The women of these villages either hide from such winds or protect their virginity by throwing stones picked on a Holy Saturday. But storms also damage crops, and against these there is or used until quite recently to be in some parts of Spain (Asturias, Castile, Seville, Guadix) a more elaborate and official ceremony. The priest came out of the church dressed in full canonicals, holding the gospel in one hand and a sprinkler dipped in holy water in the other. He then read some prayers and pronounced an exorcism, while several men stood round him and held him firmly by the skirts in case the demon of the storm should take it into its head to blow him away. In some places he ended his exorcism by throwing a stone that had been sprinkled with holy water at it. However, one condition was attached to this performance – the priest must be a virgin. If he was not, both he and the village would suffer damage.

No picture of any Spanish village can be complete that does not give some account of its popular poetry. As many people know, there is poetry of this sort in Spain which is very much

alive today. It consists of short independent stanzas of three or
four verses which are known as *coplas*. The origin of these
coplas is very remote – perhaps as remote as the agricultural
instruments and the magical ceremonies – though no examples
of them have come down to us from before the eleventh century. I speak of them as being alive because not only are they
continually sung in the house, in the fields, and on journeys, but
because new ones are still being invented and made. Anyone
who is sufficiently steeped in the medium can improvise one.

Perhaps, however, it is misleading to speak of them as
poems. Until folklorists began to collect them, they were
scarcely ever written down. They were intended for singing,
and just as Sancho Panza had an unlimited supply of proverbs
at his beck and call, so there are many people today who have
an unlimited stock of *coplas* and can go on singing them without repeating themselves for days on end. In Andalusia they
are sung in the Oriental-sounding style known as *cante jondo* or,
more vulgarly, *flamenco* – a style much ornamented with trills
and appoggiaturas, in which the accompaniment contains
intervals unknown to Western music. The Northern visitor,
whose ears are jarred by what he often regards as a disagreeable caterwauling, rather naturally supposes that this singing
has a Moorish or Arabic origin. Almost certainly, however, it
is older, and derives from a primitive type of Mediterranean
song and music.

I will not say more about the *copla* here, because the subject
is an extensive one. I have written about it at greater length in
my book *The Literature of the Spanish People*, and I have in preparation an anthology of these little songs which will contain
further explanation. At the moment I only wish to make it
clear that at Yegen they provided a constant background to
everyday life. There was scarcely a moment of the day when
one could not, sitting on the rooftop, hear someone singing
one. Across the great wastes of air a voice would rise, would
fall, would die away, and the currents of air, interrupting it,
would give it an impersonal, a scarcely human quality. It

seemed a disembodied cry, a wandering complaint, as much a part of Nature as the noise of falling water or the song of an invisible bird in a pine tree, and not to be associated with any living being. Those who have only heard *cante jondo* in rooms or on the radio can have no idea of what it is like, heard from a distance, in the open air.

The children's songs too, though in a very different way, were delightful. The best were those they sang in games of the type of 'Oranges and Lemons'. These consisted of fragments of sixteenth-century ballads joined together without too much regard for sense and ending in passages of sheer and exuberantly childish nonsense. In beauty some of them surpass anything in *Mother Goose*, and that, I think, is because while most of their material consists of real poetry written by adults, the selection and cobbling together has been done by children. The little girls, who were the principal sustainers of the bardic tradition, had also preserved, I suspect with some coaching from their elders, two complete ballads. One was called the *Romance de Catalina de Granada*. It describes in a very dramatic way the tortures imposed by her father and mother on a Moorish girl who had been converted to Christianity. We watch poor Catalina dying of hunger and thirst in forty heartrending couplets, each of which, to make the agony last longer, is followed by a refrain. The other was a ballad that begins *Dónde vas, buen caballero* and relates how a nobleman was searching for his wife when her ghost appeared, told him that she was dead, gave a description of her very sumptuous funeral, and advised him to marry again. This was not a cheerful subject either, but what chiefly made it the property of the children was its insistent, unforgettable tune. English people know it, for it is the tune of 'Clementine'. During the California gold-rush of 1849, the American and English miners grew so tired of hearing their Mexican comrades sing this ballad day in and day out that they parodied it. The tune has such an infectious quality that I have no doubt that it has by now spread round the world from Turkey to Japan.

I will conclude these brief remarks about children's songs by giving a snail verse – the Spanish equivalent of 'Snail, snail, put out your horn'.

> *Caracol, col, col,*
> *saca los cuernos al sol.*
> *Te daré una miguita de pan*
> *para que avíes de almorzar.*

> Snaily, waily, put out your horn.
> Stretch it out to the sun
> and I'll give you a crumb
> so you can cook your lunch.

The interesting thing about this verse, which children sing all over Spain, is that at Yegen it was still used as a snail charm. When rain had fallen, women and children would go out after dark with lanterns to collect the big Roman snails that fed on the grass, and when they did this they sang it. The song is presumably intended to deceive the snail into thinking that the lantern is the sun and that it is time for it to get up and show itself. But the words overreach the intention, for it is human beings and not snails that come out by day.

Baptism, marriage, and death are the three most important events in a Spaniard's life. The first of these was in our village a simple affair. The godmother carried the child to the church and made all the arrangements, while the godfather paid the expenses of the party and dance that took place afterwards. Between them, therefore, they ousted the parents and dominated the occasion. If the priest was good-looking or had *buen ángel*, that is, charm, he brought the child luck, while the salt placed on its lips would make it *salado* or witty. On returning to the parents' house the godmother would say: '*Comadre*, here is your son. You gave him to me a Moor and I hand him back to you a Christian.' Then the fiesta, with wine, anis spirit and *buñuelos* or oil fritters, as well as, if the family could afford them, sweets and sponge cake, would begin.

Before marriage comes the courtship or engagement. This

was much more informal in the villages than in the towns. The young man would 'declare himself' to a girl while they were dancing together. If she accepted she became his *novia*, and from then on she would not dance with anyone else. Since there were no *rejas* or barred windows in the villages, he would be allowed entry every evening to her parents' house, where he would sit beside her and converse with her in the presence of others, but in whispers. *Novios*, of course, often quarrelled and took up with someone else, and it was only when the young man had completed his military service and saved enough money to get married that he formally asked her parents' permission. The girl bought the furniture with the money her *novio* handed her, but she was expected to provide the bed and bedclothes. In the case of the poor the bed would be a truckle bed and the mattress would be stuffed either with rye straw or with dry maize leaves.

The decisive act took place when the young people *tomaron los dichos*, or made their declaration, in the priest's house. This was the true marriage contract. The banns followed and then the wedding. The cheapest time for holding this was in the morning, and the later it was the higher were the priest's fees. 'The rich' got married after dark, so that when the brief reception was over they could hurry off into bed. When, however, the marriage took place in the morning, it was followed by a lunch at which the two families sat down to a chicken casserole and in the evening there would be a party or fiesta. The bride and bridegroom led the dance, while the singers improvised *coplas* in honour of the bride, and sometimes in joking disparagement of the bridegroom. A gloomy note was generally provided by the older married women, who would take the bride into a corner, warn her of the danger of becoming 'loaded down with children', and offer her discreet advice upon how to avoid this. Other women, however, would tell her that children were a *fruto de bendición*, a fruit of blessings, and therefore much to be desired in moderate quantities. Then on the stroke of midnight – a figurative expression, since there

were no clocks in our village, much less one that could strike –
the newly married couple went off to their house.

Into most people's lives there comes at some time or
another a serious illness. If the doctor shook his head, the
nearest relatives would make vows for the patient's recovery:
to walk barefoot in the next procession, to offer a tress of their
hair, or even – though I do not remember this being done in
our village – to wear for so many months or years, or more
often till it fell to bits, the habit of this or that Virgin or Saint.
Some Christs and Virgins were much more effective than
others in curing illnesses. In the Alpujarra people usually
resorted to Jesús del Gran Poder, Jesus of Great Power, in
spite of the fact that he had his shrine and image at Seville and
not at Granada. This was because the patroness of Granada,
the Virgen de las Angustias, or Virgin of Agonies, was
obviously more appropriate in matters where hope had been
abandoned.

When death came, the body was buried quickly on the following day. Girls were laid out in white, with a crown of
flowers on their head and a nosegay between their folded hands,
other people in their best clothes with their leather shoes on
their feet (one pair lasted a lifetime, since they were worn only to
go to mass), and in this garb they were put in their coffins. The
night before, all the family and neighbours sat up with them.
Dirges were no longer used, though the women would give
free vent to their grief by breaking into violent laments and
praises of the departed. This was known as *dar la cabezada*. Any
widow or daughter who did not do this would be thought to
show a great lack of feeling, whereas men were expected to
show self-control. The cemetery was known as the *tierra de la
verdad*, or place of truth. When only the other day I questioned
my housekeeper about this, she replied with great feeling:
'Why, that's the only truth there is. One is buried and that's
the end. All our life is an illusion.' Rosario is a cheerful and
pagan-minded woman with few cares in the world, yet, when
asked, she gave the eternal Spanish answer: 'Life is an illusion,

because it ends.' In this country the thought of death eats into
life, and as soon as the intoxication of first youth is over,
begins to sap the taste for pleasure.

Half an hour before the funeral procession was due to start,
those who meant to attend it assembled at the dead man's
house and expressed their sympathy with the nearest relatives
in a formal phrase. 'I accompany you in your feeling', they
would say, or 'May he rest in peace'. Then the coffin – sar-
donically known as 'the guitar' or 'the violin' – would be carried on shoulder-back to the cemetery, where the burial service
would be held in the mortuary chapel. The poor, who could
not afford the usual fee, were buried in shallow graves in a part
of the cemetery known as *la tertulia* or *la olla* – 'the club' or
'the stew-pot' – while the rich were sealed up in those masonry
chests-of-drawers known as *columbarios*, which are part of the
Roman inheritance. In many places the poor were buried
naked, since their families could not afford to sacrifice the
sheet they were wrapped in, but in Yegen they wore their own
clothes and were carried to the cemetery in the parish coffin
and dropped through its hinged bottom into the grave. After
the funeral was over there came nine days of strict mourning,
when the family and friends met every evening at the dead
man's house and took turns in praying for him. This is a custom which has long been obsolete in Andalusian towns, though
it survives in many villages.

All races point their wit when death is the subject, and
Spanish villagers and workmen have some expressive phrases
upon it. Of orphans they say, 'They have nothing left but the
day and the night and the water in the pitcher'; while a poor
woman whose husband has just died will complain, 'It's not
that I miss him so much, but that he carried off with him the
key of the larder.' In the struggle for bare existence the finer
feelings count for little. To the very poor even grief is a
luxury.

CHAPTER ELEVEN

THE LONELY SCOTSMAN

*

WHEN I looked out across the great hollow of air before me, I could see through my field-glasses some nine miles away as the crow flies a small white dot. This was a farm known as the Cortijo del Inglés, and there an Englishman, or rather a Scotsman, lived. Sometimes the postman handed me his letters by mistake, and then I saw that his name was MacTaggart. He was the only English-speaking person beside myself to live – probably to have ever lived – in the Alpujarra. On any evening of the year I could watch the plume of smoke that rose from his house and which announced the cooking of his dinner.

His story, which I learned from a Spaniard who knew him well, was a strange one. Some twenty years before, a married man with a family in Scotland, he had gone on business to Oran. There he had met a Spanish girl called Lola, some said in a brothel, others serving as a maid in a hotel, and had fallen in love with her. They went off together, and after a jaunt to Madrid, to which they both took a dislike, landed up in her village, a bare hilltop place which had not even a road to it, called Murtas. Here it turned out that she belonged to one of the poorest families and had a flock of indigent brothers and sisters in need of assistance. This would have discouraged most men from lingering, but MacTaggart did not appear to mind, for he rented the best available house and settled down. Then, as he found the life to his taste, he bought a farmhouse and some land a couple of miles away, and established himself in it with his girl.

Murtas is a village which lies just below the summit of the Sierra la Contraviesa. It has little or no water for irrigation, but is famous for its figs and almonds. MacTaggart took over several hundred acres planted with fig trees and almond trees, and gave them to two of his mistress's brothers to farm for him, on the share-cropping principle. They were provided with cottages, while the rest of her family, including several small children, came to live in his house and fed at his kitchen table. Only the elder brother was omitted from the list of beneficiaries, because for some reason or other no place could be found for him.

MacTaggart was a man who liked drink. Cases of whisky reached him regularly from Almeria, and he was lavish in his hospitality. Every evening there would be parties for his friends at which they drank and played cards, and these parties often went on till after midnight. A number of the leading men of the village would attend, and since private houses where one can get drinks for nothing are a novelty in Spanish life, his farm soon came to be thought of as a sort of free tavern. He himself got drunk with great regularity, and every October when he rode down to the fair at Ugíjar he ended up so soused that he had to be tied on his horse and carried home.

All this, of course, was highly scandalous. Spaniards think badly of drunkenness, because it deprives a man of his dignity. Yet a foreigner's actions do not really count. They laughed at the Scotsman, to prevent themselves from envying him (anyone who breaks a taboo is naturally to be envied), and they flocked to his house to take advantage of the miraculous flow of drink that had broken out. Certainly he was corrupting the village, but since villages enjoy being corrupted and the priest himself sometimes condescended to take part, no one felt that any particular harm was being done. It would be folly not to relieve a rich and spendthrift *inglés* of some of his superabundance.

For indeed MacTaggart did not seem to mind how he threw away his money. His mistress had the reputation of being an honest woman, but she allowed her family to fleece him. Her brothers who ran the farm cheated, it was said, in the most barefaced way, and on one excuse or another kept back his share of the earnings. What made this the easier was that he never learned more than a few words of Spanish and that Lola never acquired any English. Between them they had invented a pidgin language – or rather two pidgin languages – in which they communicated with one another. To his boon companions he simply talked English in a loud voice helped out with signs and gestures, and drink gave him the illusion of being understood. Since he had no dealings with the British colony at Almeria and no friends of his own race to visit him, he ceased to have real converse with anyone.

He had been living in this way for a good many years when a terrible event happened. The story had got about that he kept a roll of banknotes in a box under his bed, and his mistress's elder brother, who bore a grudge because nothing had been done for him, determined to rob him. He found an accomplice in one of the municipal councillors of Murtas who was a regular attendant at the evening parties. He had gambled heavily at these and run into debt, and this gave him a grudge too. However, at the last moment Lola got to hear of what was brewing and told the Scotsman. He told the Civil Guard, they laid an ambush, and when the elder brother stole up by moonlight to the window, they shot him dead. The municipal councillor, who had lagged behind, was taken to prison, and at his trial a lot of scandalous things – all the tittle-tattle of the village – came out. MacTaggart learned for the first time how he was regarded by the neighbourhood.

These events made a deep impression on him. He woke up from the drunkard's dream of good-fellowship in which he had been living, with the suddenness and violence of a person who has had a religious conversion. In a moment his whole manner of feeling and existing changed and became the opposite of what it had been before. His previous over-confidence turned to a deep suspiciousness of everyone except his mistress, so that he gave up his drinking parties, refused to see any of his old cronies, and shut himself up in his house. I was told by a man who had worked for him that from this time on he rarely went out before sunset, when, well primed with whisky, he would take a few turns among his almond trees and fire his revolver into the air. Perhaps he imagined that he was giving a warning to future robbers. However, even before this he had been famous for his eccentricities, one of which had been a mania for punishing anything that annoyed him. If his hat blew off, he would hang it on a tree and say, 'There you stay until you learn manners.' If his coat got a spot on it, up that would go on the tree too. Once when his horse stumbled and almost fell, he shut it up without fodder for three days 'to give it a lesson'. Now, I imagine, he was 'giving a lesson' to the people of Murtas for having tried to rob him.

These stories filled me with a great curiosity to meet my eccentric Scottish neighbour. One day, therefore, I sent him a message proposing, if that was agreeable to him, to call in on a certain afternoon on my way past his farm. A verbal reply came back – he would be there. Paco's younger brother Cecilio was planning a trip to Murtas to sell some hams, so I thought I would take advantage of this to go with him. It would make a better impression if I arrived on mule-back. One morning, therefore, by the first light of day, we set off.

Our road lay straight down below the village, over the Puente and across the bare downs to the Rambla Seca. From this we climbed some low rocky hills, overgrown with broom and cistus and lavender, and dropped again to a river. Immediately above this, on the lower slopes of the Sierra la Contraviesa, lay the village of Jorairátar. Seen from the roof of my house it looked a paradisial place, its cluster of pearly houses set in a cool grey wood of olive trees. Towards evening its hundred or so chimneys sent up their plumes of smoke so straight into the sky that it seemed to be suspended from them. However, when one came up to it the impression was different. The long-branched olive trees, irrigated and little pruned, according to the mode of cultivation practised in the Alpujarra, and planted on rocky terraces that rose steeply one above the other, were all that could be wished for, but the village itself was a wretched place, with blank spaces occupied by ruined walls and tumbledown buildings that once had housed people of means, but now were given over to neglect and poverty.

Cecilio had some business to do, so I sat down by the fountain to wait. A rock rose sheer behind it, and two immense olive trees, but most of the houses in the square were in ruins. Flies crawled over the stones, the sun beat down, there was an acrid smell of urine and excreta while, as if to contradict this, out of the dust and crumbling masonry came the scarlet stab of pomegranate flowers, in colour, form, and scent pure Orient. As I sat there with the patience that Spain teaches, women came up with their pitchers under their arms, little girls in threadbare frocks and bare feet, another carrying a baby that was covered with sores, an old man with a donkey. In the square window-frame opposite an aged crone, her face parched and channelled as the hills, sat looking at me out of her beady eyes without moving. The classical Andalusian poverty. Only the olive trees seemed to tell of grander days, when one might have imagined pagan temples rising above the rubble and solemn processions of flower-garlanded girls climbing their stone stairways. But Jorairátar, which had little water for irrigation and where property was not divided, can never have known real prosperity, even in the days when some mines were worked there.

My companion rejoined me, and we resumed our journey. But the hours had gone by while I sat by the fountain, and it was nearly midday. We stopped, therefore, in the shade of an olive tree and sat down to our lunch – a bottle of wine, a cold potato omelette, and some cherries.

Cecilio was as different as possible in character from his brother Paco. He was carefree, indifferent to money-making, and a little light in the head. In every town and village in Andalusia there are one or two people who show small aptitude for practical things, but appear to have come into the world solely in order to sing *coplas*. Such was Cecilio. From

the moment of our setting out till we returned home next day
he never stopped singing for more than a few minutes at a
time, and as his stock of *coplas* was inexhaustible he scarcely
ever repeated himself. Sometimes I would prompt him with
the first line of one that I liked, and immediately he would sing
it.

> *En la orillita de la mar*
> *suspiraba una ballena*
> *y en sus suspiros decía*
> *– Quien tiene amor tiene pena.*

> On the shore of the sea
> a whale lay sighing
> and among its sighs it said
> – He who loves suffers pain.

The fact that the word *ballena*, whale, was really a corruption
of *sirena*, siren, did not prevent me from feeling that here one
had the last word upon the unescapability of love. Even the
whales knew it.

Or else he would sing an ordinary love song:

> *– Pajarito de la nieve,*
> *dime, dónde tienes el nido?*
> *– Lo tengo en un pino verde*
> *en una rama escondido.*

> – Little bird of the snow,
> Tell me where you have built your nest?
> – I have made it in a green pine tree
> on a safely hidden branch.

But his favourite songs were of unhappy love:

> *A los dos de la mañana*
> *yo me quisiera morir*
> *por ver si se me acababa*
> *este delirio por ti.*

> At two o'clock in the morning
> I wished that I could die
> to see if I could end
> this longing I have for you.

He sang them with feeling, though he had no *novia* and was not in love.

For an hour or more we climbed steadily up the Sierra la Contraviesa. This is an ancient chain of mountains, moulded by erosion into soft curves of shaly rocks and glittering mica schists. On the southern side it is planted with vines that produce the best white wine of the district, but on the northern slopes, which we were traversing, it is dotted with almond trees and fig trees. The track wound slowly round flattened spurs and rough *barrancos*, and we met no one. The only living creatures to cross our sight were the green lizards that darted off at our approach, and that little crested lark, the *totavía*, that sings a few plaintive notes from a stone and then flies in undulating, pipit-like flight away. It owes its name to the Spanish word for 'Yet a little longer', which it is supposed to repeat.

At length we came out on to the Scotsman's land and saw in front of us his farm, a low white building standing beside an ancient fig tree. I mounted the mule and rode up to it.

We were expected. The cautious female face that peeped from a window and vanished, the silence that followed the knocking on the door, the hurried steps of the girl who came to open it, all showed that something out of the ordinary was happening. I was shown in. As I turned into the parlour I caught sight of a stout middle-aged woman dressed in dark clothes of good quality standing behind an open doorway. It was the mistress of the house, who had come to have a look at me, knowing that Scottish conventions would not allow an introduction. Her round black eyes gazed at me stolidly, though her mouth remained firmly closed: what she saw in that quarter of a minute would no doubt provide her with many points of comparison between me and her lord and master.

In a small room furnished in the genteel style of the Spanish lower middle classes, with chairs that looked as if they dared anyone to sit on them, a round table covered with a worked lace cover that said 'too clean to use', and a heavily carved and knobbed and scrolled sideboard, sat a man with grey, mining-engineer's moustaches and a very red face. He wore a high, turnover starched collar round his neck and a green tweed suit that had the marks of recent folding on it. His hair was still a greyish black and there was something stiff and deliberate about his movements as though he had to think them out beforehand. He occupied the space he sat in so obstinately that it occurred to me that he would have made a good subject for a still-life portrait by Cézanne.

I began the conversation with some remarks of an apologetic kind – how I was a neighbour of his, how I hoped that I was not disturbing him, and so forth – but to my surprise he did not answer a word, but sat with his blue eyes fixed on me and an expression of suspicion and disapproval spread over his whole face.

Suddenly he clapped his hands and called out 'Ana'. The girl, who had evidently been standing just outside the door, came in.

'Bring the baby.'

Much mystified, I was about to inquire who this youthful member of the family might be when the girl returned with a bottle of whisky, two glasses, and a carafe of water. Then I remembered what I had been told. By 'baby' he meant *bebe*, the third person singular of the present indicative of the verb to drink.

He apologized for having no soda water.

'That damned Miguel hasn't brought it. He keeps on saying he's going to bring it, swears by all his saints next time he'll bring it – *mañana*, *mañana*, that's what he says to me. But it doesn't come. The people of this country are a very untrustworthy people, Mr Bremen. You can't depend on any of them.'

I said I had not found that.

'Wait until you've been here as long as I have. Then you'll see. Do you speak their language?'

I said I did.

'A great mistake, in my opinion. I said to them when I first came here: "Don't think I'm going to learn your precious lingo, for I'm not." And I never have. But I understand them all right; yes, I understand them. Better than they understand themselves.'

It was evident that he had been drinking. He was putting an effort on himself, but whenever he began to speak his resentment surged out. To keep the conversation within safe limits, I inquired about his farm.

'Farm!' he exclaimed in a tone of heavy irony. 'So they've told you I had a farm! Well, the trees grow and give their fruits in due season, as the good book says they should, but they do it without the ministrations of those whose task it should be to look after them. *Mañana, mañana*, smoke cigarettes all day, take siesta! *Dormez-vous bien, señor*! No wonder there's no profit in it for the owner.'

He refilled the glasses and relapsed into silence. I said nothing either.

'I would be glad, Mr Bremen, to have your opinion on a certain question,' he began again after a little. 'As I see it, the worrld is not what it used to be. Even in my time there's been a great decline in morality. Look at these hills – when the Moors were here they were all watered and cultivated and patiently tended, and now they only grow almond trees. The people round here are poor because they don't work. Winning a lottery ticket, that's all they think about! Running a cargo of contraband! Getting something for nothing! You read books, Mr Bremen – I would be glad to know if you can explain why this has happened.'

I replied that I could not say, because in the village where I lived the people worked hard, and the land was as well cultivated as it had ever been.

'Is that really so?' he said, and began to fill his pipe. Then, with a different intonation in his voice:

'There's another more perrsonal question I'd like to ask.

Do you, I'm wondering, find it difficult to make yourself respected in this country?'

Rather tactlessly I replied that I had never thought about it.

'Allow me to say,' he rejoined, 'that you're making a great mistake. One has to think about it. In this country a man is either respected or he is treated like dirt. There's no middle course. As a Briton I think it proper to see that I am respected whenever I am abroad.'

There was another long silence. We sipped our whisky slowly.

'These so-called Spaniards,' he began suddenly. 'They could never equip and establish upon the high seas a great fleet like that which sailed every year to the Isthmus of Panama. No, I can't see them even attempting to do it. Their nerve has gone, there's nothing left of all their past pride and spirit.'

'Times have changed,' I said.

'They have, and people, and races. This is only a little village where I live, a wee benighted place such as you might find in many parts of Scotland. But I have found degeneracy here, yes, deep degeneracy. And a most terrible ignorance. It's a sure rule, I've always found in the course of my travels, that wherever the priest goes, degeneracy and ignorance follow him. You're not a Catholic, I take it?'

'No, a Protestant.'

'Shake hands on it. Two hundred years ago these people would have burned both of us. Now all they want is our money. Have you ever in the course of your studies come across Dr Butler's work on the decline of civilizations?'

I said that I had.

'Then you'll understand what I mean. But the queer, odd thing is that these fellows have no notion of what they have sunk to. When I tell them that one little gun-boat in the British navy could blow their blessed village to smithereens, they smile and say nothing. They have a very high opinion of themselves.'

'Have you ever visited other parts of Spain?' I asked.

'I have been to Madrid, a poor sort of place, not to be compared with Edinburgh. And I have lived here. I have not been tempted to travel farther in this country.'

'And yet you like living here?'

At once the suspicious look came back into his face and he stared at me without answering.

'*I* like it very much,' I said.

'Is that so, now? Well, I won't dispute that there are worse places in the worrld than these mountains. Some would say that, anyhow, they're private. A man can be himself here.'

Suddenly there was a scream from the next room, a sound of chairs falling and of shrill female voices all shrieking at one another. Steps raced down the passage.

'Has something happened?' I asked.

Without moving he answered, 'Spaniards. That is the way they have of enjoying themselves. I shut my eyes to it,' he went on. 'I keep out of their affairs and expect them to keep out of mine. That's the only way to get along in this country.'

Another silence. I watched the sunlight warming the hill outside, the sooty stem of an almond tree against the sky, the dark glossy leaves of a fig tree. It seemed a pity to spend so lovely a day soaking whisky and listening to a half-crazy Scotsman. With my head already a little altered, I got up and said that I must be starting back. My host did nothing to detain me. The invitation I gave him to visit me at Yegen passed unanswered. Avoiding my eyes, he fidgeted with his collar. Only too obviously he was counting to himself the moments till I should go, when he would be free to hurry back to his own room – not that wretched parlour – and clap his hands for the fat woman to undo the cursed encumbrance, while the girl folded his green suit and put it away in a chest, and between them they poured into his ears a flood of gossip, which he would only partly understand, collected from Cecilio in the kitchen. So the Burgundian knights had wallowed in Oriental luxury in their harems at Barbastro, saying perhaps the very same things about the Moorish inhabitants that the solitary

Scotsman had uttered to me. It has always been the custom for those who love Spain to abuse it.

As we continued on our road, I asked Cecilio what the scuffle had been about.

'Oh, a rabbit got loose in the kitchen,' he answered, 'and they made a great fuss over chasing it. I think it was to annoy the *Inglés*. They did not seem to have much regard for him.'

'I expect that the lady of the house was annoyed at not being introduced to me. She took it as a slight on her.'

'Whatever it was,' he answered, 'they showed little *educación*. They might at least have kept up appearances in front of me.'

This was the last I saw of Mr MacTaggart. A dozen years later I heard that he was dead. The Scottish heirs claimed the property, and his mistress and all her family, who had saved nothing, were reduced to destitution. Evidently they had not made as much out of him as had been said.

The sun was getting low in the sky when we turned a corner and saw Murtas lying below us in a fold of the hills. A pale grey village of huddled, flat-roofed houses, the smoke rising perpendicularly from its chimneys. I was to sleep with Cecilio in the house of a cousin of his. As I lay on my pallet that night I thought of the last occasion when I had been in this place. I had staggered into it one October evening of 1919, weak from dysentery. After a meal of sodden rice and dried cod I had lain down on a straw mattress on the floor of the kitchen, to wake an hour later with an army of bugs attacking me. Unable to sleep, I had got up and sat shivering in the fields with my complaint heavily on me. In the morning they had refused to light the fire to make me coffee.

CHAPTER TWELVE

FOOD AND THE PHOENICIANS

*

THE great *cortijo* or farm of the Andalusian plains is a direct descendant of the Roman villa. It has the same offices and rooms, excepting only the hot baths, laid out round a spacious court. The ground floor contains the oil mills, wine vats, and store-rooms, and sometimes the stables, while the upper floor is divided between apartments for the owner, whenever he deigns to visit it, and living-rooms for the bailiff. Over the monumental entrance-gate there is a niche for a sacred image, and above the house there is a *mirador* or tower. This arrangement has been followed as far as possible in the smaller farms of the Alpujarra and in the manorial houses in the villages. It existed therefore in mine. I had the principal living-rooms with a main door on to the street, while the man who farmed for my landlord lived across the courtyard. Since, however, this door could only be opened by means of a ponderous key, I used the back entrance, which gave by an exterior flight of steps leading down from the kitchen into the courtyard. Here were the stables, the bakehouse, the cowshed, the covered porch with its stone benches placed there for the use of beggars, and the entrance into the garden.

The farmer with whom I shared this courtyard was known as *el tío Maximiliano*, Uncle Maximiliano. He was an old man with a loud voice and a strong flow of obscene and blasphemous language. Even the respect he owed to Doña Lucía's presence was not enough to check it. His wife was *la tía Rosario*, Aunt Rosario, a thin, effaced, gentle woman, prematurely aged by work and by having borne her husband half a dozen children. In her youth she had been the village beauty, and on that account had been given the nickname of la Reina, the Queen. This and her gentle, accommodating character had procured for her the post of servant to Don Fadrique's mother, and simultaneously of mistress to his father – these offices usually ran together in *caciques'* families – after which she was married off to their cattleman, who in return for his compliance was put in charge of their property in the village, which they farmed between them on the share-cropping principle. Juan el Mudo and Araceli, who at this time managed the mountain farm, owed their position to somewhat the same circumstances – the marriage of a trusted servant to a cattleman – and on Uncle Maximiliano's death they stepped into his place.

One of the more useful inventions of the Catholic Church has been the institution of godparents. In rural communities this relationship helps to consolidate the blood links formed by concubinage between the landowner and the people who work for him. Thus Don Fadrique was the godfather of Aunt Rosario's younger children and he and Uncle Maximiliano always addressed one another as *compadre*, while for the children he was *padrino*. And when he married Doña Lucía she automatically became, in title at least, their *madrina*. By this means – the dropping of the Don – the difference of rank was diminished and they became in some degree a single family. That is to say, one has here a version of the Roman *familia*, or body of domestics, in which the significant feature is preserved that the master's blood runs through most of them. His amatory exploits have been made, like his lawful marriage, to serve his economic interests, as is seen today on a prodigious scale among the caids of the Great Atlas. And this enlarged family, together with the clients who stand round it, forms the kernel of that clan system which has in all ages played such an important part in Spanish life. A useful thing in itself, the spontaneous creation of a society that distrusts its own formal institutions, it has paved the way for that much decried petty despotism known as *caciquismo*, the rule of the local big man or *cacique*. The impulse to act in this way has arisen from the

Spaniard's desire to strengthen himself by a network of human relations. The rich or powerful man needs clients devoted to his interests: the poor man needs a protector, and so a number of little clans are built up, held together by the need for mutual defence against the dangers and asperities of Spanish life. Since this is a country where purely self-interested motives command little respect, the group has to be soldered together wherever possible by moral and religious links, that is, by intermarriages, sponsorships, extramarital relationships, and personal friendships. In this way mutual obligations are given a certain sanctity.

Whenever I opened the kitchen door and looked into the courtyard I would see Aunt Rosario and her daughters busy over their household tasks, and if it was evening would hear Uncle Maximiliano's stentorian voice hurling out obscene objurgations. He was a good enough man in spite of his language, which was addressed rather to the air around him than to particular people. But he was not a communicative one. I used sometimes to sit by his fireside and endeavour to talk with him, but though he must have had interesting things to tell of the past, of the days when the wolves came down to the village, when the vines enlaced the poplar trees, and wine was so cheap that they irrigated the gardens with it, he could never be got to speak of them. His notion of conversation consisted in a loud, vociferous assertion of his own existence. How different he was in character from Uncle Miguel Medina, my landlord's bailiff – a sober, severe, reserved man who might have been born in the plains of Old Castile!

As I have said, the only effective entrance to my house lay through the kitchen. This was a smallish room with an open fireplace, a row of charcoal stoves set into a tiled shelf, and a stone sink. Cupboards of dark walnut wood let into the wall gave it a mellow appearance, and out of it opened the bake-room and the jakes. The Romans, as anyone who has visited Pompeii will know, believed in a close association between the preparation of food and its evacuation from the body, and in old Spanish houses the water-closet still opens off the kitchen. Ours – though it had no water – was an original and even a poetical place. Its seat was of fine-veined marble, and its aperture gave through an airy drop on to an enclosed *corral* or yard twenty feet below. When the wind blew, it poured through this opening with extraordinary force and with a thin moaning sound, and the place became unusable. Most of the houses in the village had no jakes at all – people simply went down into the stable and looked for a vacant spot between the mule and the tethered pigs.

Not far from the kitchen was the store-room, and this was an important place. Every autumn we hung from its ceiling two or three hundred pounds of thick-skinned grapes, which kept fresh till April, though getting sweeter and more shrunken all the time. There would also be several hundred persimmons from two trees that grew in the garden: picked after the first frost, they ripened slowly and were eaten with a spoon when they went soft and squashy. Quinces were also kept there, as well as oranges and lemons and apples, and pots of marmalade and cherry jam and green-fig jam, which I had taught Maria how to make. And there were always one or two of the famous Alpujarra hams, which kept through the summer if they were rubbed every week or two with salt. Then came the vegetables – dried tomatoes and egg plants, cut into slices and laid out on shelves, pimentoes hung from the ceiling, jars of home-cured olives and of dried apricots and figs, chick peas and lentils and other sorts of beans in *espuertas* or large frails. And upstairs in the *azotea* were onions, for *olla sin cebolla, es baile sin tamborín*, 'a stew without onions is like a dance without a tabor'. None of these things could be obtained in the shop, but must be stored through the year or bought at a higher price from a neighbour.

I was forgetting honey. This had to be fetched from a bee-keeper who lived close to the Cortijo Colorado, an hour's journey or more away. He moved his hives on mule-back up and down the mountain to catch the thyme and lavender and

rosemary and other aromatic flowers as they came out, and
every spring I paid him a visit with a donkey and brought
back two *arrobas*, that is fifty pounds, in two *orsas* or ampho-
rae. Sometimes, passing through a lonely *barranco*, one would
come on his hives – twenty or so earthenware pipes, each
weighed down with a stone. This was a neighbourhood to be
avoided, for Spanish bees are much fiercer than English ones.

Meat we got only occasionally, whenever a kid was killed.
Few people eat it except on feast days, but fish came up on
mules from the coast on most nights of the year – sardines,
boquerones, jureles, and *pulpos* or cuttle-fish – and was sold by
the man who brought it at the house door. Only in summer it
came less frequently, on account of a verse which says:

> *En los meses que no tienen erre*
> *ni pescado ni mujeres.*

> In the months that have no R in them
> keep off both fish and women.

The explanation of this adage is that in summer fish are
thought to be unwholesome because they are breeding, and
that if a man makes love to his wife then he will have less
strength for the long day's work. Or rather that is what people
tell you if you ask them, though the real reason is that, whereas
sowing and ploughing require the magic assistance of a
lecherous marriage bed, the harvest ought to be carried
through in a state of ritual purity. For the same reason women
who are having their monthly periods must not pick plants or
flowers or touch corn or agricultural implements or, if possible, cook food. If they wash their hands or faces they may fall
ill, and if they try to make bread the dough will not rise.

The merits or otherwise of Spanish cooking are a matter on
which people differ. My experience is that, taking it on its
most humble level, it contains a few admirable dishes and two
or three deplorable ones. The dish I liked best at Yegen was
known, from the pot in which it was cooked, as *cazuela*. This
was a stew of rice, potatoes, and green vegetables cooked

together with either fish or meat and seasoned with tomatoes, pimentoes, onions, garlic, powdered almonds, and sometimes saffron. The method of preparing it was to begin by frying the rice and some of the other ingredients in olive oil and, when it had acquired a golden tinge, to add water. The potatoes and green vegetables were then thrown in, and the result after twenty minutes' simmering was a sort of mess which had to be eaten with a spoon. Next to this in order of merit I would place the famous *paella*, which is the national dish of Valencia. Shell-fish, chicken, pimento, and rice are the principal ingredients, and there are no potatoes. It is cooked in a very large, flat frying-pan till all the water has been absorbed, and is then eaten elegantly with a fork.

Several stages lower in the list came the vegetarian dishes – *olla gitana*, *ropa vieja* or old clothes, lentil and bean pottages, string beans with eggs, various sorts of omelettes, and at the very bottom the national dish of Castile, which is known as *puchero*. This is a boiled affair, not unlike the French *pot-au-feu*, of which the essential ingredients are pork, chunks of *tocino* or bacon fat, potatoes, turnips, and chick peas. The chick pea, from which Cicero took his name, is a yellow bullet which explodes in the inside into several cubic feet of gas, while if the cook knows her job properly she will see that the meat is boiled till it has no taste left and that the fat, a yellowish white in colour, is rancid. A Spaniard feels when he eats this dish that he has vindicated his toughness of fibre. He has not degenerated from the breed of men who conquered a continent with a handful of adventurers, wore hair-shirts day and night till they stuck to their flesh, and braved the mosquitoes of the Pilcomayo and the Amazon.

Our range of vegetables was so large that we could play many variations on a small number of dishes. We could regale ourselves with salads almost all the year round and in summer sip that delicious salad soup, the Andalusian *gazpacho*. The winter form of this was a poached egg floating on a mixture of water, vinegar, and olive oil among small pieces of bread. A humble dish, costing at the most twopence, I found it made a pleasant introduction to a meal when one was tired. But how have I managed to forget that most characteristic of Spanish foods – *bacalao* or salt cod? Enter any grocer's store in the Peninsula, and one will see a row of flat, kite-shaped objects, a dirty white in colour, hanging like the mummified vermin on a gamekeeper's gallows or like faded, unbleached clothes on a line, from a cord stretched below the ceiling. This is the fish that when cooked gives out a smell like the lion-house in the zoo, but when well cooked and of good quality is as delicious as it is nutritive and sustaining. It is both the food of the rich and the food of the poor, but since, unfortunately for me, the poor were in the great majority at Yegen, the *bacalao* sold there was of the worst quality. Also Maria, whose natural talents ran to herb medicines and plant dyes, was little versed in cooking.

Our snow-cured hams, which were eaten raw, were famous, and sometimes we could buy rabbits, hares, and partridges. The rabbit is believed to have given its name to Spain (the Phoenician word for that animal is *sapan*), but today it is scarce. Since the forests were cut down it has had no cover from the hawks, which have multiplied in the Spanish sierras at the expense of the birds and animals that used to live on them. But when one got these rabbits they were delicious and both leaner and gamier than their northern relatives. Our partridges belonged to the large red-legged species, abundant on the dry hills and *barrancos*, but difficult to approach within gun range. They were usually shot in an unsporting manner with decoys, without any regard to the season, and this gave rise to a curious and unedifying avian display. When the decoy was a female and the approaching male was shot and killed, the caged bird would dance and crow and flap its wings in delight and triumph. But when the decoy was a male, it would droop dejectedly and remain silent.

I have passed over two dishes unknown to Western cooking, though in more primitive times they were common enough. The first of these was *gachas*, a porridge of wheat flour simmered in water, which used to be known in England as hasty pudding. In the mountain farms and at shepherds' bivouacs it formed the principal aliment, being eaten three times a day for months on end with milk. In the villages it was taken with fried sardines, tomatoes, and pimentoes. The second was *migas*, which is also a sort of porridge, but fried in olive oil, garlic, and water. It could be made either of wheat or maize flour or of breadcrumbs. The poor eat it with the invariable sardines, the cheapest and dullest of the Mediterranean fishes and often the only one to reach our village, while the rich liked to pour hot chocolate over it. My landlord, as I have already said, took it with both chocolate and fried fish, stirred up well together.

Almost everyone agrees about the excellence of Spanish bread. The loaf is very close textured, but it has a taste and sweetness like no other bread in the world. This, I imagine, is because the grain is entirely ripe before being harvested. Besides loaves we had *roscos*, or rolls made in the form of rings, and *tortas*, which are flat cakes made with wheat flour, sugar, and oil. The poor, and sometimes the rich too, ate maize bread, and in the mountain farms they ate black bread made of rye. For shepherds it had the advantage of not going stale.

There are some curious customs about bread which were strictly observed in my village, and indeed through the whole of Andalusia. Before cutting a new loaf it was proper to make the sign of the cross over it with a knife. If a loaf or *rosca* fell to the ground, the person who picked it up would kiss it and say '*Es pan de Dios*' ('It's God's bread'). Children were never allowed to strike it or treat it roughly or to crumble it on the table, and it was considered shocking to offer even stale crusts to a dog. When once I jabbed my knife into a loaf, I was reproved and told that I was 'stabbing the face of Christ'. Bread was, in fact, sacred, and this, according to Dr Américo Castro, is not, as one would suppose, a derivation from the cult of the Sacrament but a notion borrowed from the Arabs. Butter, on the other hand, was unknown. *Manteca* meant either lard or rancid dripping worked up with garlic and eaten by workmen in the coast towns with bread. This is explained by the fact that we had no milch cows. Even in the north of Spain there are said to have been none till the Flemish influence at the time of Charles V brought them in, and it is only in recent years that they have been kept in Andalusia. In the nineteenth century the wealthy families of Malaga used to import barrels of salted butter from Hamburg, and on that account they became known as *la gente de la manteca*, or 'the butter folk'. It was a luxury that set a stamp on one's social position, like having a car today.

Many wild plants were eaten in our village, and I will single out a few of them. Everyone who has visited southern Spain in the spring will have sampled the thin, bitter asparagus. This is never planted in gardens, but is picked from a tall thorny plant that grows on every mountain slope in southern Spain that is not too far from the sea. At Yegen we got it from men who came round selling it. Another very common plant everywhere is fennel. The Italian cultivated kind, which has a large edible root, is not known in Spain, and we ate the leaf and stalk of the wild species. It formed a frequent and, I think, pleasant ingredient in soups and *ollas*. Another plant which I strongly recommend is *colleja*, a sort of bladder campion whose botanical name is *Silene inflata*. The young shoots are picked before the flowering stems get under way, and eaten in omelettes. For salads the women picked *cerraja*, that is, the young leaves of the common sowthistle, *vinagrera* or French sorrel, and chicory.

At the risk of being tedious I will add that on the coast and on the interior plateaux the country people are greatly given to thistles. For example, the young stems of that superb golden thistle, *Scolymus hispanicus*, in Spanish *tagornina*, are taken in stews in spite of the fact that they make some people come out in spots, while the heads and roots of the milk thistle, *Silybum marianum*, were eaten in large quantities all through Andalusia during the famine that followed the Civil War.

Many people at Yegen had a neurosis about eating. Quite a number of women of the poorer sort seemed to feel an antipathy for food, and would rather be offered a cup of coffee than a good meal. Others were ashamed of being seen to eat, and if compelled to do so in public would sit in a corner with their backs to the room. I once knew a family of well-to-do people, of partly gipsy descent, each of whom cooked his own food and ate it at a separate table, with his back to the others. One must expect such feelings to arise in a country where for many people food is scarce and any sort of eating an act of daring and extravagance. Old women in particular developed the sort of prudery about it that in other countries they develop about sex.

The general rule, except among the rich, was for the head of the family to eat first by himself. For this he did not draw up to a dining-room table, but had a *mesilla* or little low table placed in Oriental style in front of him. His children ate on the ground, squatting in a circle round a pot or frying-pan, while the women of the house took their food last and in a hurried, scrappy manner. Sometimes, however, there would be several grown men in a family, and then they ate out of a common dish placed on a table between them. This was the custom too in ventas and posadas, and whenever parties of friends went off to the fields for a festive picnic. According to the novelist, Juan Valera, the Andalusian upper classes always ate in this way down to the middle of the nineteenth century. Naturally, as I have already said, there was an etiquette about this. Everyone selected his segment and ate till the partition separating it from his neighbours' had become thin. Those who had delicate tastes then laid down their spoon, leaving it to the coarser appetites to eat right through.

There were one or two odd customs about clothes. All through the winter months the men wore a *bufanda* or muffler which, even when it was mild, they kept pulled across their mouths. When asked why they did this, they would reply that it was dangerous to let cold air pass into the lungs. I used to suspect that there was a different reason and that the custom may have been a Moorish survival. The Tuareg tribes of the Sahara, who in the twelfth century conquered Spain, keep their mouths covered to keep out the evil spirits.

Hats were an important article of clothing, conveying dignity. When a visitor arrived he removed his hat at the door as a mark of politeness, but one had immediately to beg him to put it on again. If he saw that one had nothing on one's own head he might refuse to do so, so that I found it advisable to reach for my own hat as soon as someone was announced. This would spare my visitor the predicament either of acting discourteously or of exposing himself to the risk of catching cold. For fear of this the men at Yegen never took off their hats till they went to bed. The great social revolution of the late twenties was marked by the girls wearing short skirts and the young men going about bare-headed. What a breach with the past this made will be realized if one studies the role of hats in Spanish history. When, to give but one example, Charles III ordered that hats with broad brims should not be worn, the people of Madrid rose *en masse*, the king fled to Aranjuez, and the minister who had drawn up the decree had to leave Spain. The royal reaction to this was the expulsion of the Jesuits, who for their own ends had supported the popular hat fetish.

I did not spend all my time at home, reading and talking. I used also to travel. Since I had little money to spend on buses and liked walking, I generally went on foot. In this way I travelled as far as Murcia and Cartagena and explored the mountains I lived in and the country round them. In the summer I sometimes went down to the sea.

The nearest point of the coast to Yegen is Adra. This is a small port lying at the mouth of the river that drains the eastern half of the Alpujarra. The pleasantest way to reach it was to follow the *rambla* that began immediately below the village.

One scrambled down alongside the stream till it broadened out into a wide bed, lined with poplars and oleander, tamarisk and agnus castus. The last is a shrub which has a spike of blue flowers somewhat like those of the buddleia and whose leaves are said to have the property of making anyone who eats them chaste. This, however, I cannot vouch for, since I never heard of anyone making the experiment.

After a village called Darrical the river enters a gorge. The mule-track climbs to avoid it; but on foot, if one did not mind wading and scrambling, it was easy to get through, provided that the water was low. I used to take this way. On either side the cliffs rose sheer to a great height, fretted with holes and caves in which rock doves and jackdaws and falcons nested, as well as wild-cats and martens. It was a place of great solitude. The water ran and tumbled by under the oleanders, and the strip of blue sky overhead looked like another river.

The oleander is the most striking of south Mediterranean plants. One meets it by every watercourse, by every dry *rambla* and *barranco*. In such surroundings its corymbs of rose-coloured flowers seem mocking and sinister. They celebrate those cemeteries where the water lies dead and buried underground, too weak to rise and fertilize the parching soil. Besides, its taste is bitter and its leaves are poisonous both to men and cattle. 'Bitter as the oleander', *como la adelfa amarga*, says a Spanish *copla* when it wishes to describe the bitterness of unrequited love, and no image could be juster.

Adra is a white town set in a green sea of sugar-cane. Here the pulse of life is different. The air is languid and heavy, the vegetation is sappy and luxuriant, and a little slender plant, *Oxalis cernua*, a wood sorrel introduced from South Africa, covers the banks and edges of the fields with its sickly yellow blossoms. In the long main street one smelled decay. Walls whose plaster was peeling, flies crawling over everything, swarms of half-naked children, stench of urine and excreta. And there, where the fields ended, beyond the last row of plumed canes, lay the sea – monotonous, tideless, thumping up and down on its sandy edge, but, like the oleander, beautiful.

One year I went down to Adra with a young friend, Robin John, a son of the painter. We slept in a little cane hut on the edge of the beach over which there grew, I remember, an enormous pumpkin plant. By day we bathed, watched the fishermen tugging at their seine nets, and kept an eye open for the fisher girls. By night we listened to the twangling of a guitar and the wail of *cante jondo*, while the moon rose like a larger pumpkin over the sea horizon. From their ditches and tanks a chorus of frogs joined in, as if in protest at so much vice and rankness.

Adra has a long history. Originally, it would seem, a Greek factory (its former name, Abdera, suggests an Ionian foundation), it was taken over by the Carthaginians when in 535 B.C. they won the command of the Spanish seas from the Phocaeans. They made of it a fish-salting station. Its coins show a temple whose pillars are tunny fish, and its chief export, besides salted fish, was that famous sauce, *garon* (in Latin *garum*) which Greek and Roman authors have praised so highly. This was made out of the roes of mackerel and the intestines of tunny, beaten up with egg and cooked in brine, and after that left to soak for several months in a mixture of wine and oil.

The commercial quarter of Adra lies along the coast road and ends at the port. The old town, which occupies the site of the Arab city – the Carthaginian town lay a little way beyond it to the east – stands on a low hill at the edge of the river delta. Nothing but a few Punic sherds and coins and the graves of two Jewish children who died during the reign of Augustus has been found of its three thousand years of history, though the shrine of the Virgen del Mar, rebuilt after its destruction by pirates in 1610, perpetuates in a chastened way the rites of Astarte-Aphrodite. In Spain, unlike Greece or Sicily, it is the Virgin who has drunk up what there was of pagan antiquity. But climb the steep mountain-side, which is here as peeled and bare as if it were made of metal, and one will get a view of the whole place. The green, green delta, the white, white town, and, stretching away from these, the sea – as flat and as bright and as modern as if Picasso had just finished painting it.

When one goes westwards from Adra along the coast road, one comes every few miles to a watch-tower. Some of these are square and made of a kind of cement, and they are very ancient. Livy alludes to them under the name of *turres Hannibalis* and declares that they were built by the Carthaginians, but according to Professor Schulten many of them go back some centuries before that to Tartessian times. The more numerous round towers were built by the Arabs, but kept in use by the Christians down to the end of the eighteenth century, in order to give warning of corsairs. Fires were lit in them when suspicious-looking ships were sighted, and the mounted militia, known as *la caballería de la costa*, then hurried to the point of danger. The phrase *Hay moros en la costa*, 'There are Moors on the coast', has become a proverb.

Some ten miles on one arrives at La Rábita, which, as its name shows, was once a monastery of Moslem dervishes. Here a broad, dry *rambla* comes winding down like a snake from the hills, and a few miles up it stands the small, neat town of Albuñol. In its present form it dates from the end of the eighteenth century, for, like all the pueblos of the Sierra la Contraviesa, it was deserted for nearly two hundred years after the expulsion of the Moriscos in 1570, because the raids of the African corsairs made the coast uninhabitable. A few miles from the town is a cave known as the Cueva de los Murciélagos, where in 1857 a remarkable Neolithic burial was discovered. I shall speak of this later.

Albuñol is a centre of the local wine and almond trade, and from it a road runs over the sierra to Órgiva and Granada. The motor-bus from Granada to Almeria used to take this route, doing the journey in about ten hours. I recommend it to the motorist. When in February the almond trees come into flower, the *rambla* of Albuñol is a beautiful sight, and the climb to nearly five thousand feet, with the sea immediately below, is exhilarating. On the summit there is a venta known as the Haza del Lino and the remains of what was once a great cork forest.

I will close this chapter with a curious and, I believe, unique story. One day I went into the village shop at Yegen to buy some cigarettes and was handed back with my change some unfamiliar coins. On examining these at home I saw that they were Punic and Iberian. That is to say, they were the coins of Punic and Iberian cities, minted under the Roman Republic, and thus the first coins to be minted in Spain except in the Greek cities of Catalonia. When I returned to the shop and asked if they had more they produced twenty or thirty. An offer to buy them at a peseta apiece brought in another twenty from other people. The interesting question was – where had they come from? Had they been circulating quietly in the neighbourhood since they were first minted, or had they come from a hoard? After some inquiry I came on a man who remembered that one of his ancestors had left a collection of old coins when he died and that his family, not seeing any other use for them, had decided to spend them.

In 1940 I sent these coins to the Ashmolean Museum to be examined, and presented it with those that it had not already got. The museum authorities printed a memoir on the way in which they had come into my possession. The collection included coins from six or seven Iberian and Punic cities in Andalusia, among them several from Adra.

CHAPTER THIRTEEN

VIRGINIA WOOLF'S VISIT

*

It was in the spring of 1923 that Leonard and Virginia Woolf came out to see me. I met them at Granada at the house of some friends of mine, the Temples, who wished to discuss the African colonies with Leonard, and after a couple of nights there we came on by bus and mule to Yegen. This time the journey went smoothly, without any of the difficulties that had marked Lytton Strachey's passage three years before, and it was evident that they enjoyed it.

The first thing that comes to my mind when I think of Virginia as she was in those days, and particularly as I saw her in the quiet seclusion of my house, is her beauty. Although her face was too long for symmetry, its bones were thin and delicately made, and her eyes were large, grey or greyish blue, and as clear as a hawk's. In conversation they would light up a little coldly, while her mouth took an ironic and challenging fold, but in repose her expression was pensive and almost girlish. When in the evening we settled under the hooded chimney and the logs burned up and she stretched out her hands to the blaze, the whole cast of her face revealed her as a poet.

There are writers whose personality resembles their work, and there are others who, when one meets them, give no inkling of it. Virginia Woolf belonged strikingly to the first category. When one had spent half an hour in a room with her one could easily believe that it was she who, as one was told, had scribbled quickly in purple ink in the summer house at Rodmell that fresh and sparkling article that had just appeared in the *Nation*, and when one saw her in a reflective or dreamy mood one recognized only a little less slowly the authoress of *To the Lighthouse*. One reason for this was that her conversation, especially when she had been primed up a little, was like her prose. She talked as she wrote and very nearly as well, and that is why I cannot read a page of *The Common Reader* today without her voice and intonation coming back to me forcibly. No writer that I know of has put his living presence into his books to the extent that she has done.

Not, however, that what she said was ever bookish. She talked easily and naturally in a pure and idiomatic English, often, like many of her friends, in a lightly ironical tone. Irony, it will be remembered, plays a great and important part in her writings. There it is of a gay and playful kind, sometimes verging on facetiousness, but in her conversation it became personal and took on a feminine, and one might almost say flirtatious, form. Leaning sideways and a little stiffly in her chair, she would address her companion in a bantering tone, and she liked to be answered in the same manner. But whatever her vein, all the resources of her mind seemed to be at her immediate disposal at every moment. One felt a glass-like clarity, but it was not the clarity of a logician, but rather that of a kaleidoscope which throws out each time from the same set of pieces a different pattern. Much later, when she was, I think, working on *The Waves*, she told me that her difficulty lay in stopping the flow of her pen. She had been reading, she said, a life of Beethoven and envied his power of drawing up into his score, by constant revision and correction, themes which resisted being brought to the surface. I imagine that for her correction meant simply shaking the kaleidoscope and producing a new, more appropriate passage.

Perhaps because Virginia lacked the novelist's sense for the dramatic properties of character and was more interested in the texture of people's minds, she was much given to drawing them out and documenting herself upon them. She asked me a great many questions – why I had come to live here, what I felt about this and that, and what my ideas were about writing. I was conscious that I was being studied and even quizzed a little, and also that she and Leonard were trying to decide whether I showed any signs of having literary talent. If so, I must publish with them. Yet it must not for a moment be thought that she was patronizing. On the contrary her deference to the views of the callow and rather arrogant youth with whom she was staying was quite surprising. She argued with me about literature, defended Scott, Thackeray, and Conrad against my attacks, disagreed with my high opinion of *Ulysses* on the grounds that great works of art ought not to be so boring, and listened humbly to my criticisms of her own novels. That was the great thing about 'Bloomsbury' – they refused to stand on the pedestal of their own age and superiority. And her visit was followed by a succession of highly characteristic letters in which she continued the theme of our discussions.

I want to emphasize Virginia's real friendliness on this occasion and the trouble she took to advise and encourage me, because her recklessness in conversation – when she was over-excited she talked too much from the surface of her mind – made some people think that she lacked ordinary sympathies. I was young for my age, and rather earnest. The isolation in which I lived had made me self-centred, and like all people who are starved for conversation I was very talkative. She on the other hand was a writer of great distinction, approaching the height of her powers. Yet she and her husband not only concealed the impatience they must often have felt, but treated me as though I was their intellectual equal. Of course, one might say, they believed in encouraging young writers and spotting the winners among them. Virginia had a strong sense of the continuity of literary tradition and felt it a duty to hand on what she had received. She was also intensely and uneasily aware of the existence of a younger generation who would one day rise and sit in judgement on her. It may be, therefore, that she thought that my strange way of life and my passion for literature showed that I might have something to give. If so, however, both she and Leonard decided a few years later that they had been mistaken.

As I sit here, trying to collect my scattered memories of this fortnight, a few scenes come before me with vividness. I recall Virginia's face in the firelight, then the gaily bantering tone in which she spoke, and Leonard's easy, companionable one. Her manner at such times was vivaciously, though rather chillily, feminine, and her voice seemed to preen itself with self-confidence in its own powers. With a little encouragement it would throw off a cascade of words like the notes of a great pianist improvising, and without the affectation – born of delight in verbal mastery – that sometimes crept into the style of her novels. Leonard, on the other hand, was very steady, very masculine – a pipe-smoking, tweed-dressing man who could conduct an argument to a finish without losing the thread and who had what is called at Cambridge 'a good mind'. Moreover – and this impressed me more than anything – he could read Aeschylus without a crib.

Then, scrambling on the hillside among the fig trees and the olives, I see a rather different person. An English lady, country-bred and thin, her wide-open eyes scanning the distance, who has completely forgotten herself in her delight at the beauty of the landscape and at the novelty of finding herself in such a remote and Arcadian spot. She seemed, though quiet, as excited as a schoolgirl on a holiday, while her husband's serious, sardonic features had become almost boyish. On these walks they talked of themselves and of their life together with great frankness – to have no secrets from friends was another 'Bloomsbury' characteristic – and among other things I recall Virginia telling me how incomplete she felt in comparison to her sister Vanessa, who brought up a family, managed her house, and yet found plenty of time left in which to paint. Although I doubt if she ever lost this sense of her own inadequacy, of not being quite, in every sense of the word, a person of flesh and blood, she was practical and could cook and run a house better than most women, as well as lead a social life that often probably outran her strength.

It used to be said by those who were not invited to its

parties that 'Bloomsbury' was a mutual admiration society who pushed one another's works. This charge, which has recently been repeated, is simply not true. Virginia Woolf greatly admired E. M. Forster's novels, which seemed to her to have the qualities of 'reality' which she perhaps felt hers lacked, and she also admired Roger Fry's writings on art as well as his marvellously eager and stimulating conversation. But she had a poor opinion of Lytton Strachey's biographies, though she was greatly attached to him personally, and praised the fineness and subtlety of his mind and his discrimination as a critic. One evening, I remember, while the Woolfs were at Yegen, the subject of his *Queen Victoria* came up. Both Leonard and Virginia pronounced decisively against it, declaring that it was unreadable. Although I did not care for its flat, spongy style, which gave me the sensation of walking on linoleum, this charge seemed to me absurd: readable was precisely what it was. Yet they maintained that they had been unable to finish it. Lytton, on the other hand, greatly admired most of Virginia's writings, but could not read Forster in spite of his strong personal friendship for him. I remember him saying, after looking through his little guide to Alexandria, *Pharos and Pharillon*, that it was a pity that he had taken to novel-writing when he was so much better at history. And he disliked both Roger Fry and his work.

Virginia had much to say of T. S. Eliot, of whom she was seeing a good deal at this time. She praised him warmly as a man, and spoke of his remarkable intelligence, but seemed a little half-hearted about *The Waste Land*, which the Hogarth Press was then publishing. Like myself, she had a poor opinion of D. H. Lawrence. The boring prophetic mantle he wore, the streams of slovenly and sentimental writing that poured from his pen, obscured the sometimes extraordinary freshness of insight that showed itself in one or two of his novels and short stories. Nor had his admirers helped his reputation, for as usually happens in such cases, they had been more impressed by his bad books – those which contained his 'message' – than by his good ones. Yet she could change her mind, and when, some years later, she came across *Sons and Lovers*, she wrote an article on it which, though perhaps not very understanding, praised it highly. Has there ever been an age, one might ask, in which writers have admired more than one or two of their contemporaries?

To appreciate Virginia Woolf's brilliance as a talker, one had to see her in her own circle of friends. It was a regular custom for five or six of these to meet every week after dinner either at her house or at her sister Vanessa's, and usually one or two of the younger generation would be invited to be present. In that capacity I went several times. The aces were Roger Fry, Duncan Grant, Vanessa Bell, Clive Bell, Lytton Strachey, Maynard Keynes, and occasionally one or two people such as Desmond MacCarthy and Morgan Forster who did not, I think, regard themselves as 'belonging to Bloomsbury', though they were accepted by the others on the same footing. The arrangements were informal, yet everyone was aware of the purpose of the meeting, which was to make good conversation. With this idea, for literary people at this time they were very sober, no drinks except coffee were provided.

I very soon got the impression that these conversaziones were really of the nature of orchestral concerts. One might almost say that the score was provided, for the same themes always came up – the difference between the younger and the older generation, the difference between the painter and the writer, and so forth. The performers too were thoroughly practised, for they had been meeting every week or even more often over a space of many years to discuss the same not, one would have thought, very inspiring subjects. Thus they had each of them learned what part he must play to conduce to the best general effect and also how to stimulate and give the cue for the others. The solo instruments, one might say (both strings), were Virginia Woolf and Duncan Grant: they could be relied on to produce at the appropriate moment some piece of elaborate fantasy, contradicting the serious and persistent assertions of the other instruments. Roger Fry would drive forward on one of his provocative lines: Vanessa Bell, the most silent of the company, would drop one of her *mots*, while Clive Bell, fulfilling the role of the bassoon, would keep up a general roar of animation. His special function in the performance was to egg on and provoke Virginia to one of her famous sallies.

What one got from these evenings was, if my youthful judgement is to be relied on, conversation of a brilliance and (in spite of the rehearsals) spontaneity which, I imagine, has rarely been heard in England before. I have known other good talkers, one of them perhaps the equal of any of these, but they have always given solo performances. What 'Bloomsbury' evenings offered was the concert in which each talked, to produce himself and to draw the best out of the others. I imagine that only continual practice by people who share the same general attitude to life and who are as pleased by their friends' performance as by their own can provide anything like it.

For a young writer even a slight acquaintance with such a group of people was an education, though not perhaps a stimulus. They had standards – honesty, intelligence, taste, devotion to the arts, and social sophistication. They never, in their written judgements, let their vanity or their private friendships or their political or religious prejudices run away with them, and they were none of them out to compensate for their own weaknesses and deficiencies by attacking others. Yet it must, I think, be admitted that they lived – not singly, which would not have mattered, but collectively – in an ivory tower. Maynard Keynes and Leonard Woolf had roots outside it in the world of politics, and Roger Fry was too active and public-spirited a man to let himself be confined. The others, however, were prisoners of their close web of mutual friendships and of their agreeable mode of life and also of their rather narrow and (as they held it) smug Cambridge philosophy. Virginia Woolf, it is true, was always aware of the typist queueing for her lunch in the cheap tea-shop and of the shabby old lady weeping in the third-class railway carriage, yet she too was tied to her set by her birth, her social proclivities, her craving for praise and flattery, and could only throw distant and uneasy glances outside it. Her sense of the precariousness of things, which gives her work its seriousness, came from her private life – from the shock of her brother Thoby's death, and from her experience of madness. But the ethos of her group and indeed her whole cultured Victorian upbringing cut her off from the hard view of human nature that the novelist needs and drove her to develop her own poetic and mystical vision of things in what I at least feel was too subjective a way. Thus when one rereads her novels now one feels again the ease and beauty of much of the writing, and gets a certain muffled, Calderón-like impression of life being no more than a dream, yet one is left dissatisfied. For if one is to be convinced that life is a dream, one must first be shown, and pretty sharply, that what is set before one is life.

Looking back today, it is not, I think, difficult to see that the weakness inherent in the splendid flower of English culture thrown up by 'Bloomsbury' lay in its being so closely attached to a class and mode of life that was dying. Already by 1930 it was pot-bound. Its members were too secure, too happy, too triumphant, too certain of the superiority of their Parnassian philosophy to be able to draw fresh energies from the new and disturbing era that was coming in. They had escaped the shock of the first German war, either by being unfit for military service or by joining the ranks of the pacifists, and had not taken warning from the prophets who announced that the snug rationalist world they lived in was seriously threatened. When they should, therefore, have been in their prime, they were on their way to being an anachronism, even Virginia Woolf – the most open-minded of all except Maynard Keynes – being limited by some deep-seated doubt (connected possibly with her fits of madness) about the reality of almost everything except literature. Yet, I imagine, if the cobalt bomb does not obliterate everything, future ages will feel an interest in these people because they stand for something that the world always looks on with nostalgia – an *ancien régime*. They carried the arts of civilized life and friendship to a very high point, and their work reflects this civilization. Then, surely, two of them at least, Virginia Woolf and Maynard Keynes, possessed those rare imaginative gifts that are known as genius.

It was, I fancy, in the summer of 1923 that David Garnett, generally known as Bunny, and his wife Ray Marshall came to stay with me. I had met him in London, where he ran a book-shop in partnership with my old friend Francis Birrell, but had not felt especially drawn to him. Now he was here, and on his honeymoon.

At this time he was a slight, fair-haired man of about my own age, with rather broad shoulders, very blue eyes, and a slow way of speaking. When he addressed anyone he had a habit of swivelling his head with a deliberate Thurber-like movement round upon them and letting his eyes dwell deeply and intensely on theirs, till they became quite mesmerized by those two fathomless lakes. Then, after what seemed an ex-tremely long interval, he would begin slowly, moving his lips in a tentative way and smiling as if at his own clumsiness, to say something. At first these strange approaches embarrassed me, but as I got to know him better I came to like him very much. To begin with, he had all the pleasant, easy qualities of the extrovert. He was never ruffled, he always had his feet firmly on the ground, and there was something soothingly countrified about his manner that, if one had met him for the first time in a pub, would have suggested that he was a farmer or a local doctor. A further acquaintance showed that he had plenty of shrewd common sense, a strong sense of humour, especially about the vagaries of his friends, and a generous, very independent nature. With these qualities and the self-assurance of a man who takes it for granted that he will be liked, he got on with people of every sort and kind, and with-out ever going out of his way to please made a large number of friends. Men found him the most easy of companions – fishing, boating, bathing, at the races – while that hypnotic stare of his had a powerful effect upon women and enabled him to play with considerable success a Don Juanesque role among them. To sum up, a very English sort of man, yet crossed in an indefinable way with Russian, as though his mother's translations had played in his gestation the part of Jacob's streaked rods on Laban's cattle.

His wife Ray was a small, dark woman with a certain look about her of an Indian squaw. She had a gift for art – Roger Fry, I remember, used to praise her woodcuts – but she was so very silent that for a long time I could not form any idea of what she was like. When she began to speak the muscles of her throat contracted as though to stop her, and in the end she had to force her words out with great effort between her teeth. There was something in her appearance that reminded one of a small shy animal – a squirrel, possibly – but whatever it was, a delightful one. She lived in her own secret world, and it was by not noticing her too much that one came in the end to have contact with her. Bunny, who had just published *Lady into Fox* and had a certain amount of rather heavy animal being himself, seemed to have been attracted by this side of her, for they spent much of their time in my house looking at one another, uttering little woodland noises but hardly speaking, so that one ended by not noticing their presence.

The last time I saw David Garnett was during the final years of the war. I had heard that he had an important job in the Intelligence Service, with a suite of rooms off the Strand and several lady secretaries to wait on him, yet when I saw this handsome, well-groomed man, who carried a rolled silk umbrella on his arm and had a mass of fine white hair under his black, Foreign Office hat, I was astounded. He looked every inch a cabinet minister. However, I soon found that he was the same old Anglo-Hemingway figure: slow, humorous, amused by his own important exterior, and underneath it not changed in the least. He had learned one thing with age and official position – to tell a good story well. Yet now that I think of it, he had always, if only one gave him time, done that.

I have passed over one long visit which my friend John Hope-Johnstone paid to Yegen. Robin John, then a very good-looking boy of seventeen, joined us and stayed for some time, and after him came Robin's father, Augustus. He arrived in April and remained till the end of June, painting hard all the time, but I cannot describe his visit because I was not there. I had gone to England and only ran into him in Madrid on the way back. Sidney Saxon-Turner, a friend of Virginia Woolf and of Lytton Strachey, also came out on a short visit, and my friend Franky Birrell got as far as Órgiva with his aged father, who had been Chief Secretary for Ireland in 1915; then after waiting two nights at the posada – it was a very primitive place without even an earth closet – he returned to Granada because he could get no answer from me. I was away.

I now come to a different sort of episode. Towards 1927 or 1928, when I was living in London, I let my house to a young novelist called Dick Strachey, a nephew of Lytton Strachey's, who later developed an admirable talent for writing children's books. He came out on his honeymoon, and had a painful adventure, which I shall describe on account of the light it throws on local superstitions.

He was out walking one day in the wild, broken country of *ramblas* and *barrancos* that lies below the village, when he saw three roughly dressed men standing a little way off and beckoning to him. His first thought was to join them and pass the time of day, for that would provide some practice for his Spanish, but then a second thought occurred to him – what if they were brigands? Spain was notorious for its bandits and brigands who carried people off to their caves, beat them, and held them to ransom, and a closer glance at these people was not reassuring. He decided therefore to turn back, and since walking is a very slow method of progression and he wished to move quickly, he began to run. But gipsies – for that is what they were – can run too, and they soon overtook him.

Surrounding him with drawn knives and fierce expressions, they cried out a word which he did not understand – *Mantequero! Mantequero!*

Now a *mantequero* is a ferocious monster, shaped outwardly like a man, that lives in wild uninhabited places and feeds on human *manteca* or fat. When brought to bay it makes a shrill, whinnying sound, and, except when recently gorged with food, it is thin and emaciated. So far as I could make out, the people of Yegen, who were of a sceptical disposition, no longer believed in them, but gipsies are by nature conservative and believe in everything. And in this case there could surely be no doubt. What else could it be, this thin, tow-haired, wandering creature that had a high shrill voice, that did not speak a word of any human language, that lived alone in the *barrancos* and had run away as soon as it had seen them? The gipsies' first impulse was to kill it outright and make of its blood a magic paste useful for curing warts and for promoting fertility in women, but the oldest gipsy, who had done a term in prison for homicide and had there learned caution and prudence, said – twirling his black moustaches – No, they must keep strictly to the proper forms of law and lead the creature to the nearest *justicia* or municipal officer. They therefore tied poor Dick's hands behind his back and drove him, with occasional prods from the knife, until they came to the village of Yátor a couple of miles away, and to the house of its mayor or alcalde.

He, as luck had it, was at home and sitting in a chair, engaged in talking over some business about a lawsuit with a neighbour.

'Why, what's all this, José?' he asked, seeing the three gipsies in a row, together with a strange man whose wrists were roped together. 'What the devil have you been up to?'

The oldest of the gipsies removed his black Cordovan hat slowly, and with an air of dignity.

'Señor Alcalde,' he replied, fixing his expressionless *gitano* eyes on the major, 'with your permission we bring you a live *mantequero* which we have found skulking in the *barrancos* in

search of human blood. Will you take charge of it yourself or
would you rather we led it out and cut its throat for you?'

The alcalde inquired further, the trembling Dick explained,
mustering all the Spanish he knew in a burst of eloquence in
which, so he told me afterwards, he claimed relationship with
both King George V and 'the English Cervantes'. The alcalde,
much impressed by his speech – though how much he understood of it would be difficult to say – ordered him to be untied,
and after many apologies and handshakes sent him back under
safe escort to Yegen. Then he turned to the gipsy, who had
supposed that he was doing his country a service by ridding
it of a man-eating monster, and after rating him severely,
ordered him to be taken to the lock-up. A day or two later the
wretched man was sent in handcuffs to the police post at Ugíjar, his guards conducting him by the roundabout route
through Yegen. There, on the alcalde's express orders, he was
brought to the courtyard of my house so that the distinguished
Englishman, who claimed to be related to Cervantes, should
see him and understand 'that there was justice in Spain'. But
Dick had had enough of gipsies and refused even to look out
of the window. As soon as the money he had telegraphed for
arrived, he left for England.

The *mantequero*, or *sacamantecas*, as he is called in some districts, is known all over Spain. Only this year a friend of mine
at Torremolinos, who was making an investigation into the
subject, discovered that every housemaid in that little resort
believed in them. One of these girls even declared that her
brother, while guarding sheep in the Serranía de Ronda, had
been attacked by one as late as last summer, but had succeeded
in driving it off with his sling. As one might suppose, these
great empty sierras are a natural breeding-ground for supernatural creatures. In the towns, however, the practice of
blood-transfusion has led in recent years to the belief in a
different sort of *mantequero*, who is an ordinary human being.
He is the man who steals babies in order that some immensely
old, immensely rich, and vicious marquis may be injected with

their blood and so rejuvenate himself and commit fresh villainies. And these people really exist. In 1910 a family of gipsies was found living on the summit of the Sierra de Gádor and stealing babies, whose blood they then drank warm as it flowed from the skin or the jugular vein. Apparently they hung them on a tree and scraped them. A *curandera*, or wise woman, had told one of them, who was known as La Leona, the Lioness, that she would not only be cured of her consumption if she did this, but would live for ever – or at least for as long as she could keep up the supply of babies. And other cases of this sort have cropped up in other parts of the country. Even today there are *curanderas* who recommend human blood as the only medicine for a fatal disease, and who knows whether an officious *mantequero* does not sometimes turn up to provide it?

A recent correspondence in the *Sunday Times* (September 1954) shows that the origin of the *mantequero* is very ancient. H. J. Tarry declares that the word comes from the Persian *mardkhora*, man-eater, and that this creature had a man's head, a porcupine's quills, the body of a lion, and a scorpion's tail. As such it appears in Ctesias' *Persica* and in Aristotle's *Natural History*. Then, through a corrupt reading of the Greek text, it became the Latin *mantichora* and so spread into West European languages. David Garnett, who was perhaps lucky not to have been taken for one himself, quotes the description of it in Topsell's *Book of Beasts* as having 'three rows of teeth, the face of a man and the bodie of a lyon', while A. Colin Cole speaks of it as a familiar emblem in heraldry, and gives a picture of it, which the *Sunday Times* prints, bearded and wearing a hat. If that is so, it bore a closer resemblance to 'the English Cervantes' than it did to his nephew, who went about beardless and bareheaded.

To make an end of folk-lore, I will conclude this chapter with a word on *sabios*, *curanderas*, and *niños dormidos*. The *sabio* or *sabia* is a wise man or woman who cures by repeating spells and by anointing with spittle, and who sometimes also foretells the weather. Julian Pitt-Rivers, in his classic account of an Andalusian pueblo, *The People of the Sierra*, gives a description of one, to which I need not add anything, because I never came across one in the Alpujarra. We had, however, *curanderos* and *curanderas*, who were much the same thing. They cured by means of simples and sometimes specialized in a particular line – such as children's stomach troubles. Others practised as bonesetters. Although they had their own technique and plant-lore, they were nearly always assisted in their work by possessing some particular *gracia* or grace. A *curandera* would either be a twin or a ninth child, or else she had six fingers on one hand, or had been born on a Good Friday, or had cried out in her mother's womb. One of them was to be found in every pueblo of any size, while in the smaller villages their place would be taken by a *hechicera* or a midwife. As for the *niños dormidos* or 'sleeping children', who were merely a special type of *curandero*, there was one at Mecina Bombarón. He was a boy of about twelve who went into a trance and on waking told his mother what he had dreamed. She then interpreted. One could consult him to discover who had stolen one's hen or whether one's girl was faithful, and naturally his powers depended on his having a special *gracia*. His mother ran a separate line in simples and cured injured limbs by poultices and massage.

Another sort of wise woman, the *motera*, deserves a mention, though she existed only in large towns such as Seville. Her speciality lay in erotic matters. She possessed a store of cantharides or Spanish fly, the only aphrodisiac that is certainly effective, and applied it with massage to the genital organs of men who felt in need of such stimulus and who were ready to pay her price. But even when given in this way it is a dangerous drug, and Ferdinand the Catholic, who in 1505 had married a young wife, died of taking it. Had he lived to have a male heir, the history of Spain and of Europe would have been very different and this, I take it, is the *motera*'s claim to celebrity.

CHAPTER FOURTEEN

THE HIGH MOUNTAINS AND GUADIX

*

THE summers at Yegen were long, slow, monotonous, and, though not unpleasantly hot, drenched in an implacable light. Not a breath of thin mountain air stirred. Every day was the same. Seated in my barber's chair in the inglenook, with a book and a cup of coffee on the table in front of me, I would hear coming down the chimney, as though the village was situated on an island in the sky, a succession of slow, somnolent sounds: dogs barking, donkeys braying, bumble-bees buzzing, pigeons cooing, a voice far off singing, or perhaps the sharp twangling, suddenly interrupted, of a guitar. The shutters had been half closed to keep out the flies, and in that warmth and darkness the mind dissolved and I found it an effort to follow the book – in 1921 it would have been *Du Côté de chez Swann* or Flaubert's Correspondence – that I was reading. Then, as likely as not, I would go up on to the roof to see if anything was happening. No, nothing. Nothing but the empty trough of air billowing away and the heat-waves vibrating in front of the yellow-ochre and lilac mountains.

My bedroom looked out across open country. A single window, enclosed by an iron *reja* or grille and opening right down to the floor, let in the night air, and with it the noise of a waterfall splashing in the *barranco* below. A nightingale sang beside it, the crickets kept up their din, and as I drifted into and out of sleep I fancied that I could hear in the sound of the water voices singing together, and that if I listened a little harder I would catch the words. Then I awoke and found the sun already travelling like a bird across the sky, and began to feel that it was time for me to escape from this succession of unchanging days and to visit the high mountains.

June was too early. The slopes were still either trickling with water or covered with snow. But by July, when the shepherds went up, they were habitable. After some preliminary explorations I found a small cave, protected from the fierce night wind, in a high valley known as El Horcajo, which was approachable with a donkey. Every summer after that I went up with blankets and provisions and spent a week or two in that mixture of boredom and exhilaration which camping out alone on mountains gives.

El Horcajo contains two or three *cortijos* or farms, situated at a height of some 8,000 feet above sea-level, where rye is sown every year in September and reaped in the following August. The peasants go up with their cattle from Trevélez in July, and during the two months that they remain there live almost entirely on curds, fresh cheeses, and *gachas*, which last is a porridge made of wheat flour and eaten with sheeps' milk and a little garlic. For a small sum they agreed to let me share their *rancho*, as a common mess is called, and, though the food was Spartan, the mountain air gave me such an appetite that I ate it with gusto. These *cortijos* were small and primitive. Their walls were of unmortared stones, blackened with smoke, their roofs were of earth, and they had no furniture except for a couple of chairs and a small table. In spite of their being windowless and dark, the flies kept up a perpetual buzzing on the walls, and as soon as one began to eat settled in such swarms on the table and on the food that one could scarcely avoid swallowing a few. However, the purity of the air and water made this seem less disgusting than it would have been at lower levels.

At the upper end of El Horcajo the shepherds folded their sheep every evening and cooked their single meal at the entrance to a cave. They spent the winter on the Campo de Dalías, a great stony plain that lies between the Sierra de Gádor and the sea, and moved up here for the short summer months, leaving their wives in one of the neighbouring villages. As a rule Spanish shepherds are pleasant and sociable people, because their solitary life makes them glad of any opportunity for conversation, but these men were surly and brutish and not above robbing defenceless travellers that came their way. That, I imagine, was because they had no experience of living in a community, for in the Campo de Dalías they were as isolated as in these mountains.

Immediately above El Horcajo rises Mulhacén, the highest crest of the Sierra Nevada. It stands at 11,412 feet above sea-level, which is more than any mountain in Europe can claim outside the Alps or the Caucasus. To reach it, one ascended a valley covered with fine turf and blue gentians, and then up a steep slope to a moraine that enclosed two *lagunas* or tarns. A miniature glacier rose out of the topmost of these, under the shelter of a precipitous cirque of rocks, and pieces of it broke off and floated in the water like icebergs. An easy ascent led from here to the summit, from which one looked down over sheer precipices to screes and shaly slopes below.

There are some forty of these tarns strung out along the 10,000-foot level, all of which are regarded by the local peasants and shepherds as being of fathomless depth and even as communicating with the sea thirty miles away. This is believed to be proved by the assertion – false, of course – that whenever there is a storm off the coast the water of the tarns becomes disturbed and gives out loud reports like artillery. On this account they are known as *ojos del mar*, 'eyes of the sea', though since, according to Dr Américo Castro, the word *ojo* is derived from an Arabic word meaning both 'eye' and 'spring', the term (much used in Spain for large springs, as for example 'Los Ojos de Guadiana' in La Mancha) is evidently a misnomer. One of the largest of these tarns, the Laguna de Vacares, possesses its special mystery. Deep under its surface there is a palace built, like everything rare and unusual in southern Spain, by a Moorish king, and in this palace dwells a beautiful woman who suffers from an insatiable lust to sleep with men. This leads her to draw down into the depths any person of male sex who is so foolish as to bathe in it, and, since this must be of rare occurrence, to appear to shepherds and ibex hunters in the form of a white bird, which tempts them to the edge of the icy waters and then pulls them in. Not only this, for as soon as it is dark she walks abroad in her own voluptuous shape and, should she happen to find a benighted traveller sleeping under a rock, lies down beside him, and after she has worn him out with her caresses carries him off to her subaquatic dwelling in the hopes of further solace later on. For this reason no shepherd will linger in this spot after sunset.

On my first visit to El Horcajo I put this legend to the test. Wishing to see the sun rise from the summit, I carried up a sleeping-bag to this tarn and spent a very cold night there. But, alas – or should I say, happily – no houri-eyed princess appeared or crept between my blankets. I shivered alone and unaccompanied till dawn. Then, as I stood on the summit and the sun rose like a cannon-ball over the distant sierras, the whole coast of Africa from the Strait of Gibraltar to Oran came into view, and on the opposite side the valley of the Guadalquivir as far as the Sierra Morena. After that the heat haze descended.

A few hours' walk along the crest takes one to the Pichaco de la Veleta, more abrupt but a little lower than Mulhacén. Every year on the fifth of August, the day of the Virgin of the Snows, there is a pilgrimage to this place and mass is said there. Since the building of the motor road from Granada to a point just below the summit, a crowd of townspeople and tourists attend it, and for an hour or two wake up the lonely mountain with their laughter and cheerful conversation. Then they depart, leaving behind them their empty bottles and the paper of their sandwiches. Further on, in the valley leading to Dílar, this Virgin has a hermitage from which she may keep a watchful eye on the snows and rescue anyone who gets into trouble, and not far from this there is a dolmen which has the distinction of being the only prehistoric monument in the district. Then the Sierra Nevada drops suddenly to

a low earthy crest, the Suspiro del Moro, and comes to an
end.

One September, just before the first rains, I took it into my
head to walk home from Granada across the mountains in a
single day. Leaving the city at three in the morning, I reached
the village of Guëjar Sierra at dawn, and found a bar open at
which I was able to get a glass of coffee. From here to the col
by the Laguna de Vacares there was a steady climb of nearly
8,000 feet and, running into cloud at the top, I was lucky
enough to see the tarn under its most solemn and mysterious
aspect, with a block of ice still floating on its surface and a
raven croaking in the mists that opened and closed around.
No sign, however, of a white bird, though I sat down by the
edge of the water to eat my lunch of bread and dried figs.
Descending then into El Horcajo, I found the shepherds gone
and, after losing my way for a little in the mist, reached the
chestnut woods of Bérchules towards six in the evening. Here
I had some coffee and ham and eggs, got on to the main road
by dark, and was home by ten o'clock. It was a long walk –
scarcely if at all less than sixty miles – but on high mountains
one can keep going for ever.

As I have had some experience of Spanish mountains, I
would like to offer the prospective hiker a little advice. It is
better to wear rope-soled shoes or boots than leather ones,
because they are less likely to slip, and also – an important
point – because they weigh less. Only one must be careful to
procure strong ones, with extra sewing connecting the uppers
with the soles, the best of all being those canvas boots made
especially for the use of sportsmen. Otherwise there is a risk of
the *alpargatas*, as they are called, coming unsewn on the summit of a mountain and putting one in the position of having to
descend barefoot. It is true that if one is walking in the high
valleys of the Sierra Nevada in such shoes one will get one's
feet wet, but this should not bother one too much, because
they will soon dry again. I would also say that it is better to
carry an *alforja*, or miniature saddle-bag, such as the peasants

of the Alpujarra use to put their lunch in, than a rucksack, because it hangs loosely over the shoulder instead of pressing on the back and so drenching one in sweat. If one cannot procure one of these, a haversack will do. It should be remembered that in these latitudes the sun heat is much greater than it is in the Alps.

Ornithologists, entomologists, and botanists will find much to interest them in these mountains, for although in beauty and variety they cannot compare with those of the Serrania de Ronda, they are nearly double their height. Among the birds it is of course the hawk and crow family that stand out. Eagles of various kinds, lammergeyers, falcons, buzzards, ravens, choughs, and jackdaws abound, as on all the Andalusian sierras, though what they feed on I cannot say, since owing to the lack of cover there are very few small animals. Sooner or later, I suspect, the end of every Spanish bird of prey is death by starvation. The butterflies include several blues that are not found anywhere else, an apollo that has deep yellow spots instead of crimson ones, and the most beautiful of cinnabars, *Zigaena ignifera*, while as for other insects I can only say that in August one meets with swarms of ladybirds, which, impelled by a mysterious urge, fall in such numbers into the streams that they turn them crimson. And be careful how you sit down on that rock that rises so conveniently out of the pure, untrodden snow, for you will immediately be attacked by the most ferocious fleas that you have ever had dealings with.

On botany I can speak with somewhat better authority because, though no more than an amateur, I am an enthusiastic flower-lover, and brave all the difficulties of botanical descriptions to discover their names. I can therefore recommend the Sierra Nevada to serious collectors, for the reason that it offers a large number of flowering species, most of them alpines, that grow nowhere else. Thus a quick survey of Lázaro y Ibiza's *Compendium of Spanish Flora* reveals twenty-three plants that have for their specific name the word *nevadensis*, while approximately another thirty occur only on the Sierra Nevada and about a hundred more grow also on adjacent mountains, but in no other part of the world. To give a few examples, there are five gentians to be found, among them *Gentiana bory*, which does not occur anywhere else: a handsome pansy, *Viola nevadensis*, a shrubby mallow, *Lavatera oblongifolia*, and a honeysuckle, *Lonicera arborea*, which grows in the form of a tree to the height of twenty or thirty feet and has elsewhere been recorded only in the Lebanon. Among the true alpines I may cite a white poppy and two white ranunculi flowering on the edge of the snow, a beautiful astragalus with silky grey leaves and large violet flowers, and a minute silvery plant, *Artemesia granadensis*, with yellow flowers, which is only found above the 10,000-foot level. It has a strong aromatic smell, and under the name of *manzanilla real de la Sierra Nevada* fetches a high price at the druggist's, because a sort of camomile tea is made from it. Another striking plant of these altitudes is *Plantago nivalis*, called by the shepherds *estrellita de la nieve*, star of the snow, because it forms little silvery cushions on the green turf.

A plant that is to my mind more remarkable than any of these is *Herinacea* (or *Erinacea*) *pungens*, called in Spanish *piorno azul* or blue gorse. This is not peculiar to the Sierra Nevada, for it grows on one or two limestone mountains in the south of France and can be found on almost any bare shaly slope or summit in southern Spain above the 5,000-foot level. It is a plant of the peaflower family which forms large, extremely intricate, and thorny pincushions, and its inflorescence is a deep violet blue, which, as it fades, passes through a series of pale azure tints, so that it seems to be producing flowers of two or three distinct kinds and colours. When one comes across it for the first time, forming little islands of blue in the grim, stony waste, one cannot fail to be delighted. Yet it is impossible to pick it: it is too thorny.

Another plant of especial beauty is the Andalusian peony, *Paeonia coriacea*, which is the finest of the three or four European species. Although it occurs on the lower slopes of the

Sierra Nevada, it can best be seen on the coastal range between Granada and Antequera. Here it flourishes in great force on the mountain summits, throwing out in the first week of May thick bouquets of green leaves and golden-centred, rose-coloured flowers between the crevices of the grey limestone rocks and providing one of the most exhilarating spectacles that the aesthetic botanist can get in Europe. Finally, I would mention, for the sake of those who like strong contrasts, *Putoria calabrica*. This is a creeping, woody-stemmed plant belonging to the family of the Rubiaceae, which drapes the rocks with its starry rose-coloured flowers and whose leaves when crushed have such a strong and disgusting stench that a small piece of them will drive one from the room.

Besides these summer expeditions to the high mountains, I used to cross the range where it tails off to a lower elevation whenever I wished to reach the tableland of the Marquesado on the other side. The pass I usually took was the Puerto del Lobo or Wolf Pass – another misnomer, for the Arabic word from which it is derived is *loh*, meaning a plank and hence a narrow, flat piece of land. Since it stood at a height of seven thousand feet above the sea, it was open for pack-mules only from May to October, though men on foot could sometimes get through during the winter months, if they did not mind taking a risk.

The place, especially on a cloudy day, was sad and dreary. One approached it gradually and monotonously along shaly slopes that were rounded and featureless and almost bare of vegetation. Among the stones a little grey plant, its leaves folded together like hands in prayer, seemed waiting for something that never arrived. When one at last reached the summit one found oneself on a small narrow plain where there were several wooden crosses. Poor fish-hawkers in their thin cotton clothes, crossing the cordillera to sell their sardines and *boquerones* in the villages on the other side, had been caught here by the snow or by the icy wind, and their bodies had been found, the eyes pecked out by ravens, by the next passer-by.

Then, just before my first arrival in the country, a serious crime had been committed on this spot. Two Civil Guards were escorting a couple of gipsies with their wives and children from Guadix to Ugíjar and on the summit of the pass they stopped to have a snack. The charge against the gipsies was a small one, for they had merely stolen a mule, and in those mild days the punishment to be expected for this was no more than a few weeks' imprisonment. The guards, therefore, being kindly men, removed their handcuffs so as to let them eat and drink at their ease. All at once the elder of the two women, filled with that age-long hatred that the gipsies have for the police, threw herself from behind on one of the escort and stabbed him with her knife. The rest closed on the other and killed him too. In a frenzy of rage they then mutilated their bodies, one of the women even cutting off the men's private parts and carrying them away with her as trophies. But their triumph did not last long. Within a couple of days they had all been arrested. At the trial, which took place at Ugíjar, the woman who had incited her companions to the crime was sentenced to be garrotted, and the rest were given terms of imprisonment.

A longer but more interesting way of reaching Guadix was to cross by a somewhat higher pass, the Puerto de Rejón or de Bérchules, immediately above Mecina Bombarón. To shorten the journey I used to spend the night at Don Fadrique's *cortijo*. Then, as the sun rose, I would make my way up the valley, botanizing as I went, and climb a spur at the end. In the thin, vibrating air the boulders on the sky-line looked like caravans of pack-animals, journeying steadily on but never arriving. During the summers of 1922 and 1923 this pass became notorious for the robbers who frequented it. They were shepherds, temporarily out of a job, who held up everyone who went by and beat them if they did not find all the money they had expected. Before they were caught they made some considerable hauls, because men would be sent up from the villages to the summer pastures with a roll of notes in their wallets to buy lambs and ewes. On one occasion I ran into three of these footpads but, realizing what they were up to before I got within sling-shot, I turned off and escaped. Another time, crossing the Puerto del Lobo by moonlight on my way back from England, I met a single man who tried to stop me, but got away before he could close. On these mountains it was useful to have a good pair of legs, when one travelled alone and unarmed as I did.

The view, looking northwards from the summit of the Puerto del Lobo, is surprisingly Eastern. Immediately below one's feet lies a broad yellow plain, perfectly bare and bounded by crinkled, ochre-coloured mountains, and through the middle of this plain there runs a deep green splash, looking like ink that has been upset from a bottle, which is the oasis formed by the river of Guadix and its tributaries. One might be looking down from Mount Hermon towards Damascus. Then, if one is going on, one drops four thousand feet to an earth-coloured village, where there are iron mines that till recently were owned by an English company. No place could be more dreary to live in, without a tree in sight, yet only a couple of miles away there stands, alone and menacing, on the summit of a steep, bare knoll, one of the finest Renaissance buildings in Spain. This is the castle of La Calahorra, which was built in 1510 by an Italian architect, Michele Carlone of Genoa, for Rodrigo de Mendoza, first Marqués del Zenete.

The story of this castle is perhaps worth telling. Rodrigo de Mendoza was a bastard son of the great Cardinal Mendoza, Archbishop of Toledo, who did so much to establish Isabella on the throne of Castile and, after he had been legitimized by the Pope, his father gave him as a *mayorazgo* or entail the *llanos* or plains of the Zenete, and the Queen bestowed on him the title of marquis. The famous feats performed by him during the siege of Granada, and the great family to which he belonged, made him one of the first nobles of the day. When he visited Italy, Pope Alexander, remembering perhaps his old friendship with his father, betrothed him to Lucrezia Borgia,

and although this match did not come off – the marriage of a
Spanish cardinal's son to a Spanish pope's daughter would
have been almost too appropriate – Rodrigo, who like his
grandfather, the famous Marqués de Santillana, had a fine feeling for the arts, remained long enough in the country to be
fired with enthusiasm for the new classical architecture. On his
return to Spain, he brought with him the best Italian architect
he could find and built the castle of La Calahorra in a dramatic
situation at the foot of the Sierra Nevada, but among such
desolate wastes that neither he nor any of his descendants
cared to live in it. The building combines the Spanish and the
Italian modes in a remarkable way. Seen from the outside, its
frowning walls and massive drum towers are deeply impressive, but push open the iron gate and then the inner door, and
one will find oneself in a palace of the purest Renaissance style,
with doorways and balustrades exquisitely carved in Carrara
marble. It is the first Renaissance building to have been erected
in Spain, with the possible exception of the castle of Vélez
Blanco, seventy miles to the north-east, which the Marqués de
los Vélez put up at about the same time to the designs of a
Spanish architect. But only the shell of this castle exists today,
for in 1903 the whole of the interior was taken down stone by
stone and moved to the United States.

Today La Calahorra is the property of the Duque del
Infantado, who is the head of the Mendoza family and one of
the largest landowners in the country. I was able to see over it
in 1924, when it was more or less derelict, but at present,
though occupied by a caretaker, it is closed to the public.
Behind that there hangs a tale. A year or two ago the rumour
got about that the Duke was about to sell its sculptured doorways and fireplaces, just as his fellow grandee had sold those
of Vélez Blanco, but the Government had wind of this in time
and forbade the stripping to take place. From that moment the
Duke's agent in Granada ceased to issue permits to view it.
Even an official of the Academy of Fine Arts was, I am told,
refused entry. However, dukes no longer exert the influence

they did fifty years ago, and it is expected that the building will soon be declared a national monument, open to the public.

The plain of the Marquesado is not so entirely barren as it appears from the Puerto del Lobo, for every year it supports a thin crop of barley, which in average years grows to the height of a foot or eighteen inches. In June the poppies stain it a deep crimson – the poppy in Spain has the rich colour of blood – and the skylarks hang in the air above it and give it a ceiling of breathless, exultant sound. No doubt they thrive on the cool nights given by the altitude, for the larks most commonly met with in Andalusia are the crested lark, which lives among rocks and does not soar, and the calandria lark, which both soars and sings, but in a less ecstatic and more ponderous way. It is typical of the more earthy spirit of this bird that, unlike the skylark, it will live and sing in a cage. Then, as one continues towards Guadix, one comes suddenly to a precipitous escarpment. This is the river valley. Bordered by red cliffs, well irrigated, planted with poplars and mulberry trees, it winds slowly northwards.

Guadix is the Roman and Iberian Acci, altered by the Arabs to Wadi Ash when they moved the site a few miles to the south-east. The old city – it is ploughed over today – was the chief settlement of a small Iberian clan which worshipped the sun god Neto or Neton, later assimilated to Mars. In the time of Hannibal it acquired some importance on account of its silver mines. There was also a shrine to Isis, probably the Romanized form of an Iberian moon goddess, and an inscription that has recently been discovered mentions a gift made to her of 53 pearls, 32 emeralds, 1 carbuncle, 1 jacinth, 2 diamonds, and 2 meteorites. Another gift consisted of 20 emeralds and 119 pearls. Compare this with the 8,000 diamonds, 145 pearls, 74 emeralds, 62 rubies, and 46 sapphires that adorn Nuestra Señora del Pilar at Saragossa, and one will see that Spanish religious practices have not changed so much as might have been expected. If anything, they have cooled off a little, for I do not see any Andalusian Croesus being so lavish in his offerings to the Virgin of his native town today. However, Guadix must in those times have been a notable place, for towards the year A.D. 70 the Christians made it the first of their missionary stations in Spain. San Torcuato and his six companions, who, if we are to believe a not implausible legend, had been chosen by St Paul to evangelize that country, landed at Urci close to Almeria and spread over the neighbourhood. The mining districts seem to have attracted them – perhaps the slaves who worked in them provided good material – and San Torcuato settled in Guadix, leaving it to his junior companion San Cecilio to preach the gospel in Illiberris – that is, Elvira or Granada. For that reason the bishop of Guadix takes precedence today over all the other bishops of Spain. A miracle is reported in San Torcuato's connexion. An olive tree that grew at the door of the Christian basilica covered itself with flowers on the eve of his festival and on the following day – 1 May – bore fruit. A quiet little miracle, befitting the austere Iberian temperament, and also an appropriate one. Even then the wealth of Andalusia lay in its olive trees, and May Day was sacred to the tree spirit and to the rites of procreation. Personally I prefer it to that later type of miracle in which the sanctity of a holy person is decided not so much by his acts during his lifetime as by whether or not his corpse gives out a smell of roses and Parma violets a month after his death.

Guadix is a dirty, noisy, crowded little town with bad inns and a large population of very poor people. It has a red-sandstone cathedral built in the eighteenth century in the style of that of Granada, and an arcaded square that once was beautiful but has recently been refaced and spoiled. There are several palaces of the nobility, among them that of the Marqués de Peñaflor – an enormous, rambling building set up on an eminence with as many rooms and windows as a Tibetan convent, and now appropriately converted into a seminary. Another palace was pointed out to me in which a broken-down marquis whose name I forget was living with his mistress – so ruined by his extravagance that, if I was to believe what I was told, they had nothing to eat but dried cod and potatoes and no servant but an old crone who came in daily. But then one cannot always believe what one is told. In the popular mind of Andalusia a marquis is a semi-mythological figure who, prodigiously rich at one moment, is at the next completely burned out by his passion for women and cards, and reduced to the extremes of indigence.

There is something both harsh and sordid about Guadix which assails one as soon as one enters it. Since it is a port of call for many sorts of travelling people, there are always gipsies, mules, horses, and donkeys standing about, and rows of lorries drawn up at the entrance. The dry gritty soil gives off a fine dust, so that the men and women one meets look unwashed and dirty, spit frequently, and have loud, rasping voices. In the winter it is cold, because the city stands at a height of over three thousand feet above the sea, and the summers are hot because of the dry plains and mountains that surround it. When an old man tells one that owing to the fineness of the water the country is famous for its melons, one has the feeling that one is reading in a book of Eastern travel. For yes, the place is Eastern. With the poplars and mulberries of its river valley, with its arid steppes and wall of snow-covered mountains, this might be any town on the Anatolian tableland. Even the people with their stolid, stony faces look Turkish.

Anatolian too is the Barrio de Santiago or cave quarter, which lies just beyond the Moorish castle of Alcazaba. It contains more than a third of Guadix's population of nearly 30,000, and provides the principal and indeed the only reason for visiting the place. The caves are cut out of the precipitous, water-channelled escarpment that hems in the river valley, which is of the same alluvial formation of soft argillaceous sandstone as the broken country that lies below Yegen. Once spoken of as loess, it has been given the name of *Guadix-formation* by the German geologist Drasche. No doubt its most useful property is that it can be cut like cheese. Three-roomed or four-roomed caves, complete with their chimneys, alcoves, and cupboards, may be hollowed out of it. There are some caves at Guadix and in the villages round that have two storeys, while at Benalúa there is said to be one that has three. After being dug out, they are whitewashed inside, wired for electric light, and floored with tiles, and, as their temperature remains almost constant throughout the year, they offer the advantage of being warm in winter and cool in summer.

A cave dwelling costs less to make or buy than a house. A small one can often be bought for £5, whereas a large one may cost £70, and a luxury one, with two storeys, a balcony, and a telephone, as much as £500. Many workmen and day-labourers, however, dig out their own during the winter months when they are out of employment, and then have the satisfaction of possessing a house at scarcely any cost to them-selves and with only a peppercorn rent to pay on it. One or two precautions have to be observed. If, as often happens, the outer face shows signs of crumbling, a front of bricks and mortar must be built up. Should a vein of sand be met with, it must be stopped with lime plaster. The ceiling must be arched and the final smoothing of the walls done with a palm leaf dipped in lime. But the material is soft and easy to cut, though in the course of time the surface of the walls will become so hard that it is impossible to drive in a nail.

The special picturesqueness of the caves at Guadix, which distinguishes them from those of Cuevas de Almanzora and other pueblos of the province of Almeria, comes from the fact that the escarpment in which they have been cut has been broken up by the action of water into a series of cones, pin-nacles, and ravines, red or yellow in colour, which compose a lunar landscape. The soil is bare except where a prickly-pear sprawls over it, and the caves are sometimes piled on top of one another in such a way that one family tethers its pig or goat to another family's chimney. Their whole area covers about a square mile. Wandering through these strange sub-urbs, where sometimes a vine has been planted to form a trel-lised porch, where sometimes one passes a cave school or a

cave tavern or a cave shop, one gets a sense of being in another
world. By moonlight, in particular, the effect is startling. Yet
enter one of these caves, pass an evening with the family,
sleep in one of their beds, as I have done, and one will forget
that one is not in an ordinary Spanish house. These troglo-
dytes are very house-proud, and their dwellings are a good
deal neater and cleaner than many of those in the town.

However, it is not so easy to walk about at leisure in this
quarter. The reason is that there are at least three or four cave
children to every cave adult. Moreover, these children run
wild in gangs, with nothing better to do than to follow and
mob any stranger who shows himself among them. I in my
workman's clothes would not draw more than a dozen or so,
but let the foreign tourist appear, and he will be joined by a
shouting, pestering swarm of at least a hundred. And note
that these children have a remarkable will to survival. Infant
mortality is shockingly low among them, and when recently a
cave fell in after heavy rains, the father, mother, and two
grandparents were killed, but the ten children were dug out
unhurt. That is typical.

The various travel books I have read, both English and
French, that speak of Guadix all declare that its cave quarter is
inhabited by gipsies. This merely shows the inability of visiting foreigners to believe that ordinary working-class people
can live in such extraordinary habitations. In fact, nineteen out
of twenty of the people who occupy them are Spaniards. The
same is true of all the cave villages and cave *barrios* that I have
seen in southern Spain, with the sole exception of that of the
Sacro Monte in Granada. However, there are a few gipsy cave-
dwellers at Guadix, and if one wishes to meet them one should
climb up the narrowest ravines till one comes to the smaller
and rougher excavations near the summit. Then suddenly half
a dozen ragged creatures will throw themselves out on you
with wild and plaintive demands for baksheesh. When I first
made their acquaintance they were half naked, for gipsy
women in their own quarters are not fussy about how they

cover their bodies, and for economy none of the children under thirteen wore clothes. But today, as a little pamphlet issued by the Patronato Social of the Sacred Heart informs me, the quarter has been cleaned up, and modesty, decency, and good conduct made to prevail. And in fact all the younger women and children one sees in this district are better dressed and cleaner than they used to be.

Most of the villages round Guadix are composed of cave dwellings, those of Purullena on the road to Granada being especially picturesque. One at Benalúa has a balcony on its upper storey decorated with geraniums, and another, which I have not seen, is said to have an interior patio. All but the very poorest have electric light, and a few have running water and telephones. Yet not everyone will consent to live in them. Opinion is sharply divided on the subject of cave-dwelling, and people hold obstinately to their own views. Those who have troglodytic inclinations point out that caves are both cheaper and healthier than houses, and that it is a convenience to be able to use the same number of blankets on the beds all the year round. Those who are against them concede this, but declare that it is improper for a man who walks upright and has the power of speech to live in a hole in the ground like an animal. And so the argument goes on, those who are for human dignity at all costs standing out manfully against the utilitarians, in spite of the fact that the Church has now decided in favour of the latter.

Guadix is not a happy city. Most of the irrigated land in the valley is owned by a few large landlords, and this is generally and quite properly regarded as wrong. The land-hungry peasant has a moral right to the patch of fertile land on which he can support himself. This discontent led to many horrors on the outbreak of the Civil War. A gang of young terrorists took possession of the city, and every morning the side streets were littered with bodies, till after five months of anarchy the Republican Government summoned the courage to react and executed the leading murderers. Then when the war ended the

Nationalists marched in and celebrated their victory by a still larger purge. One may take it as a rule that in class wars it is the side that wins that kills most.

Among those who lost their lives was the Bishop of Guadix who, after being imprisoned for a time in a boat, was thrown, still living, it is said, into the *pozos* or pits at Tabernas, together with his fellow bishop of Almeria. Yet today it is a Bishop of Guadix who has done more to raise the standard of life and decency in this city than several hundred years of Spanish government had done before him. By turning his palace into a factory for making esparto mats, he has been able to employ over seven hundred men and girls at a fair rate of pay and under the best conditions, while he has so arranged things that in times of unemployment he can expand his labour force to three thousand. In this way his factory provides a model for what factories in small Andalusian towns, racked by seasonal agrarian unemployment, ought to be. Yet it would be a mistake to suppose that this admirable man had earned universal gratitude. So fanatical is the feeling against the Church in southern Spain that a person I had dealings with, in spite of his having fought on the Nationalist side and being moderately prosperous, told me that the bishop had made an excellent thing out of it for himself and his family. I can only say that the new schools erected by the Church in the cave quarter and the clean dresses of the schoolchildren show that, if the esparto factory has indeed made a profit, the money has been well employed.

I must not leave Guadix without mentioning the remarkable writers it has produced. The first was an Arab poet generally known as Shushtari. He was born in the Persian quarter of that city in or around the year 1212, and after receiving the excellent education then available to the sons of the middle classes, he obtained some sort of official post. However, his real inclinations lay in the direction of poetry, and the poets of that age were dissolute. He seems to have been particularly so. We hear of him living at Granada, at Loja, and finally in

Morocco, working presumably in a government office, and writing his lively and salacious poems on dancing-girls and pretty boys and the delights of drinking parties in imitation of those which that most talented of Arab troubadours, Ibn Guzman, had made fashionable. Louis Massignon, whose account I am drawing on here (see his article in *Al-Andalus*, vol. xiv, 1949), compares him to Verlaine.

Then, when he was a little past thirty, the great event of Shushtari's life took place. He became suddenly and violently converted to religion and, after a period of initiation, which appears to have been spent in a *zawiya* at Granada, was confirmed in his vocation by a famous Sufi mystic and philosopher, Ibn Sab'in. Taking vows of poverty, he joined one of those loose monastic confraternities which the Sufi movement was bringing into existence.

From this time on Shushtari's poetry took a new and, to Western eyes, strange turn. He conceived of God as a male force or emanation, who imposes His stamp and image on the passive and feminine soul, which in ecstasy opens itself to receive Him. The soul must abandon itself completely, must give up all desire for earthly things and have no other aim but union with the ineffable. The intoxication it will then feel will be as the wine-drinking that accompanies orgies. Now a traffic of this sort between spiritual and erotic states had for some time been almost a commonplace among Moslem mystics, and would soon spread to Christian ones, but Shushtari showed his originality by the crude and plebeian language, studded with slang and sometimes even with obscene terms, in which he expressed himself. Here he was, of course, following in the poetical tradition of Ibn Guzman. The classical Arab poetry, which had originated in the desert, had become too remote from the ordinary life of the city dwellers, and was being replaced by a more colloquial type of verse suggested by the popular ditties sung in the market place. This new style had been carried farthest in Spain, because there the Moroccan dynasties, which had ruled the country since 1100, were

barbarous, and the decline of the courtly poet left an opening
for the troubadour or jongleur. It naturally had an influence
on devotional poetry too. Just as in the sixteenth century the
religious poets of Castile were to take popular love-songs and
give them a devout colouring, so the Sufi poets took the erotic
poetry of these jongleurs and turned it to express the idea of
ecstatic union with God. But Shushtari was more than a Sufi
poet; he was a dervish who, like St Francis, had dedicated
himself to a life of poverty, and the people whom he wished to
call to salvation were the dregs of the cities, the thieves and
drunkards and prostitutes. It was natural, therefore, that since
Islam is not a prudish religion he should choose to address
them in their own language.

'I had a lover. "Come to me," I said, "and you'll get what
you want and more." What did he do? He caught me in his
net . . . he tore off my clothes . . . he beat me, taking me between my blood and my flesh . . . up to my secret locked corner. Pulling my ears, he said to me: "Now for your own good
you must open that lock. . . ." I opened it, he possessed me,
and after that I possessed him. I explored and visited his whole
Being. And now I am like a tortoise on the road, alone, without rival or company.'

Shushtari wandered across Africa, singing his verses in the
market places and converting the drunkards and prostitutes to
more sublimated forms of intoxication and love-making. We
hear of him in Egypt, where he seems to have fought against
St Louis and his Crusaders, and then we hear of him in Syria.
Returning in 1269 to Egypt with a convoy of pilgrims, he died
near Port Said. His poems are still sung all over the East,
especially among the Shadili confraternities, as a means for
entering into ecstasy.

Yet what, one may ask, has this poet of Wadi Ash or Guadix
to do with Spain? After the fall of the Caliphate of Cordoba,
the Spanish-born intellectual or dervish was at home in every
part of the Arab-speaking world, and often more so in Syria
and Egypt than in the West. That immense region, stretching

from Senegal and the Atlas Mountains to Bokhara and Sind, was at least as international in feeling as Medieval Christianity, and it is only there that his name is still remembered today. Yet Shushtari had an influence on Europe too. The Majorcan mystic and philosopher, Ram Lull or Lully, heard his verses recited and was moved by them to write his famous book *Of the Lover and the Beloved*. Three centuries later we find St John of the Cross composing his lyrics in the same city in which the Arab poet had lived and on the same erotic-religious themes. Shushtari is thus a link in a chain which reaches to our own time.

The next writer from Guadix to achieve fame was Antonio Mira de Amescua. Though little read today, for there has never been a collected edition of his works, he is one of the more interesting of the minor dramatists of the early seventeenth century. Not much is known of his life. He was born in or around 1574 of an illicit union between a hidalgo of some position and a beautiful woman whose name, Beatriz de Torres y Heredia, suggests that she may have been a gipsy. Then in 1601 he took orders, and through his father's influence obtained a chaplaincy at the Reyes Católicos at Granada, and later a canonry at Guadix Cathedral. As a priest, however, Mira was a misfit. His character was arrogant, violent, and unpredictable: we hear of him boxing the ears of a schoolmistress on the steps of the Cathedral, quarrelling with his fellow canons, and being reprimanded by his bishop on account of his prolonged absence in Madrid. This restlessness and violence in his temperament is seen in his plays. He was a romantic – for what is now called baroque was the romanticism of the time – and the extravagance and absurdity of his plots pass all bounds. Yet his language is vigorous and he had a marked influence on Calderón. The sudden and violent changes shown in some of his characters from holiness to wickedness, and then again to repentance, seem to have made a special appeal to that dramatist, who also took up and improved on several of his turns of phrase and stylistic clichés. He died at Guadix in 1644, and was buried in the cathedral.

The last Accitanian writer I have to speak of was Pedro Antonio de Alarcón, a well-known novelist whose dates are 1833–91. Among a number of books of very uneven value, he wrote one admirable short story which has achieved world fame. This was *El sombrero de tres picos* or *The Three Cornered Hat*, which in 1919 Diaghileff produced as a ballet with music by Manuel de Falla, décor by Picasso, and choreography by Massine. The mill where the story, an old legend, was reputed to have taken place can still be seen close to the main road between Esfiliana and Alcudia. The only other book which Alarcón wrote about Guadix is *El niño de la bola*, and this, though it has a dramatic plot well suited to a film, must be one of the most preposterous novels ever written. I fail to understand why Robert Graves has translated it.

Alarcón is also the only person to have written a book on the Alpujarra. He toured the country on horseback in the spring of 1872, starting out from Granada and staying with the local *caciques*. In Yegen he spent the night in the house which I later rented, as the guest of Don Fadrique's father. But as an account of the country his book is disappointing. As his novels show, he was completely lacking in the gift of observation, so that he had to fill out his pages with stereotyped descriptions of mountain scenery in the romantic style, playful passages in the manner of Sterne, and some very long accounts of the Morisco rising of 1569–70, which he condensed from contemporary histories. It may be noticed too that though he was born and brought up in Guadix he never had the curiosity to take a mule and cross the Puerto del Lobo, which he speaks of in the tone of a modern writer discussing the passes through the Pamirs. I find that typically Spanish. Not a yard of Central or Southern America would have been explored, not a settlement on its coast made, if the Conquistadors had not been driven forward by their passion for gold. Although capable when necessary of great exertions, Spaniards (if one excepts those from the rainy Cantabrian provinces) are by preference sedentary and town-loving.

CHAPTER FIFTEEN

A CHAPTER OF HISTORY

*

I HAVE now put down what I can remember of my life at Yegen up to the spring of 1924, when I returned to England, and have given the best account I could of my neighbours' habits and customs. I have still to write of Almeria and Granada as they were in those days, and to describe the changes that took place when I returned to my house in 1929. Yet this book also aims at giving a description of that peculiar region of Spain known as the Alpujarra. Would not the picture be a little more coherent if I filled in its background with a sketch of the country's history and prehistory? The subject – especially the prehistory – may not appear to be particularly inviting, yet it has a greater interest for the English reader than might be supposed, because it was from southern Spain that our island was first populated and civilized. Even for those who find the records of those nameless, shifting races of Neolithic and Bronze Age times boring and confusing, this fact is bound to strike the imagination.

To begin at the beginning, the first traces of man to be found in the Alpujarra belong to the Mesolithic Age. This comprises that long and dimly glimpsed period that followed the last retreat of the ice from northern Europe. In the rock shelters along the coast between Adra and Malaga one may pick up small flint implements of the kind known as microliths that date from that time. It used to be thought that they had been made by an African race known as the Capsians, who had been forced to emigrate northwards by the desiccation of the Sahara, but today this is less certain. All that can really be said of this people is that they lived by fishing, hunting, and food collecting and that they had domesticated the dog. They

seem to have been contemporary with a race of negroid
hunters who lived in the mountains round Valencia and
painted in rock shelters those vivid scenes of hunting and
dancing that figure in all books on prehistoric art. Only the
people of the coast painted nothing.

When we lose sight of them, some time in the fourth millennium, neolithic culture gradually begins. In the mountainous
districts of the south we come on it in the remains of a people,
no doubt the descendants of the same mesolithic races, who
lived chiefly in caves. They kept sheep, goats, and small, long-
horned cattle, wove esparto grass into rope and cloth, and
made a rough pottery which they decorated with incised dots
and dashes. For ornament they wore necklaces of shells and
coloured stones, and they buried their dead under the floor of
their caves. As a rule too the women cultivated small garden
plots. They sowed peas, lentils, barley, and spelt in patches of
ground which they had scratched with their hoes, and reaped
them with wooden sickles set with small flint blades. They also
raided wild bees' nests for honey, and made a sort of beer or
mead. But although they had bone daggers and roughly
polished stone axes, they had no warlike weapons such as
arrows or spears. We are in fact looking at a Golden – or what
is much the same thing – a matriarchal age.

As it happens, the Alpujarra can show the most splendid of
these cave burials. In 1857 an archaeologist, Manuel de Góngora, examined a cave known as the Cueva de los Murciélagos,
which lies in the side of a precipitous *rambla* close to Albuñol.
It had already been dug up before he reached it by a farmer
who was in search of bats' dung, but there seems to be no
doubt that it had contained sixty-nine bodies, dressed in tunics
of esparto and wearing caps and shoes of the same material, all
but two of whom had been slaughtered to provide their master
and mistress with attendants in the next world. In the first
group of three, lying just inside the entrance to the cave, one
male skeleton was found to be wearing a large gold diadem,
while the esparto caps that the others wore still showed – or so

their discoverer thought – some traces of blood. A second group of three, lying in a second chamber, had been buried with esparto baskets which contained grain, poppy-heads, and locks of hair. Then in a third chamber came a group of twelve young women lying in a semicircle round an older woman, who was dressed in a skin tunic laced together at the sides, and who wore round her neck a string of seashells completed by a boar's tusk, and in her ears pendants of black stones. Finally, at the back of the cave, there were fifty male skeletons, together with polished stone axes, flint knives, and of course pottery.

Here then we have the tombs of an important woman chieftain and of a chief. If it is true, as the pottery seems to indicate, that these burials date from the end of the fourth millennium, then the gold fillet found on the skull of the chief is the oldest piece of worked gold to have been discovered in Western Europe. It can only have come from one place – the streams that unite at Ugíjar to flow into the sea at Adra. The river sands here still contain so much gold that, as I have already said, a French company was recently formed for extracting it. At all events one can see that at this time the eastern section of the Alpujarra supported a considerable population, ruled by a single chief, and that women occupied an important position in it.

The scene in Spain now began to change rapidly. Towards 2700 B.C. a new and more advanced culture made its appearance on the River Almanzora in the province of Almeria. From its earliest station it is known by the name of El Gárcel. Fortified villages of wattle-and-daub huts were built on flat hilltops. The dead were buried in small cists or trenches covered with flat stones. Flint knives, arrow-heads, and finely polished stone axes are found in great numbers, together with necklaces of shells and smooth, undecorated, round-bellied pots whose originals were obviously from Egypt. Grain was stored in pits, there were small, flat stone idols similar to those found in the Aegean, and olive trees and vines were grown. It seems clear that the people who left these remains were foreigners and, seeing that their skulls are long and their bones light, most archaeologists regard them as being of the so-called Mediterranean race and the ancestors of the Iberians. They had apparently come from Libya or southern Tunisia. For us they have a special interest because a small body of them, travelling north along the Spanish coast with their flocks and herds and then up the Rhône valley, reached England and there, towards 2500 B.C., introduced neolithic culture. They were the first people to enter our country after its separation from the Continent, and their earliest known station is at Windmill Hill near Avebury.

From this moment everything in the south of Spain began to move fast. The Almeria people had struck one of the richest mining regions in Europe, where copper, lead, and silver ores lay close to the surface and silver was found – a very rare circumstance – in a pure state. Within a couple of centuries the digging out and extraction of these metals and the collection of gold from the river sands had become a considerable industry. Wealth, however, exposed them to the danger of sudden attack, so that they were compelled to expend the greater part of what they obtained from their mines on arming and defending themselves. Thus, all the settlements of this period that have been explored have yielded quantities of finely worked flint and copper weapons. One of the best preserved of these, though some centuries later in date, is at Los Millares, which lies fifty miles to the west of the Almanzora at the foot of the Sierra de Gádor, and therefore on the edge of the Alpujarra. Here one may see the stone walls and fosse that once enclosed the wattle huts of the village, a conduit that brought water from a spring nearly a mile, and – most remarkable of all – the large and impressive cemetery. Its hundred or so circular tombs, built to contain from fifty to a hundred burials each, consist of corbelled tomb-chambers approached by narrow passages of dry-walling roofed with stone slabs. Each tomb was heaped over with a cairn of earth and stones, while at its

entrance stood a circular walled enclosure in which the funeral
rites took place. The person who is versed in archaeology will
be reminded of the Early Minoan *tholoi* of Crete. Then in the
Municipal Museum of Almeria one can inspect some of the
objects that have been found here – bell-beakers of the Andalusian type as well as smooth pots of Egyptian ancestry, plaque
idols of the Mother Goddess similar to those found in the
Cyclades, ornaments of amber, jet, and turquoise, of ostrich
egg and of hippopotamus ivory, and both human and animal
bones incised with a sinister decoration of twin eyes.

The beehive roofs of the collective graves and the bell-
beaker pottery, neither of which are found on the earlier sites
in the Almanzora valley, show that the settlement of Los
Millares had come under the influence of another culture that
in the meantime had sprung up a little farther to the west. This
is the so-called megalithic culture, which at about this time was
putting up at Antequera, not far from Granada, and at Carmona, close to Seville, some of the largest passage-graves in
the world, and was roofing them with enormous stones. Its
origins are still disputed. The most likely explanation is that it
had come about through the fertilization of the old Andalusian cave culture, belonging to a race of herdsmen who lived
in the Lower Guadalquivir valley, by newcomers from the
eastern Mediterranean who had brought with them the arts of
working in metals and of putting up corbelled grave cham-
bers. At all events we can distinguish what appear to be two
early and mutually dependent centres of this culture – one
round Huelva, where the soil is poor but there are inexhaustible supplies of copper, and the other at Carmona, where there
is no copper but the land provides good pasture. From Carmona the passage-tomb builders spread eastwards to Granada
and Guadix and then stopped, because they had reached the
frontiers of the Almeria people, whereas those from Huelva
followed the supplies of ore to southern Portugal and north
along the coast to Galicia, and from there launched out across
the seas.

With the rise of the megalithic culture, we have reached one of the great moments of Spanish and European history. A new way of life together with a new religion expands with such force that within a century or so they have covered the whole seaboard of western Europe as far as Denmark and the Orkneys with their monuments. The people who accomplished this were primitive herdsmen and fishermen who took up with such zest the search for gold and copper that to discover new sources of them they were ready to undertake the most adventurous voyages overseas. But these metals were not to be acquired with impunity. Their value lay precisely in the strong magic they contained (being hard yet malleable, and the colour of the sun's rays) and for that very reason great dangers were attached to mining and working them. It was not safe to do so unless the chthonic powers which guarded them were propitiated and thus (or so it would seem) there grew up a cult of the dead which led to their being buried in great collective tombs and placated by regular sacrifices. As in the Spanish irruption into America four thousand years later, the quest for gold and the propagation of a mystery religion went hand in hand.

We have seen that in the Lower Guadalquivir valley there lived a race of cattle herdsmen who had begun to plant corn and who were closely associated with the copper-mining people a little farther to the west. They were a round-headed race with prominent brow-ridges, like the people who still live there today, and they had adopted the megalithic religion, but their characteristic product was a special type of pot, the famous bell-beaker. This was a large, richly decorated bowl, which had evolved out of the dot-and-dash pottery of the Andalusian cave-dwellers and which was used for holding the beer or mead drunk on special occasions. This beer, like the Vedic soma, was probably a sacred beverage possessed of magical as well as intoxicating properties, since its consumption evidently played an important part in their ceremonies. At a date that was round about 2400 B.C. a number of these people had emigrated to the plains around Madrid, carrying with them their beakers but not the practice (which may still have been unknown to them), of building collective tombs. From here they began to extend themselves over a large part of Spain, driving their flocks and herds before them and living in light huts or tents, but also doing a certain amount of trade in copper weapons which they obtained from Huelva or Galicia. The beakers went with them. Soon they crossed into France, and by the end of the millennium small parties of them had reached Brittany, north Italy, and the Rhine and penetrated as far as Hungary and Saxony, without altering in any way their pastoral habits or the shape or decoration of their beakers. From the Continent they crossed in three successive waves to Britain, subduing its previous inhabitants, the little dark men from Almeria, and putting up the great sun temples of Avebury and Stonehenge. This very unSpanish veneration for the sun was due to the fact that on their way through Germany they had become associated with some Indo-European peoples, but they remained Castilians at heart as may be seen from the fact that they had not yet lost that deformation of the thigh bone which their ancestors on the *meseta* round Madrid had acquired from their habit of perpetual squatting. The first sign, one might say, of the Madrileño's café habits.

We can say then that during the third millennium three entirely different groups of people left the south of Spain and settled in Britain. The first brought with them peasant farming and the arts of weaving and pottery; the second a grandiose cult of the dead and the search for metals; and the third pastoralism in large tribal units and the beaker cult. Till the arrival of the Celts our island was mainly populated by people who had come from beyond the Pyrenees. But there is one element that has been left out of this account. Concurrently with the rise of megalithic culture and of the early beakers, a new sort of art made its appearance in the mountainous regions of southern Spain. We come across it in paintings in caves and rock shelters. These remote places, which were evidently tribal sanctuaries, are decorated with designs in red ochre in which schematic signs and symbols are mingled with recognizable representations of people and animals. We can make out wild deer and domestic cows and donkeys, as well as fantastic creatures that evidently represent masked medicine men, but side by side with these are suns, spirals, labyrinths, hatchings, and other signs whose meaning can only be guessed at. We thus see that the absorption in big game which had inspired palaeolithic art, and in tribal action and drama which had governed mesolithic art, had changed with the advent of agriculture to a love of the secret and esoteric. Signs that convey meanings without visually representing them are now thought to have more magic about them than those whose sense is easily grasped – which means, no doubt, that the specialist in ritual, the priest or medicine man, has made his appearance. Although this was essentially a local and pictorial art, confined to the cave shelters of southern Spain, many of its symbols were taken over by the megalithic people and incised on tombs, plaque idols, and pottery. Thus one will find some of them decorating the big stones of the passage-grave at New Grange in Ireland.

During this time – that is from 3000 to 2000 B.C. – what has been happening to the people of the Alpujarra? This little country, shut in by its almost impassable mountains, lay at the hub of these expanding cultures we have been describing, yet it shows no signs of having been penetrated by any of them. So far as we know, it continued to develop quietly along the lines of the old cave culture, the women scratching the ground with their hoes and scattering a few handfuls of seed, and the men herding their cattle or hunting wild animals. Presumably it was able to do this because its hills and valleys were so easily defensible.

The entire region between the Sierra Nevada and the coast, except where it had been burned for agriculture, was at this time covered by forests of pine, cork oak, and ilex. There was no lack of caves for habitation, since almost every village

today can show a large one, that at Yegen being partly closed
by a fall of rock. The gold-bearing streams would naturally
have had a special importance, and here Yegen was fortunately
placed, for not only did it command one of these but it also
had a large spring of water, a piece of flat ground that could be
irrigated, and a highly defensible position. The *puente* or land
bridge, which then formed the only approach to the village,
could easily be fortified, and just by it was the Piedra Fuerte.
This, which I have already alluded to, is an immense rock, flat
on top and about an eighth of an acre in extent, with perpendicular sides that rise forty feet or more above the valley. A
narrow pathway has been cut up one of these and, since a
stream runs immediately below, water can be drawn up by
means of a rope and a bucket. In Arab times a small castle was
built on this spot, but certain crude sherds that are lying about
suggest a much earlier occupation. Naturally a place of this
kind is haunted. In the depths of the rock there lives a Moorish
princess, surrounded by her ladies, and at certain hours their
voices can be heard singing as they work at their embroideries.
However, I must warn readers that it is no use going to listen
to them during Holy Week or on Church festivals. Since the
expulsion of their compatriots they have developed leanings
towards Christianity and, though it is too soon to speak of
their conversion, they show their respect on these occasions
by keeping silent.

The next step in the advance of the Almeria people was the
discovery, brought from the East, of the value of mixing some
tin with their copper. With this the Bronze Age in Spain
begins. At the fortified village of El Argar on the River Almanzora (it stands only a few hundred yards from their earliest
settlement at El Gárcel) we see it fully developed at some date
between 1700 and 1400 B.C. This people dyed their linen
robes, which were buttoned down the side, with cinnabar,
wore their hair long and finely combed, delighted in gold, silver, bronze, and ivory necklaces and ear-rings, and, when they
were rich enough, sported silver diadems. They cultivated the

olive, had oil-lamps, carts, and threshing-boards, and – since the climate was getting drier – practised irrigation. Their houses were two-storeyed stone buildings with flat clay roofs, and they buried their dead under the floor in large earthenware jars, in the Anatolian fashion. This has given rise to a controversy. Since husbands and wives were squeezed together into the same jar, and since their burials appear to have been simultaneous, one of them must have been killed on the death of the other. But which? In this more or less egalitarian society the women would appear to have enjoyed a high position, and some archaeologists, influenced perhaps by chivalrous feelings, believe that it was the men who were sacrificed. Others, more tough-minded, opine differently.

The people of El Argar and of the other hilltop settlements near by were hard-working peasants and miners who took some trouble about their personal adornment, but otherwise showed no interest in artistic matters. Probably they had no time to spare for such things. In addition to tilling their fields, they melted out copper, lead, and silver from their ores, and hammered or moulded them into weapons, but were short of tin, which probably had to be imported from Tuscany or Catalonia. In their fortified villages of little more than four hundred inhabitants – to which we may perhaps add a certain number of slaves – they lived in a continual fear of being attacked and raided. This was an age of piracy.

The new Almeria culture spread north up the coast to the Pyrenees and inland to the mining region of Linares. Before long we find its influence in every part of Spain except among the megalithic peoples of the west. They, it would seem, had already discovered the use of tin and were fetching it by sea and land from Galicia, where there were plentiful supplies. Thus the district of Huelva and of the Río Tinto, where the largest copper mines in Europe are to be found, soon became the centre of an important bronze industry. This must be the date for the rise of the powerful state of Tartessos or Tarshish, whose chief city is to be sought for somewhere between

Huelva, Seville, and Cadiz. It spread eastwards, occupied the valuable silver mines around Linares, and in time established a sort of suzerainty over the people of Almeria. But the day of Spanish migrations abroad was over. A vigorous Bronze Age culture had opened in Bohemia, and a warlike people from Central Europe, the first wave of the Celts, had occupied the old megalithic and Beaker-folk regions of Brittany and the British Isles. Spain, which in the third millennium had exploded over western Europe, in the second became a back-water, though the slow growth in wealth of Tartessos, where the horses were reported to be fed out of silver troughs, was to provide an El Dorado for the historic peoples of the eastern Mediterranean. Unfortunately, however, not a single site in this kingdom of fabulous riches has yet been excavated by the archaeologists.

Gadir or Cadiz was founded on a sandy islet off the coast of Tartessos a little before the year 1101 B.C. The Phoenicians went there in one swoop from Tyre, setting up a half-way station at Utica near Tunis a few years later. But the legends of the travels of Hercules make us suspect that they were not the first, or at least not the only East Mediterranean people to navigate those seas. Greek writers speak of Carian and Lydian migrations to the Far West, and there seems little doubt that the Rhodians founded colonies there in the tenth century. The name they gave to Spain was Ophiussa, or Snake Land, and a whole string of names ending in *oussa* records the visits of a people speaking the dialects of the south-western coast of Asia Minor. One of these visits is mentioned by Pliny, who tells us that a certain Meidocritos passed the Columns of Hercules and reached the Cassiterides, or Tin Islands, off the Galician coast. Can this be the time at which a Greek trading-post was set up at Abdera, today Adra? The name is Greek, and was much later given to a colony founded by two Ionian cities in Thrace. If this is so, we need not be in much doubt as to the motives. The gold-bearing sands of Ugíjar provide an obvious attrac-tion, and presumably it was they and perhaps some similarity of names that led to that town being called Odysseia and to the belief that the shields and ships' beaks nailed up there in the temple of Athena and seen in the first century B.C. by a certain Asclepiades of Myrlea were 'memorials of the wanderings of Odysseus'. After this the curtain descends, and any settlements the Greeks or Lydians may have made on the coast of Spain were swept away. Was this due to the power of the Phoenicians or – more likely – to that of the pirates?

The curtain goes up again with the rediscovery of Spain by the Greeks of historical times. This is described in a well-known passage by Herodotus. At some date shortly before 650 B.C. a Samian called Colaios was driven westwards from Egypt by storms, and reached Tartessos. He returned with a cargo which he sold for the huge sum of sixty talents. The people of Phocaea, a city of seamen on the coast of Ionia, became interested in his venture and sent out an expedition composed not of ordinary merchant ships but of fast-moving penteconters. The king of Tartessos, who had the Celtic name of Arganthonios, welcomed them warmly and encouraged them to found colonies and trading-posts on the Spanish coast, of which the most westerly was Mainake, near Malaga. For the first time, then, we get some reliable information about this country. We learn that east of the Strait of Gibraltar it was occupied by a people called the Massieni or Mastieni, who had their chief town at Mastia or Carthagena, but that along the coast there was a strong sprinkling of Libyphoenices, or mixed Africans and Carthaginians, who presumably were mainly traders and fishermen. The Sierra Nevada was known as the Mons Silurus, which by the time of Pliny had become the Mons Solorius. The coastal hills, today so bare, were overgrown with pine trees. But what of the people of the Alpujarra? Did they wash their faces and teeth in stale urine like some of the Spanish tribes, and go naked in summer, or did they clothe themselves in tunics and black cloaks while their women wore high erections on their heads from which they draped their mantillas? Did they prance wildly on nights of full moon outside the doors of their houses, or did they hold hands and dance gravely in long coloured robes to the music of flutes? Were their marriages celebrated by all the friends and relatives of the bridegroom having sexual connexion with the bride, or did the men gallantly take to their beds and groan when their wives were in the throes of childbirth? We do not know, but we may be sure that whatever they were they were very conservative.

The presence of the Greeks on these coasts lasted scarcely more than a hundred years. The Carthaginians had taken over from the Phoenicians the city of Gadir and the metal trade with Tartessos, and in 535 or thereabouts they combined with the Etruscans to destroy the Phocaean fleet in a battle off Alalia in Corsica. The Greek trading-post of Mainake vanished, and the Carthaginians set up fortified factories at Adra, Almuñecar, and Malaga, where they salted fish and manufactured the Greek sauce known as *garon*. The native hold on the inland country having been weakened by the Celtic invasion, they were also able to take and destroy the city of Tartessos and to establish some sort of control over its mines. During the commotion of tribes which this led to, an Iberian people known as the Bastuli or Bastetani, whose chief town was Baza near Guadix, came to the front and took the place of the Massieni.

The conquest of southern Spain by Hamilcar in 237 B.C. was thus the climax to a long period of more or less peaceful penetration. The Roman conquest followed. Now surely, we imagine, we shall learn something of the people of the Alpujarra – but no; the six hundred years of settled rule that followed have left no trace of it in the history books, except that we gather that a road was built along the coast, following the old Via Herculea by which Hercules was thought to have travelled to the Pillars, from Urci, a few miles to the north of Almeria, to Malaga and Gibraltar. We can still follow its traces across the flats of the Campo de Dalías, and visit the meagre remains of the town of Murgi which they built there.

The Visigoths took the place of the Romans, and then in

712 the Arabs arrived to set up a juster and more tolerant system. The scheming nobles and the horrible bishops gave way before a religion that at least endeavoured to carry out the commands of its founder. The rapid conversion of most of Spain to Islam shows that a nightmare had ended. And now gradually we begin to learn something about the Alpujarra. The word is first used in the tenth century by an Arab chronicler, and is said to mean in that language 'hills of grass'. Against this interpretation must be set the opinion of some philologists that the word *alp* is a very ancient term of the pre-neolithic or Ligurian peoples of southern Europe signifying white. If so, 'Alpujarra' would simply mean 'Alba Sierra'. However that may be, the first accounts we get of the people of this country describe them as being independent and war-like. Like most mountaineers, they disliked authority and were inclined to brigandage. In all probability they had only nominally been converted to Christianity, and continued to offer the old Iberian sacrifices to springs, trees, and caves and to dance in their open places on the nights of the summer sol-stice and of the full moon. At all events, during the general insurrection that preceded the rise of the Caliphate, we hear of them supporting the Arab aristocracy of Elvira – that is, Granada – against the Christian and Jewish population of that city, who were loyal to the Emirs of Cordoba. Even the death of their leader in an ambush did not lead to their submission, for in 913 we find the young Caliph Abd al-Rahman crossing the Sierra Nevada from Guadix to Ugíjar and marching through the country. After a difficult siege he took the castle of Jubíles above Cádiar, which was defended by a mixed garri-son of *muladís*, or Spanish Moslems, and Christians who had been sent from the sierras of Ronda by that famous rebel, Ibn Hafsun. From this we may gather that the people of the Alpu-jarra were indifferent on religious matters, and were fighting solely for their independence.

A great opening came for them with the foundation of Almeria in the first years of the tenth century. It grew rapidly to being one of the chief industrial cities of Europe, a Manchester exporting not cotton but silk fabrics. To supply its looms, the slopes of the Alpujarra were terraced and planted with mulberry trees, and a mass of new settlers, mostly Berbers from northern Algeria, flocked in. At the same time the brilliant court of the *taifa* princes who ruled Almeria during the eleventh century offered opportunities to men of talent. Thus the only two writers whom the Alpujarra has ever produced belong to this time. One was Ibn Charaf of Berja, who gave up the bitter, envious world of poetry for the more decent profession of doctor, and left a book of soporific maxims behind him, while the other was a writer on Arab antiquities and geography, by name Ibn Omar, who came from Dalías. A modern figure, he earned his living by lecturing in various cities of Moslem Spain.

The thirteenth century saw another rising in the Alpujarra and then, after the capture of Seville in 1248 by Fernando III, Granada became the capital of an independent Moslem kingdom under the Nasrite dynasty. The new state, which stretched from Ronda to beyond Almeria, was carefully organized. To keep in check its unruly inhabitants, the Alpujarra was divided into administrative districts known as *tahas* or *taas*, and a tower or castle was built in every *alauz* or township. Yegen had one not a hundred yards from my house, and its site is still known as *el castillo*.

After the loss of Seville to the Christians there was an exodus of Moslems to the kingdom of Granada. Arab adventurers from Damascus, flocking in after the conquest of Spain by Tarik, had long before secured the best lands and built their country houses on them, so that the mass of new immigrants, who were mostly of Spanish descent, were obliged to pile up in the towns, where they took the place of the Jews and Christians who had been expelled a century earlier. The Berbers, on the other hand, went, as they had for some centuries been doing, to the mountains. In the Alpujarra, where there was no lack of water, the gradual extension of terraces and irrigation channels permitted a steady increase in the population, so that in time the old mountaineer stock, descended probably from the cavemen of neolithic times, became completely berberized. Thus the architecture of the houses, as well as the disposition of the villages in *barrios* and *cortijadas*, acquired a typically North African pattern. Yet the Arab aristocracy of Granada retained its links with the district and owned houses and land in many of the villages. Both Válor and Mecina Bombarón could show descendants of the Prophet.

The economic wealth of the kingdom lay chiefly in the silk trade with Italy. Granada as well as Almeria and Malaga now had factories which turned out the finest silk stuffs, and there were looms in all the villages. Jubíles, today a miserable, decaying hamlet, was then 'a mine of silk which seemed to be pure gold', and besides this had industries of furniture and jewellery. Ugíjar was the chief town, though Laujar, Berja, Dalías, Albuñol, and Órgiva were all considerable places. By the end of the fifteenth century the population was certainly larger than it is today. As a matter of curiosity it may be remarked that the Roman name for the Sierra Nevada, which was Mons Solorius, had gone through a curious transformation. The Arabs called it Djebel Sholair, but when the Christians slipped into the easier term of Sierra Nevada, they transferred the old name to the Sierra de Gádor. This then became the Sierra del Sol y del Aire, and finally the Sierra del Sol, the term Sierra del Aire being passed on to the Sierra la Contraviesa. This poetic nomenclature has, however, long gone out of use.

In 1492 the kingdom of Granada came to an end, with the capture of that city by Ferdinand and Isabella. By the terms of the capitulation, the Moors were to be allowed the full exercise of their laws, and their customs. Boabdil, the Moorish king, was given the Alpujarra as a fief for himself and his heirs in perpetuity, and on the strength of this he settled at Andarax, a few miles to the east of Ugíjar. We get a picture of him here hunting hares with his greyhounds and hawking. But the

Spaniards, now that they had gained their object, showed little disposition to carry out the terms they had signed. Apart from their reluctance to tolerate an alien religion, they feared that the Turks, whose power was rising in the Mediterranean, would use the Moorish regions of Spain as a bridgehead for attempting the reconquest of the country. Within a year, therefore, Boabdil was shipped off to Africa and, warned by her confessor that it was an offence against God to keep faith with the infidel, Isabella began to apply to the Moors a policy of forcible conversion. The consequence was that from Ronda to Baza and Almeria they rose in arms.

The rebellion was only put down after several years of fighting. A decree was then issued offering all the Moors in the kingdom of Castile the choice between conversion and expulsion. Most of them chose the first, but their Christianity remained purely nominal, because the Church made little attempt to instruct them in its doctrines. Finding it less trouble to apply force than persuasion, it proceeded to make their life impossible for them. Thus they were forbidden to bathe, to hold their festivals, to play on musical instruments, to wear their traditional clothes, to speak their own language, till at length, after a particularly severe edict, they decided once more to revolt. The date they chose was Christmas Eve, 1568, and this time it was only the Alpujarra that rose.

Their leader was a certain Don Fernando de Válor. He was of old Arab stock, a descendant of the Caliphs of Cordoba, but he had been brought up among the Spanish nobility at Granada and, though he pretended to return to Islam, he was a Christian at heart. Reverting to his Arab name of Aben Omeyya, he was proclaimed king under an olive tree, which may still be seen today at Cádiar. When a year later he was assassinated, his cousin Aben Aboó, who owned land at Mecina Bombarón, became king in his place. On the Christian side there were at first two commanders – the Marqués de Mondéjar, a man of moderation and humanity, and the Marqués de los Vélez, who believed in ruthlessness. On their failing to agree, the king's half-brother, Don Juan of Austria, was given the supreme command with new troops brought over from Italy.

The war was fought, like all Spanish civil wars, with savagery. On both sides there were commanders who endeavoured to control their followers, but the *monfíes* or brigands – more correctly the inhabitants of the high mountain villages – were fanatical Moslems who killed and tortured every priest they could catch, while the famous Spanish fury – the *Saguntina rabies*, as Livy had called it – was not found lacking on the other side. In the last stages of the fighting, the Spanish troops were given orders to kill all prisoners, including women and children, just as the English troops under Lord Grey were at that very time doing, with the approval of the poet Spenser, in Ireland. The final scene took place in a cave at Bérchules, where Aben Abóo was stabbed by his own followers.

The revolt had lasted more than two years and strained the resources of the country to the utmost. The settlement, therefore, was bound to be hard. Orders were issued that all the Moriscos – that is, Christian Moors – of the kingdom of Granada, both those who had risen and those who had not, were to be deported to the north-west of Spain and settled as labourers on the land. The only exception made to this was that two families were left behind in each village to explain the system of irrigation and the art of breeding silkworms. Then, to fill the gap caused by this immense migration, peasants from the mountainous regions of the north were invited to come in and take up the empty land and houses, on very favourable terms. Three different sizes of *suertes* or lots were granted in freehold, on the payment of a small yearly *diezmo* or tithe to the State, though production for the market was not encouraged by the tax of a third of their value on silk cocoons and olive oil. By a wise provision these lots were made inalienable, and no one was allowed to rent his lot or to possess more than one.

Within a few years, therefore, 12,542 families from Asturias and Galicia had settled in the Alpujarra in 259 *lugares* – that is, villages and hamlets. Four hundred other *lugares* were left to fall into ruin. Some of these were either very small or else had been burned during the fighting, but others lay in the coastal district – the Cehel, as it is still called today – which remained empty and uninhabited owing to the fear of pirates. The population was thus very much smaller than it had been. Strangely enough, as an ecclesiastical historian of the seventeenth century informs us, the new immigrants, coming though they did from a country that had never been occupied by the Moors, were often scarcely more Christian than their Morisco predecessors. They had been brought up in small mountain villages, and for all practical purposes were still pagans. This picture is borne out by information from other parts of Spain. The Spanish clergy were too addicted to town life to pay much attention to the remoter country districts and at the very time when Santa Teresa was founding her convents there were hamlets within fifty miles of Ávila where no one had heard the names of Christ or God. In some valleys of the Sierra de Gata near Salamanca, this remained true down to the twentieth century.

With this settlement of the land the political history of the Alpujarra comes to an end. What else remains to be said concerns its economic development. Silk continued to be almost the sole cash crop till the beginning of the twentieth century. Since cocoons weigh little, they can be transported at small expense on mule-back, and the mountains had long been thickly planted with mulberry trees. Then in 1797 permission was given to the freeholders to convert their holdings on easy terms into private property. This transformed a closed community of small and large peasants into one in which land was more unevenly divided. A similar economic policy led to the destruction of the forests. A company exploiting the lead veins of the Sierra de Gádor was allowed to cut down the pinewoods that then covered it, as well as most of the ilex and cork woods on the adjacent mountains. The mining only came to an end

when no trees were left. Then in the first years of the present
century a great step was taken by the building of roads, for
they allowed other crops besides silk to be carried to the
market. Berja, Dalías, and the valley of the Andarax embarked
on the large-scale cultivation of the Almeria grape, while the
more remote villages began to export garlic, chick-peas, and
chestnuts. Today the completion of the road system has
opened up even the most remote of the mountain villages,
though the high cost of petrol sets limits to what can be pro-
fitably sold in the city markets. A rough estimate of the present
population of the Alpujarra, including the Valle de Lecrín,
gives 150,000 persons, living in some eighty pueblos, forty
hamlets, and a small number of isolated farms and *cortijadas*.
This population has been kept fairly constant since 1870 by
periodic emigrations to South America.

CHAPTER SIXTEEN

ALMERIA AND ITS BROTHELS

*

THE nearest town of any size to Yegen was Almeria. Its distance by road was fifty-seven miles, and one could either walk or take the bus. The first time I visited it was in February 1920 when, as I have already said, I went there to buy furniture and, since I have a vivid recollection of this occasion as well as a written record to bear it out, I will begin by giving an account of it.

It was still dark as I sat by the kitchen fire drinking my coffee. The stars pin-pointed the sky and the crowing of a cock came from far away like a long arm stretched out over the hills. Then the silence was broken by a clatter of hoofs in the street. I shouldered my pack and, as the first light filtered in from the east, dropped by steeply terraced olive groves and open downs to Ugíjar. From here the road wound deviously over rocky hills scattered with aromatic herbs and thin olive trees to Berja. This is a place of some size lying under the Sierra de Gádor, and an important centre for the grape industry. The green, hard-skinned grapes, which are shipped every autumn from Almeria to London, grow on trellises which give the landscape, or rather that part of it which is cultivated, a strange flattened aspect, as though it had been covered with green tarpaulins. Around these vineyards rise low limestone hills, white and almost entirely bare, for in this region it rains little.

As I entered the town the sun was setting. A mass of rose-coloured clouds, soft and voluminous like heaped-up cushions, swam in the sky above the flat-topped mountain and threw their reflections on to the arcaded houses. Pigeons were circling in the air, the voices of the children rose into a higher key, and the fierce unreality of evening descended. There was a café in the market place, and thus I was spared the gloom and tedium of the after-supper hour in posadas.

Next morning, after covering some ten miles, I reached the coast road. Here a depressing sight met my eye. For fifteen miles the road ran in a perfectly straight line across a stony desert without, so far as I could make out, passing a single house or tree on the way. One could see it appearing and disappearing into slight hollows in the whitish ground till it merged into the skyline. This desert is known as the Campo de Dalías. Actually it is a delta of stone and rubble pushed eight miles out into the sea by the erosion of the Sierra de Gádor, and running down to it at a slight incline. Today, however, its aspect has changed. The underground springs that in past times fed the Roman station of Murgi have been tapped, and the once-arid plain is dotted with white farmhouses and green with corn and fruit trees. Only when I first saw it, it might have been the wilderness of Sinai. As I dragged my feet along in the enervating climate of that coast, the iron wall of mountain on my left glittered monotonously and I longed in vain for a venta where I could get a drink.

Then suddenly the plain ended. The mountains fell sheer and bare to the sea, and the road was cut out of them. Before long I rounded a bluff and saw before me the white, flat-roofed city of Almeria. The fishing-boats were setting out for the night catch, and the sound of their oars and of a voice singing came across the smooth water.

Almeria is like a bucket of whitewash thrown down at the foot of a bare, greyish mountain. A small oasis – the delta of the River Andarax – spreads away beyond it, green with yams and alfalfa, diversified with date-palms and waving canes, and beyond that the barren, stony landscape begins again. In the distance lilac and ochre mountains. Since rain falls on only two or three days of the year, nothing grows without irrigation.

The Arab castle and its outworks rise steeply on the bare rock above the city, as if they were meant to guard it from the wilderness beyond. In this country drought not man is the enemy. Below them lie the cathedral and the arcaded plaza, with which the Christian conquerors sought to restore the glories of the past, and around these are the narrow lanes that still follow the plan of the Arab quarter. But the Oriental character of the place is more recent, for it is provided by streets of blue or white flat-roofed houses, which have been put up within the past century. Chief among these is the Paseo, a broad boulevard sloping slowly to the sea between its dark, shiny-leaved trees, and containing all the principal shops and cafés. A disquieting street, a street charged, like everything in this city, with peculiar overtones, yet to a superficial observer merely nineteenth-century and provincial.

I found the furniture I needed, and settled down to wait for the money I was expecting to arrive. For greater economy I moved into a cheap lodging-house just off the market place and known as La Giralda. Here I got a bed and full pension for eleven reals, or 2.75 pesetas, a day. But the place was sordid. There were six other men in my room, and the sheets I was given were dirty and marked with bloodstains. I did not find it easy to get to sleep. For several hours every night I would lie awake listening to the strange sounds made by my companions. One gargled in his throat and retched, another snored, another made a loud scratching sound as though he were scraping on canvas, while a fourth – a timid-looking boy who lay with his patched coat, torn at the armholes, thrown over him – let out his breath with a sort of sigh. Yet there was a pleasure to be found in this descent into poverty and in the contrasts it offered. From the little whitewashed courtyard outside, where the door of the lavatory was always open, there came a sickly stench of drains and stale urine, but the moon swelled out the walls with light and made, as it shone, a sort of silence. Then, as the hours wore on, the crowing of the cocks became louder and more insistent. They were kept in wooden cages on the flat roofs of the houses, and across the white moonlit city they challenged and answered one another. Their questioning, announcing, prophesying voices rose like rockets into the night, and as they died away they left a sort of happiness and reassurance. Somehow, somewhen, somewhere, they seemed to say, the world would be saved and everything, including myself and these people here, with it. A future as mysterious as the crowing of the cocks awaited all of us.

A week passed while I strolled dejectedly about the town or took walks through the green lush *vega* outside, and then an adventure which I will now describe happened to me. One afternoon as I was having lunch in the gloomy eating-room of La Giralda, to the accompaniment of the din and vociferation of the market outside, there sat down beside me a thin, scraggy man who might have been about forty. He was dressed in a badly fitting, none-too-clean suit and cracked shoes, but what was remarkable about him was his deeply lined and furrowed face, so heavily pouched under the eyes that it looked as if swallows had been building their nests there. We got into conversation, and he told me that he was a *corredor*, that is to say, a middleman or broker. On learning that I spoke French, he asked me if I would do him a service by translating between him and an Arab pedlar who had just arrived from Oran and had some contraband to dispose of. I agreed, and when the affair was concluded he invited me to a tavern for a drink. Here he suddenly became very confidential. His name, he said, was Agustín Pardo, at my service, and pointing to his lined face and pouched eyes as witnesses, he informed me that his health was ruined and that the doctor had told him that he had not much longer to live. Nature had given him an excellent constitution, but for years he had been undermining it because he led a life of great vice. He could not keep away from women. He explained this by saying that circumstances had made him an agent for the principal brothels in the town and that, with the help of a few words of English and Norwegian, he met the boats that came in and led the sailors to the places where they would get what they wanted. That was how his vice had started and why he could not give it up. Then, on seeing that I was curious about these places – I had in fact never visited a brothel – he offered to take me on a tour of them. I replied that though I should like to accept his offer I could not very well do so because I was not attracted by prostitutes, but he waved this objection aside by declaring that if I went with him there would be no obligation whatever. The girls were good girls, very quiet, full of respect for their clients. The spectacle was interesting, and for a man of culture and education such as myself, it would be instructive. As for the expense, he would undertake all of that, so that if I left a small tip, say two reals, with any girl who sat by me I would be doing all that was necessary. With two reals (sixpence) she would be enchanted.

Agustín was a very boastful man, though it was not his good qualities that he boasted of but his failings. If one were to believe him, he had a wife and four children whom he loved from the bottom of his heart, but who lived in a state of destitution because everything he earned went to pay for his vices. His health, his money, his time were all spent on women, and since fate had given him that sort of nature, he could do nothing about it.

'There you have me,' he exclaimed. 'Some men are victims of circumstances, but I'm a victim of my temperament, which is the same thing as to say of my star. That bitch of a Venus was in one of her conjunctions when I came into the world, so I had to be a man of great vice. It's no use my struggling, no use my making resolutions, I'm sunk in it up to the eyes. I'm debauched to the bone. You don't need to ask what I do, you can see it a mile away on my face. Why, anyone who did not know me would take me for a marquis. Yet let me tell you that if it wasn't for these women I should be one of the wealthiest men in the city, because I have great business sense. My father – may he rest in peace – kept a grocery store, and I used to travel for him and do his purchasing. No one can arrange a confidential deal better than I, because I have a great deal of tact, and besides am trusted by everyone. "Agustín," you hear them say, "may have his weak points, but anyhow he is a

gentleman, a *caballero*." And so, because I am liked and appre-
ciated, I have good friends in every walk of life – friends in the
coastguards, friends in the customs, friends in the police –
why, with the advantages I have I could be running a number-
one line of contraband with Oran and Melilla. But what's the
use if I don't get up till the afternoon and let all the money I
make slip through my fingers? That's why I say I'm a dis-
graceful man, an impossible man. A man who can watch his
wife and children suffer as I do – just think, two of those poor
kids are wasting away from tuberculosis – is a calamity.
There's no other word for it.'

He took another gulp of wine and rubbed his nose with his
finger.

'If it wasn't for those blessed girls I should have no respect
left for myself. I should put a bullet in my head, pim, pom,
and that would be the end of it. But they understand me. They
recognize that I'm in the same boat with themselves and that
sometimes it's the noblest people who go down. The people of
greatest generosity. You'll see tonight how much they appreciate me and what a fuss they make of me. When I have no
money they let me sleep with them all the same, and sometimes
when they see that I have only a few pesetas they refuse to
accept them, and tell me to take them back to my wife and
children who have nothing to put in the pot for supper.
They're whores, of course – that's their profession, that's how
they defend themselves against the world – but they're women
too. Some of them, believe it or not, have hearts of gold. And
it's not for my good looks that they like me. Obviously not.
But they can see that I have ruined myself and my health in
their service, and that makes them feel that I'm a victim of fate
like themselves. As the proverb says, From the fallen tree
everyone cuts firewood.'

The brothel quarter, if one may call it by so ambitious a
name, lies immediately behind the Plaza Vieja. This is a small
arcaded square, whitewashed and planted with trees, and during most of the day empty and deserted. A century or more

ago it housed the cream of the merchant families, but today the wealthy have moved to more spacious quarters, and so, though it still provides a site for the town hall, it has for the most part been taken over by small workshops and bodegas. Walking in the cool arcades, looking out on the green tangle of the garden, you might think you were in a cloister, if it were not for the racket of the children who play here between school hours. But turn from this square into a cobbled lane that runs up the steep slope to the Arab battlements. On either side you will pass a row of single-storeyed houses of poor and even squalid aspect. Here on fine afternoons – and all after-noons are fine in Almeria – you can see enormous women, rouged and oiled, their black hair running loose over their shoulders, taking the sun in low chairs and being deloused by small children. Now and then a younger woman, wrapped in a faded dressing-gown and carpet slippers, will look out into the street and empty a chamber-pot. Once, taking a short cut down in the warm twilight from the castle above, I met two brown and almost naked girls, their gowns open in front, way-laying a soldier. Yet this lane, once one had got over the first impression, did not seem in any way a sinister or evil place. If a certain rankness appeared in the seated amazons, if they stared rather fixedly as one passed, they were also as quiet and peaceful as large cats sunning themselves. These were not houses which anyone would be afraid to enter at midnight with a full wallet.

The evening came round, and Agustín and I met after sup-per as had been arranged. We had a glass of wine at a tavern to put us in the proper frame of mind, and then set out for what he called the Calle de la Esperanza, or Hope Street.

'I call it that,' he said, 'because you never know what you'll find. These places are lotteries. But, anyhow, you'll see real vice. Why, some of these girls are completely worn out by the time they're twenty-five. By twenty-seven they're hags – old women.'

We reached the square and climbed the steep cobbled lane

in the moonlight. Then we knocked at a door and went in. We found ourselves in a small room which was empty except for an extremely fat woman – the *ama* or madame – who was seated in a rocking-chair and fanning herself. She was wearing some kind of a house-coat or dressing-gown over her slip, had her hair tied at the back with a scarlet ribbon, and sported a red-paper flower over her ear. On the wall behind her hung a coloured print of the Patroness of Almeria, the Virgin of the Sea. Concha, for that I gathered was her name, greeted Agustín with a casual nod and shake of the hand as though he were a member of the family whom she saw every day. He introduced me. Then two much-made-up girls, neither of whom had been pretty for some time, came in from an inner room and sat down beside us. One of them was wearing a white chemise that made a rather poor pretence of being transparent, while the other, who was called Lola, had on a loose cotton gown, not too carefully fastened in front. A carafe of wine and some glasses were laid on the table.

'Well, Concha, how's business?' asked Agustín.

'Slow, sonny, slow,' answered the fat woman, yawning into her fan. 'After Christmas nothing seems to move in this blessed town. Except when there's a boat, it's dead, and then most of them go to Teresa's. No one has any money to spend here, that's the truth, but the rent collector doesn't consider that when he comes round. Nor that monkey-face who takes for the electric light. They have to be paid even if no one else is.'

'Well, have a drink.'

'Thank you, Agustín, not tonight. I have my old trouble in the kidneys again. Whenever the moon's in the full I get it. *Ay, madre mía,*' clasping her side, 'there it is! *With God I lie down, with God I rise – with the Virgin Mary and the Holy Spirit – may this pain leave me, for I can't live with it.*'

And she crossed herself and kissed her thumb loudly.

'Why not try Mother Celestina's powders?' said Agustín, watching her with an ironic expression. 'They'd do you more good than all that sacristy stuff. And you,' he went on, turning to the girls and lifting his glass, 'here's to your health! Keep those lovely faces a little longer, and some day you'll marry a marquis.'

'Much better marry an Englishman.'

'That's just what I've brought you, lovely, only you can't marry him. He's got a wife already and two children with faces like little painted angels waiting for him in his own country. So don't start getting worked up about him, for there's nothing doing. He's not interested.'

'Then what's he come here for?'

'Because I brought him. He wants to see the things of Spain so that he can tell people about them when he gets home.'

'Will they want to know about us?'

'Of course they will, idiot. Why, this house is as typical, as typically typical, as the Palace of the Alhambra at Granada or the Holy Week processions at Seville. It's a bit of genuine folklore. It comes down from the Moors. You girls don't know how interesting you are to foreigners.'

'Are there no whores like us then in your country?'

'Yes, but not shut up in houses.'

'And what do they earn?'

'Between twenty and thirty pesetas a time.'

'That's eighty to a hundred reals. *Bendita sea la Virgen Purísima!* Why do we go on living in this place? Do you know what we get here? Two wretched *pesetillas*, if we're lucky.'

'And have you ever been told why that is?' said Agustín, bringing his hand down hard on the table. 'It's because the economic system of this country is rotten. All the money here goes into the pockets of the priests and politicians, and the poor man is left to starve. That's how things are. What we need is a republic that will sweep that riff-raff away. Wait till that comes in, girls, and then you'll see how you're paid. Those who have served their country faithfully, as you are doing, will retire on pensions, just like the colonels and the generals.'

'I don't believe you. We poor girls will never get anything, not if there are ten republics.'

'Wait and see. Do you know what the priests and the Jesuits are sucking out of the nation? Three-quarters of what it earns. When that money is properly employed in developing the country, you'll get your share. Only wait till those black crows have been plucked and you'll think you're in Paradise.'

'Now then, Agustín,' said Concha, her previously good-natured tone suddenly taking on a hard edge, 'a little less of that, if you don't mind. Surely you can enjoy yourself *como Dios manda*, as God orders, without getting on to politics. You have all the day to let your tongue flap on this and that, can't you put your thoughts on other things when you come here? You ought to know by now that we women don't appreciate these sorts of conversations. Why, look at these poor girls waiting to take your mind off your troubles – isn't it time you began to pay a little attention to them? And anyhow, let me tell you, no good can come of your ideas. These Republicans, as they call themselves, are men who don't respect even God. Now that's not the way I was brought up, nor my girls neither. Every Martinmas in my house we killed a pig and made blood puddings and, though I don't say we went so far as to go to mass, we never missed a *novena* to the *Purísima*. And till the mule died we didn't owe a cent to anyone. But, as the proverb says, whoever keeps silence wins and whoever goes with the wolves learns to howl. So that's why I say that a little more respect all round and everything would be well. Open the door, Lola, I hear someone knocking.'

A tall man with a week's growth of beard on his face came in. A muleteer. He sat down and at once a new subject came into the conversation – the price of onions and potatoes. Everything, it seemed, was as bad as possible. With prices as they were, he didn't know how people could live. The big dealers sucked up all the trade and the small man was left to starve. Yes, a change was necessary. But all changes brought to the top the same sort of gentry, so what was the use? There was no shame in the country, no shame, but he couldn't see that the Republicans were better than anyone else. No, he didn't hold with politics and revolutions. All governments were alike – no good ever came out of any of them. As the proverb said – better the known evil than the good to come. Then, finishing off his glass, he nodded to a third girl who had come into the room – till this moment he had not looked at any of them – and passed with her into one of the small rooms next door. Agustín, who by this time had drunk a couple of glasses, got up and paid the bill.

'What, aren't you going to spare a moment for me tonight?' said Lola, putting a hand up and stroking his stubbly chin, but at the same time making a face at her companion. 'You know I'm mad about you.'

'Another time, precious, another time. I can't stay now.'

'Yes, yes, just ten minutes. You're the only man who means a thing to me, you know.'

'No, Lolita, not now. I like you very much, but tonight it's not possible. Tonight I've got someone else waiting for me.'

'Someone else, have you? That's what you always say. I believe it's at least three months since you had a woman. You men who boast and talk politics are all alike. What d'you come here for, I'd like to know?'

'Give her a little present, sonny, to soothe her feelings,' said Concha. 'She's very sensitive, poor child. After all, she's an orphan. If it wasn't for me she'd have nothing to call her own but the day and the night and the water in the pitcher.'

'All right, here's something to spend on caramels. Be a good girl till you see me again.'

'A second-rate place,' said Agustín to me as soon as we were outside. 'No animation. It smells of the sacristy. This quarter is just a village. I only go to that house so as not to offend Concha. You ought to have seen her before she grew old and pious – she was a wonderful woman then. Many's the good time we've had together.'

'Why are these madames always so fat?' I asked.

'Oh, they have to be that – they have to occupy a lot of space. The girls wouldn't respect them otherwise. In these houses there has to be a lot of respect. After all, you know, these women stand in the place of their mothers.'

'How do you mean?'

'Why, just that. They get new girls because they have a look of being motherly. And indeed, they're mostly very kind women, very kind. Concha there has a heart of gold. Besides you must remember they have to deal with the police. The police respect fat women, they respect them a great deal. You never yet saw a fat woman in prison. Fat women know how to impose themselves.'

We knocked at the door of another house a short distance away. In the usual small room two men were sitting drinking with three girls, and Agustín, who knew the men, greeted them with cordiality. They had the look of habitués and, in fact, as my companion told me later, they were stallkeepers from the market who came every week. Politics cropped up again, and here everyone, including the madame, who was only a little less bulky than Concha, was for a republic. If Lerroux were president, they all agreed, he would soon set the Jesuits and the priests about their business. But the men were showing signs of drink. Their loud harsh voices rose in argument, and the girls, to calm them down and get them to the bedrooms, tried to provoke them by a show of brazenness. In the end they were successful. The men lurched out through two doors, behind each of which I caught a glimpse of a dingy bed entirely filling the little room, and of a picture of the Virgin hanging above it. Agustín who, after joining energetically in the political argument, had sunk into silence, asked for the bill. The remaining girl, who had at first directed her attention on me, made little effort to detain us, because the only two bedrooms in the house were occupied.

'Not a very edifying place,' said Agustín, whose language became more refined as he filled up with drink. 'No order, no respect. Vice has its rules like everything else. Dignity, there must be dignity. A great deal of dignity. I know these men – they are not very recommendable persons. One of them owes me two duros seventy-five centimos and won't repay it. A crook, if ever there was one.'

'Where are we off to now?' I asked.

'Well, we could go to Jesusa's establishment. They have some nice girls there, but against that you must remember that Jesusa's aunt on her mother's side works as a charwoman in the episcopal palace. That leaves a nasty taste in the mouth, doesn't it? Besides, you may be sure that every word said there goes straight back to the bishop.'

'Surely he can't be interested in what is said in such places?'

'What else should he be interested in? The Church and the police get all their information about what is going on from these madames. Abolish the brothels, I tell you, and a revolution would break out in six months' time because the authorities would have lost touch with what is being said in the country.'

'In that case . . .'

'No, we certainly won't go to Jesusa's. I don't want to see a girl crossing herself before she lies down on the bed as though she was expecting an operation for appendicitis. We'll go to Teresa's. That's a very different sort of affair – an international resort that's patronized by foreign sailors. You'll see real vice there without having to go to the expense of buying yourself a ticket to Paris. All right, then, if you agree we'll turn our backs on the houses in this quarter. They used to be something once, but today they're just dull little places, run-down establishments in search of a new management. If I had a little capital I'd acquire them and pull them together. But Teresa's – that's an altogether different thing. You'll see girls there who for two pins will eat you up, and others just arrived from the villages with faces like little sugar angels. Come on, I say, let's hurry. We don't want to miss a moment of what's waiting for us.'

But almost at once he had stopped again.

'Oh, this life!' he exclaimed, stretching out his arm with a theatrical gesture. 'This life will be the end of me. Women, women, women all the time! I can't leave off and yet it's killing me. Don Juan Tenorio – you know who he was – was an innocent compared to me. What did he know of vice? Three or four seductions, four or five false promises of marriage – why, that's nothing when one has money. I do more every month, and yet I haven't a bean.'

He turned and stood facing me, with one hand gripping my sleeve and the other gesticulating in the air.

'No, I tell you, that man was nothing, absolutely nothing. There are young bloods like him in every town in Spain, who spend their lives having their shoes polished and their faces massaged, and then take three months over dazzling a servant girl. What's there remarkable in that? In true vice there is obsession, there is self-abandonment. You sink, you sink, you discard your pride, you let yourself go on a wave of generosity. You give up everything and hold on to nothing. You die, you destroy yourself, you come down to the last truth of things. You become as God made you. I say that there is more true religion in that life than in all the sermons you hear in churches, because there is no holding back and no hypocrisy.'

He took his hand from my coat-sleeve and we resumed our progress. Soon, turning a corner, we found ourselves in a long narrow street, cut deeply as if with a knife between two façades of houses. The usual stream of passers-by had ceased, the last lovers had gone home, there were no lights in the windows. Occasionally a hurrying figure passed us, his rope-soled shoes making a soft patter on the pavement. Only the moon, throwing its bright plaques of light on to the upper storeys while the roadway remained sunk in shadow, seemed fully alive and operant.

Under the influence of the fresh air and of the wine he had

drunk, Agustín was becoming more and more exhilarated. With his face turned up to the sky, the pouches under his eyes glistened till they looked like two enormous tears suspended under them.

'See that moon,' he exclaimed suddenly, seizing my arm. 'We crawl about on earth like insects, but it rolls above and looks down on everything. And what doesn't it see? Vice in all the villages, vice in all the towns, vice and vice and vice and no shame anywhere. Look at me, I've got all the diseases a man can catch from women, but they don't kill me. I tell you, I thrive on them. They're a tonic to my system. They stimulate me to new efforts. Here, feel my pulse.'

And he held out his wrist.

'You see, leaping. My pulse is leaping. I'm in splendid health. It's only during the day that I feel ill. My true time is the night-time. My hour is when the moon is shining. Come on, I say, let's get quickly to Teresa's. Let's sample those ferocious women. Tonight especially we must finish well.'

We arrived. A substantial house, displaying an iron knocker and barred windows. The sound of voices and laughter coming through them. We rang, and a pair of eyes surveyed us through a grille; then a cord was pulled and the door opened. We stepped into a tiled hall, where a stoutish woman who was rather too heavily made-up was standing by a rocking-chair. On a table by her side an enormous black cat was lying asleep, and against the wall there were some pots of aspidistras.

'Well, Agustín,' exclaimed the woman, extending a casual hand, 'so here you are again! Who have you brought with you this time? Another German?'

'No, no, Teresa, this is an Englishman. A man of literature and science who has travelled all over the world seeing new things. He's writing a book on Spanish women, so naturally I brought him to see you. I've told him that he'll find the flower of our Almerian womanhood in your house – isn't that right? But a visit of inquiry and exploration, nothing more. He's expecting every day a money-order from his rich uncle, so till then, you understand, his interest will be purely theoretical.'

'All right. You know the way in. All foreigners are welcome.'

We passed into the lounge, if that is the proper word to use for it – a largish room furnished with small tables, a sofa, and an assortment of chairs. On the walls there was a poster of a bullfight and an advertisement of a woman wearing a black Cordovan hat and drinking a glass of sherry. A screen stood in the corner and by it sat a bored, sulky-looking girl, and with her a thin melancholy man dressed in the deepest black. He had a glass of wine in front of him, and every now and then he stared round the room and said, 'Your health, gentlemen!' He was evidently completely drunk, and Agustín whispered to me that he had been in this state ever since his wife had died a short time before.

We ordered wine; other girls and men appeared and settled at the tables. From somewhere within we could hear the sound of chinking glasses and of loud animated conversation. These came from a party that had taken the private sitting-room: for ordinary customers the lounge was good enough, and here they sat and drank till they had worked up their courage either to carry their visit a step farther or to leave. But except that the girls were lightly dressed, the atmosphere could not have been more decorous. The men talked for preference among themselves, clinging to their own sex for reassurance and paying little attention to the fancy-dress figures who sat yawning beside them. When they did address them it was in a half-patronizing, half-contemptuous tone, as though they wished to make it clear that in choosing them as partners for certain private occasions they were not in any way putting themselves on a level with them. Only those who were old enough to have grown-up daughters of their own behaved simply and naturally.

Agustín was still in his vein of euphoria.

'Look at them,' he said, pointing at the two girls who had

sat down beside us. 'You don't see women like that every day. Eyes like two car lamps fresh from the garage, breasts like cannon pointed at you, feet like the little red feet of pigeons! And they're tigers. They'll eat you up as soon as look at you.'

'What a state of mind you're in tonight!' said the older of the two. 'What's come over you? We don't usually get such fine speeches.'

'You do from me. Every time I come here I say nice things to you, because every time you're more beautiful.'

'You can keep them for your girl-friend, if you've got one. She may be taken in by them. And now tell me if you've managed to see that German sailor again.'

'Not yet, but I will soon, precious.'

'Well, mind you bring him here if you do. He promised me a pair of gold ear-rings and I'm still waiting for them. And who's this foreigner you've picked up? He seems a quiet one.'

'I've told him such terrible things about you that he's frightened.'

'I suppose then that he's a cissy like yourself. Does he know any Spanish?'

'More than you do, idiot. He's read the whole of *Don Quixote* twice over.'

'What's that? A love story?'

'*Don Quixote*,' pronounced a heavy, blown-out-looking man who had sat down at the next table, '*Don Quixote* is the national glory of Spain. No one who does not know that has the right to call himself a Spaniard. There is a monument to him in Madrid, and every year the whole of the Spanish Academy and all the members of the Government and all the principal authorities of the city put flowers on it. He was our first revolutionary.'

'That's a policeman,' whispered Agustín to me. 'Political branch.'

'You speak Ingleesh?' said the policeman to me.

'Yes,' I replied, 'do you?'

He looked at me without replying. Then –

'I am in the police force,' he said in Spanish. 'A police officer has to speak all languages, even that of the Moors. How do you like our city?'

'Very much indeed,' I answered. 'I'm enchanted by it.'

'Well, let me tell you with all frankness that it's a disgrace to Spain. I was born here and I love my city, but no one can tell me that it's not a disgrace. Do you know what other Spaniards call it? They call it *el culo de España*, "the bum of Spain", and though I regard that as an insult to me personally, because it is directed at my city, I must admit that they're not far wrong. Such ignorance, such lack of culture as we have here is a national disgrace. Why, do you know that just on seventy per cent of the population are unable to read or write? I can tell you that we Almerians who have a conscience are deeply ashamed.'

'Why not say that all Spaniards are ashamed?'

'Yes, that could be said too. Spain today is a national calamity. Once the pride and glory of the world, it is at present one of the most backward of countries. Our soil is the richest in Europe, our mountains are full of iron, copper, gold, lead, silver, aluminium, manganese, mercury, rubies, agates, and carbuncles – especially carbuncles. The people are sound, brave, noble, frank, honest, healthy, hard-working – and yet we live as you see. I say that it is a disgrace, and that those who are responsible should be made to answer for it.'

'The politicians and the priests, of course,' said Agustín. 'They keep the people in ignorance.'

'I name no one,' said the policeman. 'I am in the service of the State, and it is not for me to fix responsibility. I obey orders. If I am told to arrest a revolutionary, I do so. If I am told to close my eyes or even to place a bomb myself, I do that also. A servant of the State may have his opinions, but if so he must keep them to himself. Here – locked in his chest.'

And, tapping that part of his body, he looked round the room as if to gather in the applause, and spat quietly under the table.

'Come along, Manolo,' said the girl who was with him, tugging at his shoulder. 'There's a room vacant.'

'But some day, mister,' he said, getting up slowly, 'there will be a change, and then you will discover what Spain can do. When that comes you will see something extraordinary.'

And he walked out with the heavy step of a man leaving a room full of friends to answer a business call on the telephone.

'A fine man,' commented Agustín. 'You can see that at heart he's a Republican. And he knows how to express himself. Some day, when the Revolution comes, he will have an important position. He's the sort of person who, when one's least thinking of it, is appointed Civil Governor or even Minister.'

'But he spits like a woman,' said the girl who was with me. 'Under the table.'

'Ah, that shows he was properly brought up. He has real refinement.'

A change now began to come over Agustín. He sat staring dully at the far end of the room and saying nothing. At the same time the girls who had been sitting with us went off. I had given no encouragement to the one who was next to me, and neither of them had shown the least interest in my companion. There were other clients in the room who held out more hope of requiring their services. We might almost have been in a café, for the men were talking quietly among themselves without showing more than a sporadic interest in the girls who sat in their flimsy dresses beside them.

'Let's go,' I said to Agustín, but he showed no inclination to stir. He had sunk into a torpor and could only rouse himself enough to say '*Nada, nada*, it's still early.'

All at once there was a loud hammering on the street door, followed by the sound of raised voices in the hall. A party of four young men, sleek and well dressed, came in, their faces flushed from drinking, and demanded to be shown into the inner room reserved for private parties. But the room was occupied. After a good deal of noisy argument, which brought the madame paddling out of her rocking-chair in the hall, they

consented to sit down at a table and asked to see the new girl
who had just arrived. This led to more discussion, but in the
end she was brought in, a thin, doll-faced wench, aged perhaps
eighteen, dressed in a clean pink shift and wearing a red rose in
her hair. I had already been told her history. She came from a
small town called Tabernas on the road to Murcia; a travelling
salesman had carried her off and then abandoned her, and to
support herself she had had no alternative but to come here.
She walked across the room with the pinched, sulky expression of a schoolgirl who has just been scolded by the head-
mistress for not showing a cooperative spirit, and at once the
young men fastened on her and on two somewhat older girls
who were with her, and a loud, animated conversation began.

Agustín suddenly woke up and began to show an interest in
what was going on at their table.

'Look,' he said. 'I told you you'd see something if you
waited. *La flor de la morería*. The flower of the Moorish quarter.
Better say three Oriental pearls. You won't see such beauties
anywhere else. The new one will cost you ten pesetas for half
an hour, while the others are only five pesetas. At that price
they're thrown away, for I can tell you they give their money's
worth. After a night with one of them you wouldn't be able to
walk home – they'd have to send you in a carriage. Did I tell
you that only last year a man died in this house? He had just
won a lottery prize, so he felt he could let himself go. The
older of those two girls we were talking to killed him.'

'Really?'

'Yes, a very respectable man who went every evening to the
Casino. Don Indalecio Buzón. Stout and quite bald. He kept
that pastry shop in the Plaza San Martín. He left behind him a
wife and three grown-up daughters, so you'd have expected
the police to arrange an alibi and tell his family he'd died while
performing an act of charity to a poor cripple and so gone
straight to Paradise. But no, they had a grudge against him
because he had refused to pay certain little sums, so they just
blurted the truth out to his widow like that. She took it badly.

In her indignation she couldn't contain herself but told everyone. "Just think," she screamed out, "that husband of mine
never even let me know he'd won a lottery ticket. I only hope
that at this moment he isn't suffering torments for his deceit-
fulness to me." At that time the eldest girl, Satisfacción, was
engaged to the son of a man who keeps a religious-image shop,
but when his father, who by the way I've sometimes seen in
this house, heard of what had happened, he made him break it
off because he was afraid the scandal would affect his business.
However, to make up for this, the pastry shop suddenly began
to do very well because everyone went to it to hear Doña
Maria Josefa telling the story, and many of those who went
became regular customers. Quite a lot of people had kept away
from it before, because the old man, who liked to stand behind
the counter himself, had very bad breath, and that in a pastry
shop is not nice. But now it was the girls who served the pastries, and they smelt of rose-water and cough lozenges. Then
a new fiancé turned up for Satisfacción in the person of the
hairdresser's son from the Paseo, who of course was a far
better match than her previous one. His father strongly
approved of the match because he was anticlerical and wanted
to snub the image-shop owner, while his mother, who was very
fond of pastries, thought that it would be nice to be connected
with a place that made them. He himself was in love with her
because he had long been crazy about her hair. It was very fine
hair, a pale brown in colour, and ever since he had left school
he had dreamed of the happiness it would be to spend the rest
of his life combing it and stroking it and making it up into new
and extraordinary hair-do's. He had even written poems about
it, and one of them had been published in the *Almeria Echo*.
However, this wasn't the end of the family's spell of good
luck. In the general excitement over the affair the other
daughters, who were decidedly plain, suddenly found fiancés
too, while, to put the last touch to their happiness, it turned
out that the old man hadn't had time to spend more than a
fraction of the money he'd won in the lottery. Even after the

madame here and the police had helped themselves to what they thought fair and just, there were nearly eleven hundred pesetas in notes in his pocket-book. That was a very pleasant surprise, I can tell you. After paying for the funeral and for some masses to help the old boy through his troubles in the next world, there was quite a nice bit left over that more than paid for the wedding trousseau. So in the end the affair turned out well for everyone except poor Don Indalecio, and even he died happily. In fact, he died of happiness.'

The young men at the next table were laughing and talking loudly and scarcely seemed to notice that the new girl was not responding to their sallies. With her small tight mouth and sulky expression she looked the image of cornered and resentful adolescence. Clearly it was the word 'new', and not anything in her physical appearance, that had cast such a spell over them. But for some hours I had been drinking steadily, and now the wine was beginning to produce an effect. I heard the voices, saw the faces, but did not properly take in what was happening. Agustín, too, after his burst of loquacity, had again fallen silent and was staring gloomily at the wall in front of him. Then, after how long I cannot say, the sound of loud voices and scraping chairs roused me. The party from the inside room had come out and were having a dispute with the madame over the bill. When at length they left, the room was empty because, while they were arguing, the young men and the girls with them had moved inside.

I got up and pulled Agustín to his feet. He was as drunk as I was, and hiccupping loudly.

'All right,' he said, 'now that the feast of beauty is over, we'll go. At once. Certainly. Tell them to call my carriage.'

Just then a girl passed through.

'Still waiting for me, darling?' she said jeeringly to Agustín, and poured the dregs of a glass of wine down his neck. He did not seem to notice her existence.

In the hall the madame was dozing quietly, with the black cat asleep beside her. The blue lines of make-up that covered

her eyelids suggested to me the shadows of pine-clad mountains, perhaps the Carpathians, but before I could do anything
about this she yawned, and her yawn disillusioned me. I paid
for the drinks we had had, and we left. A quarter of an hour
later I was in bed.

Next morning I woke up late. The little room in which I lay
was empty, and the faint smell of the lavatory in the courtyard
next door seeped in with the cries of the market and with the
sunlight. But my head was clear, and after a cup of hot barley
coffee and some fritters fried in oil, I got out a notebook and
began to write down the events of the previous evening. The
day passed without my seeing Agustín. On the following afternoon, however, he came into La Giralda where I was writing,
sat down at my table, and called for a glass of wine. He seemed
in very low spirits, and after remaining there almost without
speaking for some time, he began in a not very convincing
tone to tell me of a wonderful deal that had been offered him.
He could make several hundred pesetas within a few days if
only he could put up fifty now. Could I lend him the half of
that – that is, twenty-five? He would swear on his honour to
repay me, and besides that he would arrange for me to have
the new girl – he had noticed that I had been strongly attracted
to her – at a specially low rate. At Teresa's they were always
ready to accommodate him.

As I was by this time almost through with my money, I
refused to lend him anything, but he persisted so much that in
the end I parted with two pesetas, say half a crown, and the
promise of more when the money order I expected arrived. He
pocketed them without comment and went off.

'I see you've made a friend,' said the owner of La Giralda
when Agustín had left.

'Yes, who is he?'

'Oh, a poor devil who has ruined himself through drink. He
came of a good family too. His father kept a grocer's shop in
the Calle de Granada.'

'He has a wife and four children, I understand.'

244 SOUTH FROM GRANADA

'A wife, yes, but no children. He's not the sort to have them.'

'How's that?'

'Well, I only know what people say. But it's the general rumour that he's – you understand – not a complete man.'

That evening, on counting up my money, I found that it was almost all gone. When I had paid for my bed and supper I should have less than a peseta left. However, on calling at the post office I was told that the letter I had been expecting so impatiently had at last arrived. Opening it in haste, I found that it contained a refusal on my relative's part to lend me anything. This was going to make things difficult for me, and it was also going to be hard on Agustín. I felt that I owed him a great deal – not so much for taking me round the brothels, which were completely boring, as for displaying to me his remarkable self. When I ran into him again on some future occasion I should probably be feeling less generous.

As I lay in bed that night, mixing in a Baudelairean way the brightness of the full moon with the smell of the lavatory bucket, I thought that I would call the story I meant to write about my new friend *A Don Juan of our time*. For who else was Don Juan but a man who was prepared to brave great obstacles to satisfy his ruling passion? In the past the obstacles had lain outside in the defences of a society which had studded itself with duennas and barred windows and menfolk armed with rapiers, but today these hazards had grown so trifling that the man who wished to be a hero of love must conjure them up within himself. For no one could suppose that he could become a person of that sort by a mere Casanova-like display of amorousness. Now the peculiarity, I said to myself, of Agustín's situation was that, while he could not overcome his obstacle in an ordinary or practical sense, he could sur- mount it by rising above it into that other dimension of the imagination. With his gift of impotence he could conjure up a marvellous region where the humdrum man is purified and ennobled by vice, just as Don Quixote could create out of his intrinsic dullness and ordinariness his noble career of knight errant.

I was in the middle of these casuistical reflections, which seemed to explain why such a man as Stendhal, whose life had been a succession of amatory fiascos, should have come down to us as one of the great exponents of the art of love, when I fell asleep. But daylight brings more positive ideas. As I trudged along the interminable road that runs as straight as a surveyor's tape across the Campo de Dalías, I decided that my whole conception was absurd. No one, not even Dostoevsky, could bring off a love story of which the hero was impotent. Even the comic muse drew back before that.

CHAPTER SEVENTEEN

ALMERIA AND ARCHAEOLOGY

*

DURING the next few years I came to know Almeria pretty
well. It was so easy to reach – a mere nine or ten hours away –
that I used to visit it whenever I wanted a change from village
life. Even the journey by motor-bus had its excitement. One
bumped in a cloud of dust across the great stony plain, hugged
the yellow cliffs where they dropped to the sea, and suddenly
saw the white city spread out before one like an illustration in
a book of Eastern travel. Then, after a wash and brush-up in
the hotel, I would take a seat in front of one of the cafés on the
Paseo. Up and down, up and down the people passed, in endless leisurely perambulation. I began by picking out the blind
woman led by the child, the blind man led by the old woman,
the energetic man with one leg, the girl who had a face like a
sleep-walker, till after a little half the people in the street were
familiar.

Each part of the day had its characteristic feature. In the
mornings, for example, as soon as one came out of the hotel,
one would hear from the direction of the market a roaring like
a cascade. On going closer one would distinguish the wailing
nasal voices of the street vendors, making the air throb as they
cried their wares and rising above the general gabble and argument of the throng of people. There was something exhilarating in this bonfire of exotic sounds (it no longer exists today,
since all market cries have been forbidden), and one left the
place feeling one had had an electric massage. Then the city
emptied for lunch at about two, and this suspension was
followed by the spectacle of a seated population, consisting
entirely of men, who filled every chair in the cafés. A little
later the procession I have spoken of began. It grew and grew,

till by late evening the whole roadway was occupied by a gently milling stream, the girls walking in groups in their flower-coloured dresses, their swinging gait and dark floating eyes setting up waves of excitement in the air around them, and the scents they used leaving a trail behind. Although individually few of them, I fancy, were particularly pretty, by taking here a nose, there a neck and there a head of glistening, cascading hair, one made up a collective picture that dazzled.

Two things combined to give Almeria its special character – animation and monotony. It was a hurdy-gurdy. Every morning and every evening the miraculous act would be put on – but it was always the same one. The Spanish pattern of culture is so tight and rigid, and the need for keeping up appearances so strong, that in a small provincial capital such as this there could be no variations. Courtship led to marriage, marriage led to children, and children landed the parents in a groove of narrow economic restrictions from which there was no hope of ever emerging. The monotony that descended like the sunlight was untempered by even the ghost of an illicit love affair. So it came about that the individual with his hopes and daydreams had withered by the time he was thirty, a cog in the chain of births and deaths, and by the time he was forty looked like a pressed fern in an album. The only gainers were the children, because the parents put all the illusions of their own youthful days on to them, and treated them like heirs to a kingdom. Thus the spectacle of heightened life and animation, which so impressed the person just arriving from his village, was a mirage. The routine of a peasant, with its quiet variation of crops and weather, was a good deal more satisfying than that of a white-collar worker in this city of *ritournelle*, though the peasant was the last person to know it.

At all events I can say that I myself never came down to Almeria without a feeling of excitement such as Granada, with its far larger population and therefore greater complexity of life, did not give me. It was like a fair or an opera, and everything that happened in it had happened a great many times

before. Was it this that gave such a curious richness to the
overtones? Certainly it seemed that the sea was doubly Mediterranean here, and that the city, spread out in the bright
coloured light, contained within it echoes of distant civilizations.

Another feeling that, arriving as I did from the mountains, I
found it hard to resist was that a delicious vice and corruption
lay hidden under the surface. The climate was so relaxing that
when I had walked the length of the Paseo once or twice, I was
glad to subside into a chair. If in a fit of energy I forced myself
out for a stroll into the *vega*, I found a succulence and luxuri-
ance in the vegetation, a sappiness in the flopping, creeping,
nerveless plants that seemed to infect my own system. Then,
coming back in the late evening through the crowded streets,
with the dust rising from the roadway and the palm trees waving and a crimson cloud floating in the sky overhead, I passed
the women standing in the doorways of their houses or waiting to fill their pitchers at the fountain. Their dark, velvety
eyes, their brown bodies thinly concealed by their cotton
frocks, and their languishing stances and gestures could surely,
one imagined, be nothing but a deliberate invitation. Yet such
suppositions were groundless. The more subversive the
climate, the more carefully the women are hedged in and
guarded, and the less opportunity there is for casual love
affairs.

Above the flat roofs of the city stands the Arab Alcázar, or
castle, with its outlying fortifications. This large building,
which dates from the tenth and eleventh centuries and has
today been converted into a museum and public garden, was
at this time occupied by an Army signal station, but the
Castillo de San Cristóbal, which crowns a different hill and is
of the same age, lay open to anyone who chose to visit it. One
scrambled up past the hovels of the poor and the sprawling
prickly-pear plants and dried excreta, and came to a flat place
that looked out over the city and the sea and towards the
distant ochre or rose-coloured mountains.

The castle, or what was left of it, consisted in a long crenel-
lated wall of pisé, faced with yellowish plaster that had peeled
off in places, and strengthened at intervals by square towers.
In the upper chamber of one of these towers there lived an old
crone who supported herself by begging. The access to this
chamber was difficult and, since she was crippled as well as
blind, there was no means by which she could get down. Few
people except the children of the *barrio*, who came up to play
or to eat the fruit of the prickly pears, ever visited the place, so
that it was surprising that the old woman could make enough
to keep herself alive. She was only able to do so because she
had an acute sense of hearing. Whenever this told her that
someone was passing she would come hobbling out on her
crutches on to a little platform outside her room and cry in a
piercing voice:

'*Por el amor de Dios, una lismonica,* an alms. *Por el amor de Dios
y de María Santísima, una lismonica, caballero, una lismonica.*'

The boys mocked her. 'There is no *caballero* here, it is only
us, and we have nothing to give you.' This made her stop and
listen again. Then, in a more discouraged and whining tone,
scarcely believing that her ears had reported the truth, she
would begin once more:

'*Caballero, una lismonica. Dé a una probe anciana una lismonica.*'

When one gave her something – and it was necessary to
climb up a broken staircase to do so – she poured out a stream
of blessings.

'May the Blessed Virgin give you everything you wish for!
May she give you and your father and your mother long lives!'
Then, after counting the coins, 'May St Gabriel and St Michael
and the holy choir of the angels come down through the air
and carry you up to Heaven!'

Such blessings bring good luck, and often, I think, coins
were given her not so much out of kindness of heart as to
obtain the *baraka* which might help one to pick a winning
number in a lottery. The wretchedness of the old woman
could be judged from the fact that a *perra chica*, or halfpenny,

drew from her a flow of language that, measured by the standard of the beggars in the town, was worth at least three *perras gordas*, or pennies. But perhaps this undercutting paid. I would not be surprised if she had quite a clientele of gamblers who made the steep climb up the hill to visit her because her good works cost a halfpenny less than those of the church-porch beggars in the town.

One day I climbed up the broken stone staircase that led to the summit of the wall, and made my way into her den. I found that it stank horribly and had nothing in it but a jar of water and a heap of straw and rags. Since she had forgotten how to converse and could only utter screams or whine, it was impossible to learn anything from her about her life. Later on, however, I met a ragged little girl who was carrying her weekly ration of bread, bought with the money she had begged, and a can of water. For doing this the old woman gave her every now and then a halfpenny. Who she was or how long she had been there the child did not know, but she informed me that in the next tower there was an old man who could no longer even move.

'They're going to let him die now,' she said. 'He's lived long enough.'

I went in and found him: he was lying on some straw, and paid no attention to me beyond making some incoherent mumblings. Next day I brought him some bread and wine, but he did not seem to understand what they were, and I expect that the children, who lived in a state of permanent hunger too, got them as soon as I had left. As the little girl had said, there seemed no point in prolonging such an existence any longer. However, the old woman lived for many years: whenever I went to Almeria I would visit her, and her loud, shrill voice calling out in the sunset from the ruined tower while the clouds turned scarlet overhead was always an eerie and macabre experience.

During the dictatorship of General Primo de Rivera a large monument to the Sacred Heart, illuminated by night, was erected on this hill to overlook the city and the port. It was built of such shoddy materials that it began to crumble almost as soon as it had been put up, and when the Republic came in all the saints' heads moulded in plaster on it, with the exception of that of the Virgin, were mutilated. It was pulled down during the Civil War, but has now been re-erected on a much larger scale and with better materials.

Almeria has had a typically Oriental history, consisting of one brief period of *Arabian Nights* affluence, followed by a long slow decline. The city was founded during the first years of the tenth century. A confederation of Spanish-Arab merchant seamen, who had set up a factory on the African coast near Oran, decided to move their headquarters to Pechina on the River Andarax, a few miles inland from Almeria and close to the old Roman and Iberian town of Urci. But the river was not navigable except for small boats, so that their fleet was obliged to anchor off the coast under the shelter of the Sierra de Gádor. Here arsenals were built and a settlement grew up which took the name of Almeria or 'The Watch Tower' (and not, as is usually said, 'The Mirror of the Sea') from an old tower that stood on the seashore. It rapidly outdistanced Pechina. Abd al-Rahman III gave it a port, a mosque and a castle, and when the Caliphate of Cordoba fell in 1008 it became an independent kingdom ruled by a dynasty of 'Slav' kings, drawn from what would in a later age be called the Caliph's janissaries.

This was Almeria's brief period of splendour. Its five thousand looms supplied Europe and Africa with rich silken stuffs – cicaltoun, camlet, sendal, georgian, damask, the costly *tiraz* – and with those fine-coloured gauzes known as *almajares* and *alguexís*. It had shipbuilding yards and a powerful navy, iron foundries and potteries, while its foreign trade was so extensive that it boasted of having a thousand inns and public baths to accommodate the merchants who visited it. With a population of perhaps 300,000, it was for a time the wealthiest and most commercially active city in Europe, after

Constantinople. But this prosperity did not last. The Christian armies were pressing down from the north, and to repel them the small kingdoms into which Moslem Spain had broken up invited the Saharan dynasty of the Almoravides, who had just conquered Morocco, to cross the Strait and come to their assistance. They did so and, after winning a great victory, decided to remain. In the year 1091 they marched into Almeria with their tom-toms beating, and its great days were at an end.

During the next four centuries Almeria maintained itself as a town of moderate size by its manufacture of silk stuffs. Then in 1489 it was surrendered to the Catholic kings after their successful siege of Baza, and declined still further. Its Morisco population driven out, twice shaken by earthquakes, and without any trade, it sank to being little more than a village, supporting itself by smuggling. Then, during the third quarter of the nineteenth century, its revival began with the building of the railway and the port. A considerable mining industry sprang up, with the help of British and Belgian capital, and when this declined the grape industry took its place. The city as one sees it today dates chiefly from the last decades of that century, and its characteristic architecture of one-storeyed or two-storeyed houses of almost double the normal height, with plaster mouldings framing the windows and doorways, bears the stamp of Queen Isabella's reign. Really bad street architecture in Spain does not begin before the nineties, when the *art nouveau* style was introduced from Vienna.

To the east of Almeria a huge semi-desert region stretches away as far as Murcia and Carthagena. The Romans called it the Campus Spartarius, because only esparto grass grew here. Actually the soil is good, but the rainfall is meagre and uncertain, and sometimes there is none at all for several years on end. Most of the male population emigrate to Barcelona, while the women earn what they can by lace-making. However, the traveller who has a feeling for landscape will find that this is one of the most rewarding regions of the Peninsula. It is composed of small plains traversed by low ranges of barren hills

that are so channelled and fretted by the storms that occasionally fall that they look like their own skeletons. According to
the hour and soil they turn from chrome or cadmium yellow
to rose, and from lavender to blue, and in that dry deceptive
light seem sometimes to be almost transparent, as though they
were made of molten glass or crystal. Then one comes suddenly to a little escarpment and sees below one a river-bed,
where the deep refreshing green of the orange trees and of the
alfalfa make a complete contrast to the high, light tones of the
plains and mountains. Oasis and desert, cave villages and date
palms: one could suppose oneself in Africa, if this country was
not on a much smaller scale, with the detail sharper and better
defined and the composition more pictorial than anything to
be found on that rolling, space-drunk continent.

Níjar, twenty miles to the east of Almeria, is a good centre
from which to explore this region. It is a place of some size,
lying like a large white cow on the slope of a denuded hill, and
it has a good posada. It lives by its potteries, which, with those
of near-by Sorbas, are so far as I know the only ones left in
Spain that have not adopted aniline dyes. The men make the
pots, and the women paint them in the three primitive colours
of manganese, copper oxide, and cobalt. Since the lead glaze is
soft, it wears through quickly, and on that account they are
sold for very low prices to the labouring classes. For the same
reason, and because the Spanish poor are naturally careless and
destructive, it is rare to come across pieces that are more than
a few years old, though at Níjar itself some of the pottery
owners have kept early specimens.

These pots, which are so despised in their own country,
sometimes find themselves occupying posts of honour in
foreign collections by reason of their Oriental design and
facture. Until 1936 the British Museum displayed two of them,
a wine jar and a bowl, both quite modern, which were labelled
Samarra, 8th century and *Egypt, 18th century*. On my pointing
out this error to my friend William King, who was then the
Keeper of the Pottery Department, they were, I regret to say,

removed. Yet some of this Níjar ware is attractive. I myself possess two wine-jars, dating from perhaps a century ago, which any museum of Oriental art would be glad to possess, provided that they did not know where they came from.

About a dozen miles to the south of Níjar is the Cabo de Gata, the cape which shelters the bay of Almeria from the easterly winds. Its name, Cape Cat, is really a corruption of Cabo de Agata, Cape Agate. Its red, waterless rocks are volcanic, and since Phoenician times have been famous for their supply of various sorts of precious and semi-precious stones, among them carbuncles and amethysts. On the seashore a little to the west of the cape, at a place known as Torre García, there is a small chapel which marks the spot where the Virgen del Mar, who is the patroness of Almeria, appeared to some sailors in the year 1502 and showed them where her image lay buried in the sand dunes. Actually the cult of this Virgin goes back many centuries beyond this, for we are told that the confederation of merchant seamen who founded the city in the ninth century set up her statue above the gates of Pechina. Since it is evident that most of these people were Moslems, we may suppose that she had taken over the role of Isis as the protectress of Mediterranean sailors and fishermen. Indeed, even today the devotion to the Virgin transcends creeds, for in the years before the Civil War the Andalusian fishermen, who were almost without exception of anarchist affiliations and therefore violently anti-Catholic, invoked her in storms, and when churches were being burned protected the one in which her image was kept.

The Cabo de Gata is also of interest to botanists, because of its unique flora. In the square mile of marshy land that lies at the foot of the headland are found some twenty plants that grow nowhere else in Europe. Most of them are ordinary enough, except to the specialist's eye, but one of them, though small, should please flower-lovers who like to find something rare. This is *Melanthium punctatum*, a sort of colchicum with striped blue-and-white petals which flowers in December.

However, one may say that the whole of this very arid coast has a flora that is more African than European. Like that of the Atlantic coast round Agadir, it depends as much on the heavy dew as on rainfall.

The botany of extreme climates has its special fascination. There is a thrill to be got from plants that surmount great natural difficulties, especially when they do so with excess and bravura. Thus I shall never forget climbing one afternoon up a dry hillside not far from Almeria, where the soil could scarcely support more than a single woody, almost leafless plant every few yards, and coming suddenly on a cluster of long pendent racemes of rose-coloured flowers, each about two feet in length, surrounded by finely cut leaves. They belonged to a statice, whose second name very appropriately was *insignis*. Then I might mention the colocynth or colo-quintida, the Dead Sea fruit of the Bible. If one walks on the seashore in the early autumn, one may come on some small yellow melons lying just beyond the reach of the waves. They seem to belong to no one, and it would be delicious, one imagines, to relieve one's thirst by sampling them. However, cut the ripest of them in two with a knife and let the tongue just touch the juicy interior and the whole of one's mouth will shrivel up as though one had tasted a solution of hydrochloric acid. The colocynth is the bitterest thing imaginable and would be a deadly poison if one could find a way of swallowing it.

The herbalist may be interested in two rather unobtrusive plants that grow along this coast. One is a thorny shrub with white flowers of the same family as spindlewood and known as *Catha europea*. It is a close relation of the *Catha edulis*, in Arabic *kat*, which is cultivated in Yemen and in Abyssinia on account of its rich supplies of caffeine. A delicious drink, something between coffee and camomile tea, but with, I am told, a slight flavour of ostriches' dung, is made from it. Seeing that the price of coffee in Spain is at present 13s. a pound, one wonders that no enterprising chemist has thought of putting this at present useless shrub to some use. The second plant to be noted is a woody, leafless dwarf growing on the cliffs that overlook the sea and known as Ephedra. It is the plant from which the drug ephedrine is made, but it is also of considerable botanical interest. Its primitive flowering organs show that it belongs to the once-extensive but today very small family of the Gnetaceae, which form a link between the flowering plants and the gymnosperms and include that most remarkable of vegetable extravaganzas, the Welwitschia of South West Africa.

There are other interesting plants to be found along the coast, though those I will mention are neither rare nor peculiar to the province of Almeria. Thus, anyone bathing from the sand dunes in August is likely to be struck by a group of large, white, fragrant lilies with frilled petals. Their name is *Pancratium maritimum*. Even more lovely, I think, is *Urginea scilla*, which flowers in September. Its tall, tapering rod of white flowers, delicately marked with lilac stripes, rises straight without foliage from the ground, for the green strap-like leaves, which are very conspicuous in winter, have withered before the flowering stem appears. In general appearance it closely resembles that towering Himalayan plant, the Eremurus, which one sometimes sees in English gardens, except that it is shorter and more elegant. One of its conspicuous features is the enormous papery bulbs, projecting from the earth, which are known in Spanish as *cebollas albarranas* and in English pharmacy as squills. Since classical times they have provided a valuable cough medicine and cardiac stimulant, and the invention of oxymel of squill is attributed to Pythagoras. During the Roman and Arab periods the collection of squills was an important Spanish industry, especially on the island of Ibiza, but in the ignorance of the Christian Middle Ages the bulb was sought chiefly as an aphrodisiac and kept for home use.

There is not much that I need say of the other plants of this coast, except that they are most of them a little sinister. That prickly-leaved yellow tomato is the *Solanum sodomaeum*, or apple of Sodom, and will kill you if you eat it in a salad, while the tall uninviting shrub with small yellow flowers and glaucous leaves is a Peruvian Nicotiana, or tobacco, which made itself at home here in the eighteenth century. Again, it is better not to smoke it. The scarlet plumes of the castor-oil plant will be familiar to most people, and nearly every one of those coarse yellow umbelliferae has a long medicinal history, coming down from Theophrastus. I will therefore conclude these botanical notes with the aloe. The indigenous aloe, in Spanish *zádiva*, has yellow flowers and is becoming scarce, because its place has been taken by the more showy scarlet species from South Africa. But it was once an important plant. The Arabs introduced it from the East, not only for its medicinal virtues but because, through its ability to live for long periods without water, it became a symbol for patience. For this reason it was planted on graves: the dead, awaiting the day of judgement, require all the encouragement they can get. In Christian times its commercial value was so great that Ferdinand of Aragon found that he could pay for the upkeep of the Alcazaba, or castle, of Malaga by a tax on its cultivation.

Beyond Níjar and the Cabo de Gata the province of Almeria stretches away as far as the Almanzora, which is the only river in a hundred and fifty miles of coast to contain a little moisture. Sorbas on the main road is a savage-looking place, built in the angle of two gorges, and Mojácar, on a hill overlooking the sea, is a little corsair settlement where the women still wash clothes in the Moorish fashion, by treading them with their feet, and partly veil their faces. Then one comes to Vera, which was the Roman Baria, and a few miles on to Cuevas de Almanzora, which till sixty years ago was known as Cuevas de Vera. These two little towns detest one another, and it had long rankled with Cuevas that its name suggested that it was a mere cave suburb of its rival. Finally, after years of agitation, the Cortes took pity on its sufferings and passed a special act changing it to Cuevas de Almanzora.

I have sad recollections of this place because once, not so long before his death, I spent an afternoon and night here with Roger Fry. Greatly taken by the Moorish castle and the cave quarter, he sat painting them till the sun sank and the light faded, and then suddenly, as always happened to him at this hour, his interest in the visible world went out. Although he was strongly susceptible to landscape and had an almost Greek sense for the *genius loci*, he was too much of a painter to think of Nature except as a subject for pictures and, unless one wished to incur the reproach of being a romantic, one could not ask him to look at anything by moonlight. He spent the evening, therefore, playing chess at the Casino, surrounded by a crowd of gloating *aficionados*, whom the presence of a new performer roused to such enthusiasm that before long the schoolmaster, who had passed a week in Paris and spoke a little French, was begging him to stay and make his home among them. This hospitable suggestion was at once taken up by the entire company and, as a proof that it was genuine, an elderly gentleman who was sitting there, sucking the silver head of his cane, at once offered him a house. On our way back to the inn we were taken to see it: it proved to be a villa lavishly decorated with horseshoe arches and pseudo-Moorish tiles, and Roger Fry's struggles to combine truth with politeness – for he was a man who, in spite of his great urbanity, could not bring himself to say anything he did not feel – were amusing to listen to.

A few miles down the river at a place called Herrerías there lived a Belgian engineer called Louis Siret, who was a famous archaeologist. He was employed as manager of some small silver mines, and his knowledge of metallurgy had enabled him and his brother, who had died some time before, to make the most surprising discoveries upon the beginnings of the Copper and Bronze Ages. Since my wife and I were anxious to meet him and see the collections, we drove out to his house one evening in 1933.

The road led through a dismal region of red and yellow

earths, pitted and scarred by millenniums of desultory mining, and ended in a solitary grove of eucalyptus trees in which all the sparrows of the neighbourhood had collected and set up a deafening chirping. In the middle of this grove stood Siret's bungalow. After ringing the bell we were shown into a room in which every available corner was taken up by trays of flints and shards, and by stacks of books and papers heaped in what appeared to be great confusion. Soon their owner joined us and began to speak in French about his discoveries. He was a man who at first sight suggested a *Punch* cartoon of a foreign professor. Flying locks of silvery hair and untrimmed wisps of snow-white beard and moustaches stood out round his face, and taken with his bright pouncing eyes and rapid nervous speech, made up a picture of slightly crazy enthusiasm. But it soon appeared that there was nothing soft or gullible about him. His voice slid easily into an ironical tone and his eyes then had hard twinkling points to them. In the intervals of showing us over his museum and expatiating on his finds, he told us something of his life. It appeared that he had lived in this house, which he had built himself, for more than fifty years – the first twenty-five with his brother Henri and the remainder alone. Fifty years at Herrerías! That took some imagining!

Siret was an intelligent and well-educated man, whose solitary life had bred a few very active bees under his bonnet. He was devoted to Spain, which he declared to be the original land of the Sirens. Those who had once felt its charm could never, he said, accustom themselves to living anywhere else. Yet he railed against the middle-class Spaniards, whom he called ignorant and lazy, and spoke well only of the *pueblo* or common people. They had great qualities, but let no one think that he could help them by improving their lot, because their merits depended on their remaining what they were. In every attempt to raise their standard of life he saw the hand of Moscow.

His work had, of course, been outstanding. He could claim that on the small salary of a mining engineer, without financial help from anyone, he and his brother had excavated more sites than all the Spanish archaeologists of their day put together, and that in doing so they had found and fitted into its place an entirely new and unsuspected piece of the jigsaw of prehistory. Here in the remote third millennium the men of the Eastern Mediterranean had possessed a sort of Potosi, where they smelted out copper and extracted silver by a complicated process of heating together two separately obtained ore-bodies. In his opinion, most of the silver used in Minoan and Mycenaean times had been mined in this place, and this was a proof of how early the trade routes to the west had been opened up. Yet he himself had thrown a doubt upon the value of his discoveries by his insistence that all this had been the work of the Phoenicians. The learned world, which held that that people was then living on the Persian Gulf, refused to accept this view and had even for a time questioned the genuineness of his excavations. I found that this still rankled. As he took us round his museum, gaily crowning a neolithic skull with a pink lampshade or caressing an engraved ostrich egg with his fingers, his irritation broke out. Denigration of the Phoenicians, he declared, had become a mania with some people. One could call it the anti-semitism of the learned. And it was useless to argue about it. The only facts to which archaeologists paid any attention were their own envies and jealousies. '*Ce n'est pas une science, l'archéologie, c'est un combat à mort.*'

When we had finished looking at everything, Siret came out with us to the porch to see us off. Shouting so as to be heard through the fearful din made by the sparrows, 'This is what happens,' he said, waving his hand in their direction, 'when you think you are burying yourself in some peaceful, solitary spot. Every year they get worse, and every year I decide I will have them destroyed. *Mais que voulez-vous?* When one lives alone it's not so easy to turn on one's only neighbours.'

A year later we went back to Cuevas to see Louis Siret. He had promised to pay us a visit at Yegen and to make some excavations at the Piedra Fuerte and at Ugíjar, and I wanted to remind him of this. But as we drove into the main street we were stopped by a funeral procession. The splendid old man had died the day before.

The country round Cuevas is one of the richest archaeological regions in Europe, for it has been mined continuously for copper and silver from the middle of the third millennium B.C. to the present day. Where a mile or two below Siret's house the Almanzora trickles into the sea, one may still fill a basket with fragments of Samian ware and walk over the sites of the Punic, Roman, Byzantine, and Arab cities that once stood on this shore, beside which not a building nor a blade of grass are today to be seen. Or else one may visit, close to the village of Antas, the sites of neolithic El Gárcel and of Bronze Age El Argar or one of the many others – El Oficio, Gatas, Fuente Alamo, Fuente Bermejo – that lie within a radius of half a dozen miles. Yet the casual traveller should be warned that there is little to be seen above ground at any of these places, and that without a previous look at the Sirets' plans and descriptions he is not likely to get much out of them. The only excursion, therefore, that I would recommend to the non-professional is of a purely sentimental kind. Let him drive, as I once did, to El Gárcel, and stand on its bare, flat hilltop, because there in all probability took place an event that, incredible though it will seem to most people, marks the beginning of English history.

Put back the dial on the time machine to a date that is round about four thousand six hundred years ago. The Great Pyramid of Cheops has just been completed, and the people of Crete are emerging from the Neolithic Age into the first Minoan culture. On this hill there then stood a walled settlement inhabited by a short, long-headed, dark-haired people (the men were under five feet in height and the women an inch or two taller), who sowed and reaped corn, smelted down a little copper, and kept goats, sheep, dogs, and small long-horned cattle. They dressed in linen garments and baked

smooth, dark, round-bottomed pots of a type that had been
made in the Nile delta a thousand years before. But the pasture
was poor, and new immigrants kept arriving from Africa, so
that one day a small party of them set off with their esparto
sacks of seed corn and their domestic animals in search of
better-watered lands. Following the east coast, they passed into
France, then drifted northwards through the oak forests,
where a scanty population of hunters still lived in caves, till
they reached, perhaps after several generations of wandering,
the English Channel. This was narrower than it is today; and
led on perhaps by the hope of finding a virgin country that
would be safe from the arrows of the forest peoples, they
crossed it with their cattle in skin coracles. Here at last their
travels ended. They settled in small palisaded villages on the
chalk downs, to cultivate the soil, spin their linen garments,
bake their smooth-bellied pots, herd their sheep and cattle,
and now and then, after the proper ceremonies had been
observed, to eat one another. In this manner they introduced
the arts of civilized life to England. And how long, one
wonders, as they sat in their damp huts looking out on the
driving rain, did the remembrance among them persist that
their fathers had travelled here from a land of perpetual sunshine? Did they ever dream of returning again?

The sun sank as I stood among the ruined huts on the hilltop, the long shadows vanished, and a cold rosy glow flooded
the western sky. From the village below came the harsh rapid
tinkling of a church bell, and the evening, becoming suddenly
a picture by Ingres, took on the appearance of a young corpse
laid out in a mortuary. I scrambled down the slope to the dry
river-bed and made my way up it to where my car stood on the
road. In that warm milky air, in that clear marmoreal light, I
seemed to be a long way from the chalk downs and the elm
trees of England.

There is one other archaeological site in the province of
Almeria to which I should like to call attention. This is the
rock shelter known as the Cueva de los Letreros, or Cave of

the Inscriptions, which contains some of the most interesting prehistoric paintings of the schematic sort to be found in Europe. To visit it one must go to Vélez Blanco, a pueblo just off the Granada–Murcia road and where, as I have already said, there is a Renaissance castle that, in spite of the loss of its marble decorations, is still worth looking at. The cave stands high above the village, just under the summit of the mountain, and its paintings are thought to be roughly contemporary with the settlement of El Gárcel, though carried out by a different people.

The most remarkable of the pictures on this short panel of rock is the figure of a masked magician, horned like Pan, holding a sickle in either hand, and from one of whose horns dangles what appears to be a large fruit or flower. Clearly he represents a vegetation spirit analogous to those shown on Early Minoan seals, and the ceremony he is got up to perform is the plucking of a sacred bough or sheaf. Of the pictures that accompany him, some seem to repeat in a more abstract or abbreviated form the same theme, while others employ different symbols. Anyone interested in these strange hieroglyphic paintings should consult the volumes which the Abbé Breuil has dedicated to them – *L'Art rupestre schématique de la péninsule ibérique*, 4 volumes, 1933.

CHAPTER EIGHTEEN

GRANADA IN THE TWENTIES

*

GRANADA in the nineteen-twenties was a quiet, sedate, self-contained country town, little troubled, except during the month of April, by tourists, and very different from the busy, expanding place it is today. Its charm lay, of course, in its situation – the immense green plain, the snow-covered mountains, the elms and cypresses of the Alhambra hill, the streams of noisy, hurrying water. These made up something one could not expect to find anywhere else. But the city was also attractive for its own sake. Its streets and squares and vistas and public gardens might be too unobtrusive to catch the passing tourist's eye, but they had plenty in the way of character and variety to offer the resident. And then beyond them there was always the flat green countryside with its great glittering olive trees and its clear racing streams bordered with blue iris and its groves of poplar poles by the river. There was a lyrical quality about the place, an elegance of site and detail, of tint and shape, that evoked Tuscany or Umbria rather than the harsh and tawny lion-skin of Spain.

Not everyone will agree with this picture, because there is a tradition in English and French travel books, handed down from the early Romantic writers, by which Granada represents the height of the exotic and Oriental. Yet one has only to visit it to see that in spite of its latitude it is far more northern in character and climate than Naples. A glance at the guide book will confirm this by showing that it stands at a height of well over two thousand feet above the sea and that its winter rainfall, measured in inches, is greater than that of southern England. Even if that glorified gazebo, the Palace of Alhambra, calls up during a few months of the year the boredom of dancing girls and the flicker of light and heat, the first autumn rains will quickly erase that impression. Already by December the visitor finds himself surrounded by northern things – the cold touch of air under the sunshine, the chestnut roasters huddled at the street corners, the yellow leaves lying fossiled in the roadway, the morning mists rising from the plain. And then, as the new year comes in, the snow falls, icicles hang from the eaves, and the Alhambra takes on an aspect which, for all its picturesqueness, is not allowed to figure on the picture postcards.

The citizens of this poetical city are a long way from conforming to the usual idea of the Andalusian character. Unlike the Sevillanos and the Malagueños, they are a sober and conventional people, rather more puritanical than are most Spaniards, little given to laughter, who dress as much as possible in black. They are independent and high-spirited, obstinate in defence of their rights, and very hard-working. Indeed so well provided are they with what is known as 'character' that they could easily pass as Castilians but for their love of gardens and pot-plants and other sorts of aesthetic refinement, which the people of the *meseta*, living like Anatolian peasants in their mud-walled towns and villages, are pleased to despise. But this difference can be accounted for by the fact that they have in their possession one of the richest irrigated plains in Europe, where wheat and beans and potatoes and tobacco and sugar-beet and maize grow to perfection among pomegranate bushes and huge olive trees.

This plain or *vega*, as it is called, is of course the reason for Granada's existence. In Moorish times it supported more than half a million people. Then the Moors were expelled, the Christians took over, and the population began to fall. By 1800 the city, together with its thirty or so circumjacent villages, could not muster a hundred thousand. Yet the *vega*, indifferently cultivated though it was, possessed so much natural fertility that it continued to grow almost as much food as before. Since the state of the roads and the remoteness of the markets did not allow any produce other than silk to be exported, the cost of living therefore fell to an extraordinary level. Granada became known as *la tierra del ochavico*, the land of the farthing, because almost nothing in it cost more than that. To quote from the novelist, Juan Valera, a family could rent a good house with servants and horses and eat the best obtainable food for six hundred reals (five or six pounds) a month, while the most expensive hotel charged only six reals (a shilling) a day. This was the state of affairs when, in the spring of 1807, Chateaubriand paid his famous visit and put the Alhambra on the Romantics' map, and it continued without very much rise in prices till 1870, when the railway to Malaga was completed and a journey that till then had taken three days by diligence could be made in one. After that farming gradually began to pay, and during the first German war small fortunes were made out of sugar-beet and the quick-growing balsam poplar.

On my first visit from Ugíjar to Granada, I stopped at the Posada de San Rafael in that street of inns and cheap lodging-houses, the Calle de la Alhóndiga. This was the place to which the village carriers from the eastern Alpujarra always went, and had, it would seem, been going since the seventeenth century. The bedrooms, which were little windowless cells, opened off a wooden balcony that ran round the patio, and cost a peseta a day. Then my landlord Don Fadrique, who had been staying at Yegen, invited me to return and spend a week or two with him and his wife's family at their house in a village close by.

It was the August of 1920. To escape the heat of the day, we set out a little before sunset and travelled a good part of the night, he seated on his scraggy grey horse among various rolls and bundles, and I walking by his side. The moon shone, the nightingales sang almost within reach of our hands from the tamarisks and poplar trees, and a freshness rose from the river each time we forded it. We lay down for a few hours at one of the roadside ventas that then stood every three or four miles

along the principal roads and mule-tracks, and reached our
destination hot and dusty on the following evening.

The house in which Don Fadrique lived was a substantial
building standing at the end of the village street. Its front door
gave on to an interior patio, covered by a movable awning, in
which the family spent the summer evenings, and off this there
opened on one side a dim and shuttered drawing-room where
carved and gilded chairs, loosely wrapped in muslin, gazed at
their reflections in dusty mirrors, and on the other a small
dining-room with adjoining it a still smaller room, a sort of
dark cubby-hole, in which, as I later found, the family passed
the winter days, clustered round the *mesa camilla* and its
brazier. In large Spanish houses, where heating is so difficult,
the cold months produce a general contraction, a snail-like
withdrawal into the last and smallest cell, while the first breath
of summer brings an expansion. I noticed too that although
there was a slatternly servant, Doña Lucía did all the cooking
herself. The well-to-do families in Andalusia dress with care
when they go out, and often have fine houses, but they live in
an economical style. Till a century ago they did not know
the use of plates, but ate out of a common dish, like the
poorest villagers today. Naturally there is no entertaining.

I shall never forget the kindness and hospitality with which
this family received a young man who dressed like a workman
in corduroys and rope-soled shoes and spoke in execrable
Spanish. There I was, put in the best bed – a magnificent
polished brass affair – in the best bedroom – decorated in blue
and rose – and served with weak but rather medicinal tea four
or five times a day. If they could have provided me with a
London fog as well, they would have done so, to relieve me of
the homesickness which they imagined I must feel. But by
'they' I mean chiefly Doña Lucía. Her husband, as he rolled a
cigarette, turned on me his usual amused and cynical eye. No
doubt it gratified him to think that his private Englishman had
turned out to be true to the eccentric type. Her mother and
brothers, disturbed perhaps by my clothes, were on this

occasion no more than polite and friendly. It was my hostess alone who poured out for me that generous warmth and goodness of heart which later experience taught me to believe was characteristic of Andalusian women.

Unfortunately, however, I cannot count among these paragons her mother, Doña Ana. She was a coarse, fire-breathing example of the elderly matriarch. A delayed masculinity had made the hairs sprout on her upper lip and chin, and when, as often happened – in fact whenever she felt left out of the conversation – her ego mounted up and overflowed, she shouted and waved her arms, while her short, plump body throbbed all over like an engine. Her sons kept out of her way whenever she was in this state, and all the weight of her demands for attention fell on her daughter. Yet even she had interesting things to tell. Every Andalusian woman of her age could remember cavalry charging in the streets and revolutionary militiamen searching the house for arms, and her stories gave me my first contact with nineteenth-century Spanish history. Her end was fearful: some years later she threw herself out of an upper window in one of her fits of excitement, and was killed.

Doña Lucía had two brothers, one of whom lived in the house and was called Tancredo, while the other was married and lived a few doors away. Although they had both taken law at the university, it goes without saying that neither of them had ever dreamed of practising. They were Andalusian *señoritos*, and their lives were therefore fully occupied in living on the rents of their lands, which they let, sometimes on the share-cropping system and sometimes outright, to peasant farmers. In appearance and character they were different. Jaime, the married brother, was a man who had deliberately sacrificed his personality to a great ideal – that of being a perfect and finished gentleman. For the perfect gentleman, as he saw it, is a man who cannot allow himself any deviation from the norm. He must be as indistinguishable from all the other perfect gentlemen of his club as a pebble on the seashore is from the other pebbles of its beach. This meant that he was obliged to suppress whatever inclinations to self-assertion he may once have had and to pursue the narrow road of correctness in dress, conversation, opinions, manner, calligraphy, way of spending time, acquaintances, and everything else. Only in his letters (I have some that are more than twenty pages long) did he let himself go, reaching heights of sublimity and eloquence on the subject of the restoration of the monarchy – and, what is more, in a faultless and eloquent hand without a single erasure – which it would be impossible to convey here. Yet this man, in spite of the relentlessness with which he pursued his aim of self-perfection, which suggested to me sometimes the austere single-mindedness of the great Spanish ascetics and mystics, had nothing about him of the common or pretentious. He could have spared himself all that industrious polishing, for he was by nature as well as by determination a *caballero*.

The other brother, Tancredo, was a man of coarser and more ordinary type. At first sight one would have put him down as a retired officer, or even fencing master. He had a special feeling that came over him in the presence of women, which made him bow and smile a great deal and raise his thick eyebrows and twirl his waxed moustaches and let his black pupils exude a sort of moisture that made them gleam, and the women, to show that they could do it too, replied in the same manner. At the parties and dances he went to in Granada this gallant air of his gave him a sort of avuncular popularity with the girls. But he was not marriageable, because, quite apart from the question of age, he had a mistress. This was a middle-aged woman, the wife of a retired officer, who had deserted her and gone to the bad and by whom she had had a son and a daughter. Tancredo spent part of every day with them, and nowhere could you find a more respectable *ménage*. The lover fussed and fumed incessantly over the manners and upbringing of the two depressingly dull and model children, and wore their mother out with the exuberance of his paternal sentiments. She could not put him in his place, as any Spanish wife would have done, because, since they were not married, she was economically dependent on him. Yet, to do him justice, he was ready and anxious to marry her, and when the Republic came in and legalized divorce he took steps to obtain her freedom. His family, whose feelings of humanity were stronger than their obedience to the Church, supported him in this, but before the matter could be concluded the Civil War came and the divorce law was abrogated.

The *querida* or mistress plays a somewhat different role in southern Spain from what she does in other countries. For the married man she is a luxury – as expensive to keep as an American car, and much less satisfying because he cannot show her off to his friends. In provincial towns there are few men rich enough to be able to support such a burden. But for a bachelor she is a second-class wife, and so long as he goes on living in his parents' house and visiting her in the cheap flat he has rented for her, an economical one. The situation usually arises in this way. A young man puts off marrying either because he cannot afford to or because he does not want to lose his liberty. So long as he has a little money in his pocket, he will find plenty of girls of a more or less respectable sort to keep him amused. Then he grows older. The desire for a settled life comes over him, yet he does not want to renounce the privileged position he has hitherto enjoyed with women through their being financially dependent on him. Besides, he may have grown accustomed to the idea of his sex life being secret and furtive. If he is living with his mother and is emotionally fixed on her, this is especially likely to be the case. What usually then happens is that he comes across some young woman of the lower or lower middle classes, falls a little in love, and installs her in a flat in a popular quarter. If she has children by him their relation is likely to be a permanent one, and on his death-bed he may marry her. Such arrangements, be it said, often work well. The mistress will be faithful, if only because she knows that she is watched by a thousand hostile eyes and will be given away at once if she compromises herself. The lover will be kind, because he will have the whip hand and will only need to visit her when he feels the inclination. Both will consider that they have got something which a marriage to a person in their own station in life would not have given them.

Granada was such an obviously habitable city – its waters so clear, its views so beautiful, its *pâtisseries* so good – that it was only to be expected that it should contain a small but long-established British colony. They lived, not in the town among the noise-loving, crowd-delighting Spaniards, but perched above it on the southern and therefore more sheltered edge of the Alhambra hill. Here they occupied a row of modest *carmens* or villas, each provided with its strip of terraced garden and its slice of view over roofs, streets, churches, river, plain, and distant whale-shaped mountains. Standing outside one of their doorways in the evening, the cries and noises of the city rose up to one's ears like something that was moving off and no longer had any connexion, and the lights one by one came out.

The first of these *carmens* to catch the eye belonged to William Davenhill, the British Vice-Consul. Here he lived with his delightful family – a mother, three sisters, and a brother – exercising a hospitality that many passing visitors will remember with pleasure. It was a hereditary post, for his father had come here as a young man and been vice-consul before him, and it was one of the family's feats that, while they were completely and utterly English, they could mix in Andalusian society as though they were Spaniards. Their misfortune was that, after the site of their house had been chosen for its view, the vast Hotel Palace should then have been built immediately in front of it.

A hundred yards farther along the terrace stood the Pension Matamoros, with its attractive garden. It was kept by a rather fierce and gruff Scottish lady, Miss Laird – short, white-haired, always dressed in black – who in her young days had been the Davenhills' governess. And next door to this pension, in a tiny

single-storeyed house that was said to have once belonged to
that famous soldier of the Renaissance, Gonzalo de Córdoba,
the Great Captain, lived the senior member of the colony, Mrs
Wood.

This old lady – she was born in 1840 – was a remarkable person. In her youth she had been a famous beauty, and she never
ceased to dress as though she was one still. An invitation to tea
with her was therefore an event. One began by ringing a bell
in the iron gate that gave entrance to her demesne and, after it
had been opened, caught sight of a tall erect figure clad in a
white linen dress that swept the ground, a high lace collar, and
a Leghorn hat. Chains of heavy amber and silver beads hung
round her neck like amulets, and her face, which held one by
its enormous, softly-glowing eyes, was heavily painted and
rouged. On seeing her visitor she would put down the long-
spouted watering-can she was holding and, after removing her
glove, shake hands. Then, talking in a rapid voice which sometimes dropped into a Spanish that on account of her American
accent and garbled syntax was quite unintelligible, she conducted one into a very small room crowded with antiques and
bric-à-brac and smelling of potpourri and flowers. Her niece,
Miss Dillon, a handsome white-haired woman, made tea, and
there was a lavish supply of hot cakes and sweet pastries.

After the meal was over Mrs Wood, still keeping up a
breathless patter of conversation, would lead the way into the
garden. A line of cypresses ran along the edge of the escarpment, and under them, if it was in April, grew freesias, jon-
quils, stocks, and yellow wallflowers. Between these trunks
one looked out over a panorama of green plain and grey olive
trees stretching away to distant mountains. Then the path
ended at an ivy-covered wall and a gate. Opening it, one saw
in front of one another garden and another terrace, belonging
to another house known as Los Mártires. It was here, in a Car-
melite priory of which only a few blocks of masonry remained,
that St John of the Cross had written *The Dark Night of the
Soul*.

Mrs Wood was one of those heroic women who put up a determined resistance to the assaults of old age. She spent a good deal of time dressing herself and making up her face, and most of the rest in quiet employments such as reading and gardening. Conversation tired her more than other things, possibly for the reason that she felt obliged to do most of the talking herself. This was not because she had so much to say, but because listening tired her even more. With her gabble of words she kept the dangerous, dissonant, contradictory voices at a distance. Her niece told me that she had worked out a system of behaviour to meet all situations. Its key word was 'Dissimulate, always dissimulate', by which she meant that it was only by concealing one's thoughts that one could keep one's freedom and peace of mind. She was evasive about her looks too, and her large, dark, deeply-shadowed eyes moved restlessly over the ground or table, but avoided one's own.

I came across the other day a number of tense, neurotic letters from her niece, pouring out her thoughts on the subject of this society of a dozen or so people, most of them unmarried women, to whom something was always going to happen but to whom nothing ever did happen, and whose feelings on that account frequently ran disproportionately high. As in the novels of Dostoevsky, the tiniest events had a way of blowing up into prodigious dramas. Scandal always lay close to the surface. However, none of this affected Mrs Wood. Her feelings were only seriously aroused by the affairs of her own generation, which in practice meant only by Miss Laird, whom she had set up in a pension to provide meals for herself and therefore regarded as her particular creation. And Miss Laird was always mutinying. She was dour and crimson-faced and fiercely independent, and she had, or so it was rumoured, a secret addiction to gin and whisky. Long retreats in her bedroom would therefore be followed by dark and cryptic pronouncements in the dining-room or by dazed and dishevelled appearances on the stairs. It was then that Mrs Wood, trembling at what she took to be a personal threat to her authority, intervened. 'She's trying to frighten me,' she declared to her niece. 'But you may tell her from me that if she dares to get a stroke and die before I do, I shall never forgive her.'

Like all the very old, Mrs Wood was an exile in the present age. Although she rarely spoke of the past, her mind went back freely to her childhood in Mexico during the troubled times of the war with the United States, and then to the American Civil War, when her beauty had been in its prime. She remembered visiting Paris before the boulevards had been made, but what she had done since, or who Mr Wood, to whom she owed her British passport, had been, no one any longer seemed to know. She lived on to 1935 with all her faculties unimpaired, and my wife and I had tea with her on her ninety-fifth birthday. That morning she had staged a demonstration against her age by walking down alone to mass in the town and taking the tram back. But then she had always done these things. When she was near eighty she had gone off by bus and mule to that posada at Cádiar which had so horrified Lytton Strachey, hired a mount, and ridden about the country in a white hat. Seven or eight years after that, she took my house at Yegen for the summer during my absence in London, braving the long journey there and back in the heat. She had spirit, and never complained of anything, and that, I imagine, was why she lived to be so old.

Very different in every way from the British residents who had made their homes along the edge of the Alhambra hill were a married couple who in the year following the war established themselves in a new, expensive house high up on the bare spur that adjoins the cemetery. These were the Temples. He was a tall, thin, handsome man in his early fifties who, after prospecting for rubber in the Gran Chaco, had entered the Civil Service and risen rapidly to being Lieutenant-Governor of the Nigerian Protectorate. Then, after only three years in this position, he had retired, broken in health by the blackwater fever he had caught in Paraguay, and settled in Granada. His wife was Scottish – the daughter of Sir Reginald

Macleod of Macleod of Dunvegan Castle in Skye, Under-Secretary for Scotland at the beginning of the century.

Their marriage had come about in a remarkable way. Olive Macleod had been engaged to a romantic young soldier called Boyd Alexander, who lived like her in a Scottish castle, wore medieval clothes, and had a passion for ornithology. Then he took to exploration. In 1905 he led the first expedition to cross Africa from Lake Chad to the Nile, and a few years later, on a second expedition, was killed by natives in the swamps that surrounded that lake. His fiancée, who had been much in love with him, resolved to carry out a block of their native granite and lay it on his tomb. Her parents gave their consent, and she set off with a married couple who had had some experience of West Africa. The easiest route would have been through British Nigeria, but since the Governor of the Northern Provinces, who was Temple, refused to allow them to pass, on the grounds that the country was not safe for white women, they went in by a longer route through French Congo. After a difficult journey across previously unexplored country, which she has described in her book, she found the tomb and laid the stone on it. Then she returned by Nigeria, where she met the man whom she had defied – and married him.

Charles Temple was a man who would have drawn attention anywhere. His great height, his lean handsome face, and his air of authority imposed themselves. One could see him as a great feudal lord, charming his enemies at one moment and at the next – for he was capricious and impatient – ordering their heads to be struck off. But there was no place for him in modern Europe. Here his habit of stalking around like an eagle among sparrows and his too-obvious indifference to what people thought of him, created a bad impression. Besides, his long years in the wilds had really made him an eccentric. Thus in summer he would walk about the streets with two felt hats, placed one on top of the other, on his head, because he had found that they were just as good as a topee. This led to his being followed about by troops of little boys with rags or

broken pots on their heads, which caused him intense irritation. Then, when his attacks of fever required him to wear an
overcoat in the house, he put on one that was covered with
stains of paint and oil from his workshop (he was proud of
being a trained engineer who worked with his hands) and
stuck to it. He wore it over his evening dress when the
Ambassador came to dinner.

Temple had besides peculiar ideas in architecture. He did
not see why the only angles used should be right angles. They
made the building, he thought, too rigid and uncompromis-
ing, and prevented it from following the natural lie of the land.
The Mongol (later Taoist) notions by which the tent should be
pitched in a spot where it would have a harmonious relation
with the countryside so that it might not offend the *genius loci*
or attract the attention of evil spirits, seemed to him a better
approach to the subject. He also had a theory about fireplaces.
They should never, in his view, be set on the ground but
rather four feet above it on a level with the face of a seated
person. Thus when he built his house on the site of an old
French redoubt on the hill above the Alhambra, he saw to it
that many of its angles should be obtuse or acute, and that the
fireplaces, of which there was one in every room, should be in
little alcoves half-way up the wall. Here they looked pleasant
enough, but did not keep one's feet warm.

Mrs Temple was completely unlike her fascinating, capricious, restless husband. She was slow in speech, but when she
had spoken one felt that she had put the whole force of her
character, the whole range of her experience behind her words.
She had a specific gravity, a weight of being, greater than I
have met with in anyone else, and when she had once decided
that she ought to do a thing, nothing in the world could deflect
her from carrying it through to the end. But if these granite
qualities did not make her very entertaining to talk to, they did
make her admirable as a person, for she was liberal, broad-
minded, almost painfully honest, and endowed with the
strongest possible sense of responsibility. One saw this in her

married life, for she had subdued her will and personality
entirely to those of her husband, whose chronic ill-health and
impatience of temper made him a difficult person to live with.
Night after night she sat up till two or three in the morning
reading aloud to him.

Both the Temples belonged by birth and training to the
Edwardian governing class. They were unusually fine
examples of it, for they had the largeness of view and sense of
principle of the Whigs as well as the devotion to the public
interest of the higher grades of the Civil Service. Yet they
were somehow remote and bleak. In their well-ordered country houses and colonial Residencies, these people breathed a
different air from ordinary mortals, and this and their con-
sciousness of their own ability and integrity gave them an
aloofness from what seemed to them the petty and frivolous
affairs of others. One might see them as a sort of supermen,
bred exclusively to bear the white man's burden and whose
only faults were that they had so few weaknesses. In a feudal
warlike country such as northern Nigeria this would not matter, but in an ancient civilization such as that of Andalusia their
incompatibility stood out. This was immediately evident to
anyone who, fresh from the Spanish world, was present at the
sunset ceremony.

To explain what this was, I must begin by saying that the
Temples had built their house on a hill high above the city so
that it might command a view of the snow mountains. Every
evening after tea, at the hour when the sun was getting ready
to set, Mrs Temple would marshal her guests towards the
veranda, or if it was cold to the large window facing south,
and pronounce in her slow, emphatic, careful voice: 'I don't
think it will be long now.' We looked and waited. Gradually
the smooth, undulating summits, which up to that moment
had seemed remote and unterrestrial, began to turn a pale rose,
just as though the beam of a Technicolor projector had been
turned on them. 'There,' she said. 'Now.' At once a silence fell
upon all of us, and we sat without moving, watching the rose

flush deepen and then fade away. As soon as it had completely gone everyone began talking again with the sense of relief felt by people who have just come out of church, and without any allusion to what they had just witnessed.

I had become so accustomed to this little ceremony that I had ceased to think about it, until one afternoon I met at the Temples a Spanish friend of theirs, Fernando de los Ríos. He was a professor at Granada University, who in spite of his charm and culture had made himself disliked in that conservative place for his very mild socialist views. After tea we left together.

'Can you tell me,' he asked as we walked down the hill, 'what was going on when we all sat without speaking, looking at the pink spot on the mountain?'

'We were watching the sunset.'

'Yes, I know, but why was everyone so serious?'

I hesitated for a moment. No one likes to give away his country by revealing its secrets. However, there seemed no alternative, so I explained that this was a mystical rite confined to the higher levels of the British Raj.

'Here it's the sunset on the snow,' I said. 'But in other places it may take the form of watching through field-glasses some rare bird, a siskin, for example, or a peregrine falcon, alighting on its nest. Our viceroys and Foreign Ministers draw strength in difficult moments from such things.'

'I don't understand,' he said.

'No,' I answered, 'it's not really explicable. We must wait for someone to write a book upon it. Till then I can only say that some people have compared it to Zen Buddhism.'

Don Fernando did not answer. He was a simple, gentle man who had not seen enough of the English to take in their absurd side. All he felt was that the political scene in his country would be the better for having people like the Temples in positions of influence. What he did not realize was that their efficacy lay entirely in their dealings with colonial peoples.

CHAPTER NINETEEN

COURTSHIP AND MARRIAGE

*

GRANADA, with its cypresses and its poplar trees, its running water and its airy situation, seems designed like Florence to be a city where the arts of poetry and painting and music take root and flourish. Yet in fact this has never, except for a short spell before the Civil War, been the case. Till 1571 it was a Moorish town, not altogether unlike Tetuan today, and after that it was eclipsed by Seville, to which the trade with the Indies had drawn all the life and wealth in the country outside Madrid. The Golden Age of Spanish culture therefore passed without its being able to claim any painter or sculptor of importance, except Alonso Cano, or any writers other than the aristocrat Diego Hurtado de Mendoza and the preacher Luis de Granada. Later the nineteenth century gave it a political thinker in Angel Ganivet, but one cannot speak of great figures, or of a society mature enough to nourish a vigorous art, before the 1920s. Then two names stand out, the composer Manuel de Falla and the poet Federico García Lorca.

Falla had come down from the north during the European war and settled in a house next to the church of the Alhambra. He was then in his early forties, and the production of *The Three Cornered Hat* in London in 1919 had laid the first steps of his international reputation. He was deeply interested in Andalusian folksong and music, and the Fiesta de Cante Hondo, which he organized in 1922 in the Palace of Charles V, helped to put this style of singing on the map by teaching people to distinguish between *cante andaluz* or *jondo* and the debased and vulgarized version of it known as *flamenco*. García Lorca had also shown an interest in this festival. He was at this time a young man of twenty-three, who spent the summers in his parents' house just outside the city and the winters at the famous Students' Residency at Madrid. He was very musical and, folk-lore being in the air, he fully shared his friend Falla's enthusiasm for the popular singing and guitar-playing of his province.

I should like to be able to describe this ambience of music, *cante jondo*, bullfights, walks about the Albaicín or the Alhambra by moonlight, and literary conversations, out of which García Lorca's plays and poems have sprung, but unfortunately I cannot do so at first hand. I never met Falla, and my two meetings with Lorca were so slight that only a vague impression of them has remained. Yet when many years later I read his *Romances Gitanos*, I felt how strongly saturated these poems were with the Granada of those days, which has changed so greatly in mood and feeling since the Civil War.

The twenties were a period of economic prosperity following on a decade or two of civic improvement and renovation. The electric tram was in its first glory, sailing like a swan along the streets with far less creaking and shrieking than it makes today, and throwing out thin tentacles across fields and olive groves to the neighbouring villages. Of the same age was the electric light, which of all the inventions of the nineteenth century was perhaps the only one to be really welcomed by the Spaniards, because it enabled them to do something they had always longed to do – turn night into day. However, there were still no motor-cars. Then the dictatorship of General Primo de Rivera dropped out of the sky, the roads which previous governments had built were surfaced, and the motor made its appearance.

Yet though Granada had all the outward aspect of an up-to-date city (its new principal street, cutting through an old quarter, was of a genuinely modern ugliness), it continued to belong spiritually and by force of inertia to the past. Children still played their round games in the squares, water-sellers hawked their water from the Fuente del Avellano, the goats climbed the staircases to be milked, the *pastelerías* had not yet learned to make French pastries, the ice-cream makers continued to fetch their snow on mule-back from the summits of the sierra just as they had been doing since Arab times. From morning to night the Plaza Bibarrambla, which is today so dead, was filled with peasants dressed in black corduroy suits and black and purple stuff dresses and head handkerchiefs. This was the sober, all-the-year-round costume of the country people, which contrasted with the melodramatic cloaks faced with scarlet silk which the men of the middle classes wore during the months of winter. And who were those young men one saw as soon as darkness fell, pressed like moths against the bars of the ground-floor windows? They were the *novios* discoursing on love and marriage to their *novias* within.

One of the things that had least changed in Granada was the manner of courting. It went back to the eighteenth century and was a more interesting thing than its picturesque aspects suggest, just as the bullfight is more than the costumes of the toreros and the ceremonial parade. To understand how it worked, one must start off from the idea that the sexes were rigidly separated. A girl could not be seen out of doors with a young man, even if she was properly chaperoned, without creating a scandal, while she could scarcely expect to meet and talk to one in a private house, unless he was the brother of a school friend, because except on very rare occasions, there were no dances, no parties, and no entertaining. She was, however, allowed to exchange passing words or glances with one in the street during the afternoon promenade and, on taking a *novio*, to spend every evening up to midnight talking with him at the *reja* or iron grille of her window.

The words *novio* and *novia* mean, of course, boy friend and girl friend. A girl could change her *novio* several times, though she might lose some reputation by doing so, because a *noviazgo*, as the relation between the two is called, only became an engagement when the parents formally gave their consent and the date of the wedding was fixed not too far ahead. When this happened the *novio* was invited into the house, made friends with the girl's brothers, and was treated (except perhaps by the father, who might not soften till the wedding day) as a full member of the family, whereas until this time he had been a potential enemy to be kept beyond the bars of the street window. A girl's male relations, as they came into and out of the house, were expected to pretend not to notice him.

This system of courtship had its advantages. To begin with, no introductions were necessary. A young man could make the acquaintance of any girl he caught sight of in the street simply by staring at her as he passed, following her to her house, and walking up and down in front of it: then, if she was free and liked the look of him, she would make him a sign and appear that evening at the *reja* of her window. If his conversation pleased her, he could become her *novio*, and after that he would be the only man outside her own family whom she could dance with or even, if she took a strict view of her obligations, look at. *Novios* also had their duties. They must arrive every evening just as it was getting dusk at their girls' windows and remain there, with a short interval for dinner, till midnight or later. This was known as *pelando la pava*, 'plucking the turkey'. It was not for nothing that among the working classes the act of asking a girl to become one's *novia* was known as *pedir la conversación*, requesting conversation, since the whole life of two *novios* lay in talking endlessly together.

Under these circumstances the girl who could dispose of a window on the ground floor was obviously in a fortunate position. If she lived on one of the upper storeys, she tried to arrange for the use of that of the family downstairs or of some neighbour or relative in whom her family had confidence. Failing that, her *novio* had to stand in the street and shout up two or even three storeys. Till laxer customs came in, in the thirties, and young people were allowed to go to the cinema together, high blocks of flats could not be built, because no one would have rented them. A girl living on one of their upper floors could never have got married.

Andalusia is often regarded as a land of romantic attitudes, but it is also, like Ireland, a land of absurdities. Thus the classic picture of the girl seated at her barred and embrasured window, with the gallant standing cloaked and stiff-hatted outside, can be paralleled by a very different spectacle. In the street doors of most old houses in Spanish cities there is or used to be a small hole cut close to the ground for the use of cats. (Convents are especially given to them, and at the Encarnación at Ávila, where St Teresa spent so large a part of her life, there was one which opened into the door of her three-roomed flat-let or cell.) These *gateras*, as they are called, were in some districts used by *novios* in the place of windows. The man lay or crouched on the pavement or cobbles, and the girl took up a similar position inside, but – this was the point of the arrangement – invisible to passers-by, and thus protected from glances which might have hurt her modesty. I have seen this method of courtship in use in the Albaicín of Granada, but its real home was in certain large pueblos of the provinces of Cadiz and Seville, where old-fashioned habits lingered late. Here on any night of the year one could see in one of those long, empty streets of the country towns, dazzlingly white by moonlight, a row of cloaked and prostrate figures discoursing in whispers to their *novias* within.

I can speak of the rite of courting at *rejas* from my own experience. Once in the late twenties I was staying at a small pension at Almeria, and feeling, as I often did in that beautiful city, a little bored, I decided to go for a walk. Returning through dusty lanes an hour or two later, at that disturbing hour when the sky above turns crimson and the whole street seems to be melting and dissolving in the dusk, I became aware of a pair of dark eyes looking at me through the bars of a window. I made a circle and walked past again. The eyes were still there, a pale Byzantine nose and mouth appeared beneath them, a smile drifted over them, and after another turn or two

I found myself fixed to the spot and even holding on to the *reja*. The girl was called Carmen, and before I knew what had happened I was her *novio*.

My hours of duty were from seven to nine-thirty and from ten to twelve. I gulped down my dinner and had to cut out my usual coffee. There she would be, framed against the darkness of the room behind her but with the lights of the street catching her face, and a sweet but rather formal smile stamped on it. And then I would take up once again the task of making conversation through the bars of a window with a girl to whom I had absolutely nothing to say.

As a person Carmen did not make a clear impression on me, because her feelings were always masked by the role she was playing. In much of what she said she seemed to be carrying out a ritual. I never, for example, arrived at her window without her exclaiming, 'How late you are!' or left without her asking, 'Why are you in such a hurry to leave?' These phrases and many others seemed to be part of the formal language of *novio*-ship: we were playing at being lovers just as people when they paid an official call played at conversation. And finally when, at the stroke of twelve, half-dropping with fatigue, I tore myself away, she would smile and say in what was, I suppose, meant to be a roguish tone: 'Now, mind you don't go off to one of those naughty places.' It seemed as though the convention required that I should have been so worked up by these hours of *tête-à-tête* at the *reja* that I should be unable to resist that sort of vicarious satisfaction.

Carmen's parents kept a grocer's shop which specialized in hams, garlic sausages, and dried cod. When one passed the door, which was in a street parallel to that in which I had my station, one could see them hanging in grey, rather uninviting rows from the ceiling. In her family there was an uncle who had once been a bullfighter, and several brothers who were *aficionados*, and she made a point of representing them as fierce and touchy people, full to the brim of pride and *pundonor*. Had they, she declared, the least idea that an unknown man was talking to their sister at her window, why then – 'What?' 'Oh, I can't imagine what they would do.' It seemed that I was meant to get a picture of seven brothers ready to defend some very strict notion of her honour, although in fact I knew enough of Spanish things to feel sure that her family were well aware of my courtship and were probably at that moment considering – though of course in the most gentlemanly way – how many thousands of reals or duros I might be worth as a son-in-law. But to Carmen, with her old-fashioned ideas (she had learned to play the guitar instead of the piano and could sing in *cante jondo*), the convention of the gallant in the role of a burglar, which gave such a zest to courting, had to be kept up as long as possible.

My *noviazgo* came to an end in an abrupt and painful manner. I had been courting Carmen patiently and with circumspection for a couple of weeks, and had got to the point where I was allowed to hold one of her fingers in my hand, when the crude Anglo-Saxon idea came to me that it was time to take another step forward and give her a kiss through the bars of the cage. But when I attempted to do this there was an immediate reaction. Drawing back several feet into the room she declared, though with a smile to soften the harshness of her refusal, that no man's lips had ever touched hers, nor would they be allowed to do so until her husband bestowed his on her upon their bridal night. Then, seeing that these words had a chilling effect upon me, she made an offer. She would meet me on the following afternoon at a certain place in the public gardens accompanied by her younger sister, and we would walk up and down a little. Only I must understand that this was an extraordinary concession which she would never have agreed to if I had not been a foreigner, accustomed to greater freedom than Spaniards in these matters.

The hour came and I approached the rendezvous. And there, at the end of the alley, I saw two girls dressed in black shiny silk, standing with their hands folded in front of them under a white-flowered trumpet tree. One of them was young, a mere child, while the other, who might have been twenty-four, was short and squat, almost a dwarf. She had the face of Carmen – it was a handsome and distinguished face and by no means a stupid one – but oh, that body! In an access of panic I turned and fled, unable to face the ordeal of meeting her and pretending that nothing had happened, when in fact her short-ness had made my tallness seem a deformity.

After this the situation was naturally beyond explanation. That night I had several drinks before I could summon up the courage to confront her at her window. As I came up to it I could see her strongly boned white face and dark, heavily arched eyes looking out through the bars. She had not changed out of her unbecoming black dress, but her lips were more thickly made up than ever and she had put a red lily in place of a carnation in her hair. There was a stronger smell than usual of jasmine water, and she seemed, I could not exactly see how, to have grown tall and slim again. Hurriedly I gave her the box of chocolates I had bought and, without mentioning my failure in the afternoon, told her that I had had a telegram saying that my mother was ill and that I was leaving next morning for England. She offered her con-dolences – pretending was what she was good at – and I promised to write. Gently, and as if believing me, she smiled. But that facial cast, severe and melancholy as of a lady-in-wait-ing at the court of the Paleologues, did not exist for nothing, and I knew that she was proud and incredulous underneath. Then I said good-bye. As I bent to kiss her hand a door opened behind, letting in some light, and I saw that she was standing on a low wooden platform. No, I had not been mistaken.

This story of my brief *noviazgo* is naturally little more than a caricature of a Spaniard's relations with his girl. But one thing about it may be observed. Since in those days there was no future for Spanish women who did not get married, and since by the time they had reached the age of twenty-five it was generally too late, they often became quite desperate to find a husband. What was the best way? Beauty, charm, position,

money, all counted, but with some men a reputation for reserve and modesty counted more. A girl who was suspected
of having been a little free with her *novio* – for example, of having given him a kiss – might find it difficult to acquire another
one if she lost him. Then among the small shopkeepers and
peasant farmers there were men who demanded a standard of
intangibility in their future wives that was almost Oriental. In
their view a girl who was known to have danced with a man
or to have had a *novio* on even the most distant terms had put
herself out of the running. These ideas were especially current
at Granada, and to cater for them a class of severe and recluse-
like girls arose who boasted that they never looked out of the
window or lingered on the balcony, and even that they did not
take part in the afternoon *paseos* or promenades. The only day
in the year on which one could be sure of seeing them was the
feast of Corpus Christi, when they all came out and walked
about in their new dresses. And they were not necessarily
plain. One of them, who was pointed out to me on that day
and who had the reputation of being unapproachable by men,
was one of the most beautiful girls I have ever seen. She was
the daughter of a well-to-do farmer, never went out except to
early mass, and had five brothers to guard her.

Cases of this sort, however, were exceptional. Most girls
were intensely and actively concerned in the capture of a
husband. This was where the balcony came in. Till a *novio*
turned up and had been brought to the bars of the *reja*, a balcony on the first floor of a rather old-fashioned house offered
a girl her best chance of finding one. Here, raised just sufficiently above the street, framed by pot-plants and green win-
dow-blinds, holding a piece of sewing in her hand, she looked
more easy and natural than she thought it safe to look down
below. The young man who stared up at her as he passed felt
that he had caught a glimpse of her as she was in the intimacy of
her family, as she could some day, if only he chose to speak the
word, be in his. For the girl, on the other hand, the balcony
was a breathing hole, a looking-out point on the world, from

which she could see and be seen by everyone who passed, without the risk of being compromised. This made it a poetical place, as the fireplace or hearth is in the north, a focus round which desires collected, because it was a frontier of the house, which is women's territory, overlooking the street, which belongs to the men. Also, though no one any longer remembered this, it represented a victory that the women had won when in the eighteenth century they had torn down the *celosías* or latticework that covered the windows of their living apartments, as it still covers those of convents, and established themselves, chairs and all, in the air above the street. The liberty of the *tête-à-tête* at the *reja* followed later.

If we ask how such a pattern of sex relations can have come into existence, we shall find that, though no doubt there has been some Moslem influence, in the main it was a development of the classic pattern of the Mediterranean peoples. It was based on the very ancient assumption that the two sexes are possessed of entirely different magical powers and aptitudes, and that for that reason their roles in society must be kept distinct from one another. To make sure that this happened, there were certain severe taboos which prevented men from doing women's work and women from doing men's, even at the cost of great inconvenience. Anyone who broke one of these taboos would suffer a loss of self-esteem, because from childhood men were taught to put their pride in being as manly as possible, and women to put theirs in being womanly, and to feel that any dabbling in the affairs of the opposite sex would lead to a sort of contamination. That is to say, each sex had not only its own sphere of life, which might never be departed from under any circumstances, but its own ethical standards.

The next step came when these two halves of society, which had such different habits and rules of conduct, had to be brought into relation with one another. There was no sexual *apartheid* as in Arab countries, because the young men and women, though separated by physical barriers, were given ample opportunities for seeing and speaking to one another in

privacy. Indeed, the bars of the *reja* were so far from being a
real obstacle that it might be said that they actually increased
the strength of the forces that played across them, in much the
same way as a barrage increases the strength of the current in
a river. Love was generated, as it always is by difficulties,
while the fact that the two *novios* could never be together on
the same side of the fence allowed them an ease and naturalness in conversation that was unknown to our Victorian
ancestors. Such was the system that in the years that I am
speaking of gave Andalusian life its distinctness and clarity
and, in the Greek sense of the word, beauty. How different to
the state towards which we seemed to be moving in England,
in which, in the name of justice and equality, men and women
were to be as like one another as possible!

We may thus say that what distinguished the pattern of
sexual relations in southern Spain from that of northern
Europe was that it raised a strict physical barrier between the
young men and the girls, but at the same time made it easy for
them to see one another both in public and in private. The
streets took the place of the ballrooms of other countries, the
girls appearing in them combed and scented, with their hair
freshly set, their high heels giving them a slow, deliberate gait,
and their heads and torsos held back, as though they did not
know what their legs were doing. Much of their parents' sav-
ings had gone to produce this result, because the man must
be dazzled, allured, fascinated, if he was to be got to the point
of declaring himself and so renouncing the advantages that lay
in continuing a bachelor. But, if we consider the already
married, we shall find that the situation was entirely different.
Here men and women did not, could not, must not meet. The
jealousy of husbands lay like a cloud in the air. The respectability of wives saw in even the most unlikely males a risk to
their chastity. With one accord the neighbours put the worst
interpretation on the most innocent things. For Eros was
powerful, Eros was strong, and had besides an absolutely
limitless appetite, and no sense whatever of discrimination. All

K

men and women were capable – this at least was the theory – of rushing into one another's arms at a moment's notice, so that whenever any two were present alone together great risks and dangers would be run.

Yet that did not at all mean, as such writers as D. H. Lawrence have supposed, that the sexual life of these peoples – using the word here in its narrower sense – was stronger or more free from guilt than that of the Anglo-Saxons. If anything, the contrary was the case. Young Spaniards approach love in a romantic and puritanical spirit which allows very little scope to sensuality. Even after marriage the women often remain cold, having been brought up through the influence of Catholicism to regard the sexual act as something unseemly which they must submit to patiently for the sake of keeping their husbands attached to them and of having children. And then these arrive. Almost at once the wife begins to dress in dark clothes like an older person, leaves the house less and less, and turns, to her husband's deep satisfaction, into a mother-figure. This is what he has always wanted, this is what he has married for. The happy home of his childhood has been created again, and he is at the same time his own father and the eldest of his children, bound by a law that does not admit of divorce to a mother-wife. The curse has been lifted off sex, and under the grand matriarchal system of the country his children grow up to carry on the same tradition. He himself, without much feeling of disloyalty to his wife, can look about for real sexual adventure and satisfaction outside his home.

If, however, one wishes to consider the attitude of Spanish women to physical love from some other angle, one can look outside marriage. As one would expect, there are always a good many surreptitious affairs going on in the cities. These take place between men of a certain class and women who as a rule, though by no means invariably, come from a lower one. Excluding Madrid, where there is all the variety of a metropolis, one may say that in nearly every one of these cases the women, however respectable they are in other ways, give themselves for money. As a Spanish friend of mine put it, a Don Juan always has a few hundred peseta notes in his pocket. Now a woman who gives herself to a man who is not her husband is sacrificing an asset that, whatever may be thought of it today in England, is still highly regarded in Spain – her honour. Even though she may privately attach no importance to it herself or treat it as a matter that concerns only her reputation, she will expect to get something back in return for giving it, and not only her purse but her sense of her own value will suffer if she does not. The suggestion a modern Englishwoman might make that she was being paid in fun and pleasure would seem to her utterly inadmissible, because it contradicts the Spanish belief that on these occasions it is always the woman who gives more than the man. Even the Civil Code sanctions this view, by making the adultery of the wife a justification for divorce, but not the adultery of the husband unless it is public and scandalous. But what if the woman is in love? Then, of course, she will refuse all material recompense, and the only thing that needs to be said about such cases is that in the provincial towns and cities they are rare. Here the opportunities for getting to know married persons of the opposite sex are so few that real love affairs are scarcely possible, except between members of the same family. And there is no idealization of such situations. I am not sure that, in the lower middle classes at least, most married women would not regard it as more respectable to give themselves for money than for love, especially if that money was to be spent on buying better clothes and so raising their social status. The moment one leaves the really indigent levels, the standard of appearance is what counts and not, as in England today, the standard of living.

One must bear in mind in any study of sexual relations in the south of Spain the influence of the Church. It is itself a sort of mother-figure. It envelops all, except the working classes, who have broken loose, yet often it seems to be the private society of the middle-class women, providing them with a magic which enables them to hold their own in their passive struggle with their men. For everyone who knows Spain will be aware of the frequency of the marriage in which the wife is deeply pious and the husband is irreligious. This is indeed a fairly normal situation. The man's sense of *honra* or self-esteem conflicts sharply with the teachings of the Church, especially in the sexual field, while he is irritated by its many small, fussy rules and regulations which treat him, he feels, as if he were a child. Except in Ireland, where drink and violence take the place of sex and sexual pride, Catholicism produces anticlericalism by an almost chemical reaction. Yet in ordinary times one need not attach too much importance to this division in families, because at bottom the husband nearly always approves of his wife's devoutness, is aware that he is only playing truant and that, after a life spent in attacking or shrugging his shoulders at the Church, he will return to it in time to receive its last sacraments.

This playing truant is such a characteristic of the Spanish male that one may, without too much exaggeration, explain many of his activities by it. It accounts for the persistent Don Juanism of all those middle-aged or elderly men who can afford to pay cash for their conquests. It accounts for his absurd, usually revolutionary politics, which end either in fiascos or disasters. It accounts for his lack of a sense of social responsibility. He is a spoiled child – all boys are spoiled in Spain – who sees life as an adventure story in which he, of course, plays the leading role. On the other hand the strong framework of Spanish cultural life, which holds this otherwise anarchic society together, is the work of the women. After the revolution is over, their unchanging conservatism will bring the country back to its centuries-old mode of living and make the men's speeches and manifestations seem little more than a froth on the surface.

It is just here that the influence of the Church has come in. As its hold on the men weakened, it began to pay more attention to the women. The bishops thundered against immorality, by which they meant short sleeves and low dresses, modern bathing-suits, and sometimes even ballroom dancing. Through their Church sewing-parties and social gatherings the women took this up, and their naturally strong reserve and modesty were strengthened. 'Do you know why,' a Spaniard once said to me, 'so many Castilians in the Middle Ages married Jewesses? It was because they were sensual. Our women never give themselves, either to their husbands or to anyone else.' Yet there can be no doubt that in spite of or even because of this deep reserve and pride in the wives, a great many marriages in Spain are happy. This, a Spaniard will say, is because they are not built on *amor*, that is passion, but on *cariño*, which is a strong and tender affection. That is to say, on the *amicitia* recommended by St Thomas Aquinas. If later on the husband, in search of a little excitement, takes to adventures, his wife, should she suspect it, will usually console herself with the thought that that is how men are made and that, though it is very disagreeable, one must put up with it. Unless her marriage has been a failure from the first, she will have no temptation to imitate him.

The Spaniards, then, have not been affected by the formal *galanterie* of the French or by the casual looseness of the English. In the eighteenth century the Italian system of the authorized lover or *cicisbeo* was taken up for a short time in court circles, but did not survive the Peninsular War. All their feeling and thinking about love has been focused on the courtship of two young people who, if all goes well, will bring their romance to a happy conclusion by getting married. Long ago this courtship became fixed in ritual forms such as the lover's watch below his *novia*'s balcony, the midnight serenade, and, most important of all, the nightly conversation at the *reja*. With the help of a fine climate these things gave a sharpness and an edge to life because they provided love-making, which is essentially a private thing, with an element of drama and display. Then in the thirties, or a little before, the atmosphere began to change. New ideas about the independence of women seeped in from abroad, and with the proclamation of the Republic the political tension began to rise. The Civil War came, and by the time it was over nothing was left of the rite of courtship through windows. And it has not been revived. The *novio* of today takes his *novia* openly and unchaperoned to the cinema or to a chic bar or café. Yet underneath it would seem that very little has changed. The iron chastity of Spanish girls has been strengthened by the religious revival, so that while the two young people sit in the darkened cinema or walk home by secluded alleys the ghost of the window bars falls between them. And it may be noted that it is precisely the girls of the upper middle classes, those who are most likely to be under the influence of the Church, who are allowed most liberty. In working-class families they will have less, because there the parents will expect their daughters' suitors to seize any opportunity that presents itself to seduce them. If they do not, these young men will run the risk of appearing soft, for in this formal Spanish world where everything is organized so as to produce and maintain tension, the man has the obligation to press forward and the girl that of resisting him. If she fails to do this, she is ruined, for then her *novio* will despise her for not preserving her chastity, and refuse to marry her.

I had finished writing these pages on Andalusian customs in courting and taking mistresses, when a Spanish friend with whom I was discussing them put forward an ingenious idea on a subject that, I admit, had not occurred to me before – the connexion between love and politics. With the help of a glass or two of wine this idea grew between us till it had acquired a certain consistency and verisimilitude. I will give it, more or less in his words, for what it is worth.

Politics, according to my friend, is the primary and funda-mental passion of all Spaniards, the frame into which they pour their unconscious aggressive energies. Love is quite unable to compete with it, and in fact has never done so in any age of Spanish history. Thus one may say that the real Don Juan was a man who went about breaking voting urns and that that famous Renaissance novel, *La Celestina*, is an allegory showing how a notorious boss or *cacique* encouraged the beginnings of a starry-eyed left-wing party but was destroyed together with it when the gunmen were refused the wages they had asked for. It is for this reason that the ages for love in Spain have always been the ages of political stagnation or repression. Every dictatorship is born under the sign of Venus, and those winged patent-leather hats of the Civil Guard that shine so brightly in the sun are, as any sixteenth-century poet would have seen, *las alas de Cupido*.

How does this happen? One morning the *pronunciamiento* is made and at once the era of parliamentary debates and of nicely worded insults and of bombs going off and of churches being burned comes to an end in a depressing silence. The newspapers become too boring to read. The speeches of the sole victorious Party are even more insufferable. Except on the days of bullfights – and since Manolete's death even they have been bad – life seems too tedious to be endured. And then one fine spring afternoon, just as the first ice-cream kiosks are coming out in the parks, the men wake up to the fact that there is another sex in the world known as *las mujeres* or, to use our less demonstrative English word, 'women'. What a delightful discovery! How is it that we have never noticed them in all these years? Surely they are the most beautiful and the best natured and the liveliest and the most seductive in the whole world! And they are not, oh no, like the hares or partridges of the sierras, to be walked after and stalked for hours on end: on the contrary, they are all round one, everywhere, with their high-heeled shoes and their eyes like acetylene bicycle lamps, and their hair like the aurora borealis. Each evening *paseo* is a mannequin parade, where one goes to admire and choose, not the dress, but the girl inside it.

Let us therefore do something that few liberal-minded people have ever done before, and praise dictatorships. To large sections of society they are periods of compulsory happiness when *homo hispanicus* is forced to turn away from the pursuit of power and the aggrandizement of his self-esteem, to which his nature spontaneously inclines, to the cultivation of pleasure, which he rates low. Love and staring and keeping one's shoes polished become the order of the day, so that for many people Utopia would have already arrived if it were not that to provide for these things more money has become necessary. The standard of living has risen with the close season on politics, but the standard of wanting has soared, so that no rise of salaries and wages can keep pace with it. In the general discontent the dictatorship falls and the democratic orchestra strikes up again, every instrument magnificently out of tune, while the streets are littered with discarded *novias* and mistresses.

'Such,' said my friend, making a sign to the waiter, 'is Spanish history. Say what you like about it, but anyhow it has the rhythm of life. Do you really think that can be said of your system?'

CHAPTER TWENTY

LAST YEARS AT YEGEN

*

IN the spring of 1929 I returned to Yegen after a five years' absence. I had looked forward to seeing it again, yet I remember that as I drove up from the coast my first impressions were disappointing. Through visiting picture galleries I had acquired more of the painter's and less of the poet's or airman's eye, and thus the vast scale of the Sierra Nevada and its flat, sagging outlines struck me as monotonous and devitalizing. I wondered why I had chosen the only undramatic mountains in Andalusia to make my home in. However, as I drew in sight of the village this feeling vanished. The grey jumble of boxes seen in the slanting light, the familiar faces, my house with its peasant furniture, the shelves of books, my chair, and the round table with a meal set out on it filled me with surprise and elation. Was all this mine? Had I really this pure and calm existence to fall back on, after the squalor and racket of London? I saw stretching in front of me the long uneventful months, interrupted only by the occasional visits of friends, in the serene and timeless atmosphere of this village.

For serenity was the word. I had not been there a day before the old impression of height and stillness, of fields of air stretching before me, and channels of water running behind came over me again, and I saw that Yegen had a quality that was unlike anything else. The moment for seizing it in its greatest intensity was on the nights of full moon. Standing then on the flat roof, one saw the earth falling away sheer on every side, as though one stood on the prow of a ship that was sailing off across a petrified ocean. Or else the ship was a plane which was gliding out over the chaos of dark and grey, till, brushing perhaps that thin wisp of cloud, it would tilt up its

wings towards the stratosphere. And then, what silence! A
silence so deep, so widespread that it needed to measure it the
sound of water falling or the occasional inviting strumming
of a guitar. Apart from this, no sign of human life, except for
the lights of the distant villages – Jorairátar, Alcolea, Paterna,
Mairena – lying like constellations in the vague immensity.

By day the aspect was, of course, very different. One saw
then a tilted mountain slope ascending and descending in
terraces, upon which the wheat grew as high as the armpits,
while the olive trees drooped their branches till they almost
touched the ears. Fig trees, mulberries, pomegranates, and
apricots were planted along the edges, there were vines on
trellises and clumps of poplars, and everywhere one went one
heard the sound of water running and passed the channels in
which it flowed, swift between its banks and clear. But this
slope faced emptiness. Through the branches of the olive trees
one looked out on a welter of blues and reds and lavenders
that changed as the sun rose to a dazzling bath of yellow and
pale brick ochres. This was the backdrop, above which the
distant mountains floated as thin and as unreal as strips of
painted cardboard.

Washed by the ocean of air, cut off by the precipices and the
height, the village hugged its life to itself. Even its noises
were muffled. No dogs barked, no children screamed: no
harsh metallic conversations could be heard, or loud raucous
croakings such as grate on the ear of foreigners in Spanish
cities. The speaking tone was soft and, if anyone shouted, if a
cock crowed or a donkey brayed or a hawker cried his wares,
the sound was at once sucked up into the silence. This gave the
place an air of peace. Rough, simple, primitive, rich only in
crops and fruit trees, but distilling in its customs many centuries of history, Yegen seemed to be full of echoes of the
Golden Age.

Yet even in ideal places things must continually, if their
character of life is to be kept up, go a little wrong. Thus it
happened that scarcely had I been here a couple of days than

I found that the situation in my household was no longer what it had been. My servant and housekeeper Maria Andorra had had the sole run of it during my absence, and she had greatly changed. Some time after my departure her sister Pura had died, apparently of under-nourishment brought on by a neu- rotic inhibition about eating, and leaving no direct heirs, because her son, who was a consumptive, had already pre- deceased her. On her deathbed she had made a gift of her pro- perty, which was worth at most a hundred pounds, to Maria, in order to elude payment of the tax on the registration of wills, but had forgotten to include the goats and the cow. This omission had led to a lawsuit with the Justicia or municipal authorities, which she had just lost. The sum involved was no more than thirty pesetas, but urged on by Cecilio, that glitter- ing-eyed, hawk-beaked evil genius of those who in our village considered going to law, she determined to appeal. Ever since she had come into her sister's strips of land her head had been turned and she had lost all sense of reality.

One effect of this change in Maria's circumstances was that I no longer had my house entirely and in peace to myself. I had to submit to my kitchen being taken up every evening by Cecilio and his friends, discussing lawsuits and the best means of paying out the Justicia, to seeing the stables on the ground floor occupied by cows and goats, hens in the patio, a braying donkey under my sitting-room, and every room infested by the tribes of fleas they brought with them. Through all this Maria paced to and fro in her dingy black bodice and skirt, her features worn and haggard, her complexion yellow, her eyes now sad and dull, now lighting up in a sort of cunning frenzy, her entire nature given over to her obsession. At moments she was so far above herself that with a sweep of the hand she would claim that the whole house was hers, and that I should pay to her the rent, because Don Fadrique had willed it to her on his deathbed.

Those who have lived for long in villages in the south of Europe will have noticed how many of the petty dramas of peasant life recall those of classical Greek tragedy. The Fates, the Furies, catastrophic lusts and hatreds, examples of hubris and of demonic possession all find their place, though in sordid dress and on a greatly diminished scale, in these communities, because the passionate disposition of southern people, finding no satisfactory outlets in the poverty and narrowness of their lives, allows their desires and resentments to accumulate till they become obsessions. One example of this was the case of my servant María. But if I am to tell her story I must begin by going back some six or seven years, to the time of my previous residence at Yegen.

Of the various people who then took the trouble to pay me formal visits, the most persistent was a tall, good-looking man in his late twenties whose name was Paco Cobo. He was a peasant farmer, who with his father's help worked the small plot of family land, but in the evenings put on a fairly clean suit and a very clean shirt and became the gentleman. In those days there was a political group or party in Spain known as the Young Mauristas, who had anticipated some of the attitudes of fascism, and Paco, on the strength of an occasional glance at a Granada paper, regarded himself as one of them. Striking his marble-headed cane on the floor, he would say: 'The stick! Give them the stick! What the Spanish workman needs is a good thrashing!' And he would describe with gusto how General Martínez Anido was dealing with the strikers in Barcelona. Since I took little interest in these matters, I found this stupid and conceited young man who never laughed or smiled a great bore and, as he seemed to find me the same, wondered why he paid me so many visits.

A year or so later I discovered. I had been on a short trip to England, and when I got back I found that in my absence Maria had given birth, in squalor and secrecy, to a seven-month child. Whose was it? Don Fadrique's, she said, and at first I believed her, because I had seen him tiptoeing into her room late at night. But scarcely was this out than the news came from Granada that Don Fadrique was very ill with typhoid. He was not expected to recover, then he was dead, and on his deathbed he had sworn upon the crucifix that this child was not his. Since there are no secrets in Spain, though a great deal of reserve and discretion, the word began to be passed round that it was Paco Cobo's.

The funeral was barely over when Doña Lucía, draped in the deepest mourning, arrived in the village and settled into a room reserved for her across the courtyard in the house of Uncle Maximiliano and Aunt Rosario. She had come in such haste in order to take back from Maria the keys of the store-rooms and of the depot of furniture which she had in her possession. Many of the things and much of the olive oil had already gone, for Maria had been up for two nights in succession removing them, and without calling in the Justicia and so starting an action and a scandal, there was nothing Doña Lucía could do. But she showed in every word she addressed to her late servant the hatred and contempt she felt for her, and Maria's only answer was to hang her head and slink away.

During the next week or two I came to know my landlord's widow a good deal better than I had previously done, because every evening she invited me to a cup of coffee in her room, and we sat up talking. She was a slim, bird-like creature of about forty, rather Japanese in the cast of her face, who had seen her six children and then her husband die one after the other, and had besides suffered a deep humiliation over his mistress. These things had left her without hopes for herself, yet where other people, and especially the young, were concerned, she had kept all the illusions and romanticism of a schoolgirl. Brought up on Walter Scott's novels and on Zorrilla's poetry and only moderately susceptible to religion, she saw their future *couleur de rose*, because she put her own youthful dreams of happiness into it. One of these dreams concerned Angela, Maria's daughter by Don Fadrique. She had long wanted, she told me, to adopt her and rescue her from the life in which she was being brought up, yet every time she got to the point of doing so she drew back, because she feared to put herself in the power of the girl's mother.

'And now that vile woman, by her lies and thievings, has exceeded herself. How cruel, how monstrous that she should have the power to ruin her daughter's prospects!'

'But surely,' I said, 'if you adopt the child legally, Maria will lose her rights over her.'

'Yes, that's what they tell me,' she said with a sigh. 'But how can I be sure that if I leave the girl my dear Fadrique's property, she will not let some of it fall into the hands of that creature?'

Six years passed after this conversation, and I was back once more at Yegen. My first shock on entering the door was to see that Angela had changed from a plain, rather prim and proper child, into a pretty and sweetly smiling young woman of seventeen. She kissed me warmly. Watching us impassively from a corner by the kitchen fire I became aware of a peasant youth whose name I was told was Angel. Every evening he arrived and sat there in a heavy, sulky silence till bedtime, so that I naturally concluded that he was her *novio*. But no, said Maria, not at all. This was just a child's affair they had grown out of. Angel was a poor boy who would never inherit anything, and her daughter had prospects. Wouldn't she come into the whole of her father's property, mountain farm and all, on the death of Doña Lucía? And this idea suddenly taking hold in her head, she rushed into the kitchen, began violently abusing her daughter, drove her out of the room, and, muttering insults under her breath, turned her back on Angel, who continued to sit as motionless as a log of wood in his corner.

For the first few weeks I was too taken up with my own affairs to pay much attention to those of these two young people. During the years I had spent in England I had led a fairly full life, and now I found my Spanish home a vacuum. The novel I was writing refused to make progress, and I began to look around me for some stimulus, which, of course, could only take the form of girls. A new crop had grown up since

my last stay in the village, and on the whole it seemed a pretti-
er, gayer, and more conversable one than the last, who were
now all married and loaded, as the Spanish phrase has it, with
children.

'We are going to give a dance tomorrow,' I said to Maria.
'Go out and make sure that Antonia and Paca and Lolita and
Carmen and Dolores all come to it. And get two bottles of anis
instead of one.'

I was determined that if I had to put up with my servant's
cows and goats and hens, all the racket of her legal affairs and
her execrable cooking, she should serve my interests in a role
which, as I knew, she understood perfectly.

And then something that I had never thought possible happened. I realized that Maria was pushing her daughter towards
me in the same way in which her mother, the midwife, had
pushed her towards Don Fadrique, and that this was the
reason for her annoyance with Angel. I was being offered the
girl. I had a sufficient understanding of Angela's situation and
character to be shocked by this, though on Maria's behalf it
might be said that she was merely acting in the good old-
fashioned way in trying to 'place' her daughter in the big
house. For generations every village *cacique* in Spain has had
the prettiest of the widow's daughters for his mistress, just as
the English squires of a previous age had the pick of the
village girls, and the southern planters down to the American
Civil War the flower of their Negresses. That was one of the
more kindly ways in which this run-down feudalism worked.
But before I could guess what the girl's feelings on such a
proposal might be, a still more unexpected thing occurred. A
letter arrived from Doña Lucía in which she said that if, as she
hoped, I found Angela the sweet and lovely creature she was
reported to be and, what in that case would not be surprising,
fell in love with her, I need not let myself be restrained from
marrying her by her lack of sufficient means, for she would
make over to her on our wedding day the whole of her property at Yegen, including the mountain ranch or farm. This,

she continued, was an offer she would not upon any account extend to Angela if she married anyone other than myself. And since she repeated this to her bailiff, who at once told it to Juan el Mudo and Araceli, it reached the ears of Angela almost as soon as it reached mine.

There is something very intransigent about the sexual instinct in men: it refuses to compromise or make a bargain with other feelings. Thus, though I was romantically drawn by the idea of becoming the principal landowner at Yegen, of marrying not so much a woman as a place I loved, I was not sufficiently attracted to Angela to be able to do it through her means. Under her pretty, rather pathetic face I saw ready to break out the tight, sour look of a woman of the shopkeeping class who has grown up in the knowledge that she has had a rough deal. If I were to have anyone, it must be a village girl pure and simple, who would make up for what she lacked in schooling by being a symbol, a point of condensation, for this untutored poetic life in which – or so I sometimes thought – I wished to sink myself. Thus I refused Doña Lucía's offer, and was careful to show Angela that my affection for her was of a very different sort.

Today I am more aware than I was then of her feelings. Angela hated her mother because she felt degraded by what was base and cunning in her disposition, and also for being the obstacle to her adoption by Doña Lucía. In taking Angel as her *novio* she had been consoling herself with an orphan whom she had played with as a child and who like her believed that he had been defrauded of his rightful inheritance. For Angel was the youngest son of Uncle Maximiliano and of Aunt Rosario, and his older sisters (though no one now alluded to this) were Don Fadrique's half-sisters: not only had he disliked his coarse-tongued father, but he resented the way in which his mother, la Reina, with her 'notorious love of luxury', had dissipated the wealth – perhaps as much as five hundred pesetas or twenty pounds – which in the days of her beauty had been lavished on her by her *cacique* lover. The inno-

cence, therefore, of the two young people in a world of wicked
adults, and the similarity both in their circumstances and in
their names – angels, as it were, encompassed by demons –
had been the link between them. Then I had come along, and
for a moment her prospects, diverging from his, had seemed
to open out in a miraculous way. Women are too sensible not
to put escaping from poverty before everything else, and
Angela would no doubt have accepted me upon any terms, in
the hopes either of my eventually marrying her or of Doña
Lucía making her some compensation. But this possibility had
no sooner shown itself than it had vanished again, and so she
had gone back to her *novio*, though with resentful feelings
towards me which she suppressed at the time, but which were
to come out later.

Meanwhile another situation was developing. Maria was
becoming more and more insupportable. Her head had been
so completely turned, first by her inheritance and then by her
lawsuit and finally by Doña Lucía's offer, that she could no
longer give any attention to the cooking and housekeeping or
allow her daughter, whom she scolded continually, to do so
either. On the smallest occasions her noise and rantings filled
the house and, as if this was not enough, she had developed a
strong and unpleasantly pungent smell. Every time the door
of her little bedroom opened an overpowering whiff came out
– sour, sulphurous, with something of a fox about it and something of a tanyard, and besides a decided flavour of anis spirit.
Yet, as she swung from one pole of her temperament to the
other, from a sort of sly, buffoonish gaiety to a silent gnawing
concentration or a rasping anger, she could suddenly delight
one by a display of pure extravagance. At the end of a party,
when all the guests except one or two friends of the house had
left, she would dance by herself, with light and whirling movements and faster and wilder gestures, her private version of a
malagueña, which itself is the most bacchanalian of the Andalusian dances. Then she would collapse and, though sober, lie
prone on the floor without speaking or moving, while her

daughter's face became tense with shame and disapproval. On the following day her temper would be worse than ever, and her loud, angry voice drove me mad.

At length, on my return from a visit to Seville, I decided that I could stand no more. Reluctantly – for in spite of everything I liked Maria, and felt that she had served me loyally – I told her she must leave. She took it quietly, with that meek hen's face of hers, and at once began to move out her personal things, among which she included, as if by right, a few of the less noticeable among mine. But the moment she had completed this operation her attitude changed and, putting her head out of the window of her house, which was just down the street, she let herself go in a flood of loud, angry, rhythmical vituperation on the subject of myself and my doings, with allusions, scarcely to be avoided on such occasions, to the supposed disreputable profession of my mother. This outburst – which like all public declarations made in our village was couched in purely conventional terms and contained no personal revelations – was repeated every morning and evening with great monotony for a week or two, after which she moved to Pura's house in a different part of the village. There she kept so effectually out of my way that I never, except from a distance, saw her again.

There was a cruel sequel to this quarrel. I had promised Angela a small sum of money when she married, to give her some slight independence of her mother. Doña Lucía, whose daydreams were always more generous than her actions, had also spoken of making over to her some strips of land. But when Maria left me in a rage, her daughter broke with me too, because she could not forgive me for having been the means of her losing her father's property. Since I now needed this money for another purpose, I said to myself that her behaviour had released me from my promise, while Doña Lucía also changed her mind. Angela therefore married her Angel on nothing, and my private resolutions to help them later on remained, like most good intentions, unfulfilled. The pair,

who had settled down with her mother, gradually became
more embittered. He was a simple, stubborn man who, like his
father, concealed his sensitiveness under a mask of mulishness,
and her repeated disappointments were turning her into a
shrew. But no son-in-law could live for long with such a
mother-in-law. Squeezing some money out of her, therefore,
by threats, and giving up all hopes of Doña Lucía's interven-
tion, they set off with their two children for Barcelona, where
they are still. And what of the other characters in this story?
Before 1940 Maria had died mad, while Doña Lucía was killed
by the explosion of a kitchen stove which set her clothes on
fire and burned her severely.

To return now to 1929, I need scarcely say that before dis-
missing my servant I had made certain that there was someone
who would take her place. Maria Martín – for she was a Maria
too – was the daughter of a tall, gaunt, sad woman, always
dressed and hung in black, who kept the village posada in the
lower *barrio*. The family was poor, because the inn brought in
little money and they possessed only a strip or two of land, so
that the two girls had been obliged to go out to service while
they were still in their teens. The elder sister Rosario, who was
both handsome and clever, had found a good place at Cádiar,
while Maria, who was neither, had been left to take an indifferent one at the poor village of Lucainena, which lay in the
opposite direction. Here she had met and married a young
man who had touched her by the tale of his misfortunes, only
to find out when it was too late that he was a bad hat and a
thief, and to see him carried off to jail. She left him at once
and for ever, and returned to her mother's posada with her
child, which was not yet a year old. After a year or two there,
doing odd jobs of field work and living badly, she came to me.

My new Maria was a short, snub-nosed young woman with
straight rather thin hair pulled back over her head, a smooth
rounded face like a seal, and a fine skin. One would have called
her plain, if her expression had not been so open and pleasant
and her movements and carriage so dignified. When she sat by

the kitchen fire with her child in her arms and her head a little bent, she looked like a Flemish Madonna, all pensiveness and resignation, but when she got up to walk one noticed her air of self-possession. Then it was always a pleasure to talk to her. Most Andalusian women of the peasant class mix into their speech a good deal of what they think you want to hear, but Maria did the opposite. She enjoyed telling home truths to people she liked, and the gay, ironical tone in which she did this, the natural honesty and frankness which brought everything that was in her head tumbling out, were very refreshing. She never acquired a trace of the servility or false pride of the servant.

Peasant women from remote villages, when brought for the first time to the towns, often show an amusing *naïveté*, restrained only by their fear of giving themselves away. Thus, I shall never forget the occasion when my wife and I took Maria in a çar to Almeria. We arrived at the sea and had pulled up beside it before, in a voice full of doubt and hesitation, she asked what it was. 'Why, the sea, Maria,' I said. 'The same sea you see every clear day from the village.' 'In that case, how can it possibly be so big?' she asked with incredulity and then, gradually convinced that it could be nothing else, she explained that, though people had told her that one could not see across it, she had never believed them, but had supposed it was just a large pond. 'And what can you do with it?' she went on, her voice hardening in annoyance. 'Can you irrigate with it?' We told her no. 'Can you wash clothes with it?' We said one could not. 'Then what use is it?' And she turned her head and refused to give another look in its direction.

A few minutes after this we came to the long straight stretch of road that crosses the Campo de Dalías. Accustomed to roads that continually turned and twisted, and imagining that such turns were an intrinsic part of their nature, she refused at first to believe that it was a road at all. Then as we drove on over it she made the adjustment, but the knowledge that she had a second time given herself away led her to determine that when she got to Almeria she would be astonished by nothing. We arrived. Steamers, sailing-boats, rowing-boats, carriages, trains, paved streets and shops with plate-glass windows, hotels, porters, bootblacks, hairdressers, lamp-posts, were all with a hundred other things new to her. She had not even been prepared for them beforehand by illustrations in books or newspapers, and her natural scepticism and lack of imagination had closed her mind to any talk about them she may have heard. Yet from the moment that she got out of the car she walked along in her usual cool and self-possessed manner, with as much apparent indifference to the things around her as though she had been brought up among them. Then as we came down the Paseo I saw people looking up and pointing. There, immediately above us, quite low down above the houses, there circled an enormous fish-shaped object, gleaming silver against the blue sky, which took my breath away by its beauty and its unfamiliarity. 'Look, Maria,' I cried excitedly, 'a Zeppelin!' But she, true to her new precepts, after a casual glance upwards, continued impassively on her way, as though she had been seeing Zeppelins all her life.

Perhaps Maria's most original feature was the way in which her strong belief in herself as a person was combined with an obstinate disbelief in her capacity for doing almost anything that she had not done before. One might say that she had carved out and defined her own character by her firm rejection of the things she thought were beyond her range. Thus it was impossible to teach her anything. Although I spent hours giving her reading lessons, and although Spanish is the easiest language to spell out in the world, she made no progress. She was one of those born illiterates of whom the Andalusians say that 'the black in their eyes gets in their way'. Yet if she was left to her own devices she was capable of surprising one. When some years after this my wife and I left Yegen for a larger house near Malaga, we took her with us as our *ama de llaves* or housekeeper and her elder and much abler sister Rosario as our cook. We never regretted this choice. In her new situation Maria blossomed out in a remarkable manner, laid the table, though always with one mistake, as though table-laying were among the fine arts, developed a nice taste for arranging flowers, and, in whatever she did, displayed a natural style and dignity. Every act in life was important, her step and port seemed to say: every detail in the organization of a household had its weight and value, and we too had to fall into line. Myself in particular. In an Andalusian house a man is a constitutional monarch in a government of women: that is to say he is waited on hand and foot, but his advice, if he ventures to offer any, is disregarded. Tactfully, with good-natured irony and a ready supply of sayings and proverbs, I would be headed off if I showed an inclination to have things my own way, while if I did anything that turned out badly, '*A padre quién le pega?*' 'And who beats father?' would be the beaming, scornful comment. But the task she took on with the greatest unction was that of being my wife's champion. Women hold strongly together in Spain, and though I knew that Maria was genuinely attached to me, I could see that she felt that this was one of the things she had been engaged for. The only pity was that my wife and I gave her so few opportunities for proving her mettle, because on matters that were within her competence we rarely disagreed.

We had not been long in our new house before the Civil War came, and we returned to England. For years we could not send money, and as Maria's brother-in-law had the garden, she had to fend for herself. She began by selling vegetables in the square, was drawn into black marketeering in foodstuffs, and thanks to her manifest honesty and respectability, which impressed the police who controlled this traffic, made a success of it. Before long she had bought a house and a shop, and through her daughter's marriage to an energetic young Alpujarreño was launching out into larger transactions. Yet to this day she has never learned to read and cannot write the numerals. To make up for this last deficiency, she has invented a script of her own, not unlike the Linear B script of Ancient

Crete, with a perpendicular stroke for 1, a horizontal stroke for 10, a circle for 100, and so on. In this she is able, by manipulations invented by herself, to add, subtract, multiply, and divide with more speed than I, who took higher mathematics at school, have ever been able to achieve. Yet, I must say again, by any accepted standards, in any branch of life, Maria would be classed as stupid. She has risen in the Castilian way, by building on her own modest pride in self and by saying no to everything else. This has given her both her lovable nature and her great integrity.

My second period at Yegen lasted a year, and when I returned again in 1932 I was married. The road to Granada had been completed, and I had bought a car, so that the place, though still remote by any European standard – it was nearly five hours' driving from that city – was less inaccessible than it had been. Various friends came to see us, among them Roger Fry and Bertrand Russell, but I will not describe their visits as I have done those of Lytton Strachey and Virginia Woolf, because this book is coming to an end. Indeed, all that remains to be said is that in December 1934 my wife and I packed up the books and furniture and left for a house we had bought near Malaga.

CHAPTER TWENTY-ONE

A POSTSCRIPT

*

More than twenty years have passed since I left Yegen, and
the reader may wish to know what has happened to it in the
meantime, and in particular how it fared during the Civil War.
Politics, as I have said, had a purely local character in the Alpujarra. This continued to be the case even after the establishment of the Republic and the rapid spread of left-wing ideas
through large areas of the country. Although I remember
Maria telling me in 1933 of a certain man who had returned
from working in a factory at Malaga that 'he was one of those
who were paid so many pesetas a day by the Government for
not believing in God', it turned out that the most radical idea
he had brought back with him was vegetarianism. No one in
Yegen except the shopkeeper, the priest, and the doctor had
ever heard of socialism, anarchism, or communism, and their
feeling about the Church was not hostility or anti-clericalism,
but simply lukewarmness.

However, as the political tension in Spain increased, the
trade-union movement extended its centres of propaganda to
hitherto unaffected places. Thus in 1934 a local centre of the
Socialist trade union, which was strong in Granada, was set up
at Cádiar, while the Anarcho-Syndicalist trade union, spreading west from Almeria, invaded Berja and Adra. Then, on 18
July 1936, the Civil War broke out. The military garrisons
which were maintained in the capitals of every province rose
against the civil administration, and the first day's fighting
decided whether they had won or lost. Very soon it became
known that the Republican authorities had defeated the risings
in Malaga and Almeria, but that in Granada the garrison,
which was the stronger for including an artillery unit, had

come out on top. That night and for two nights in succession all the sandy water-courses and steep mule-tracks of the Alpujarra, from the outskirts of Almeria as far as the sugar-cane plantations of Motril, were filled by convoys of horses and mules loaded with men, women, children, and piles of bedding. They were the leading people of the region, the landlords, doctors, priests, and shopkeepers, all the *gente gorda* or *de categoría*, fleeing for protection to Granada; and none of their fellow villagers opposed their leaving. Then on both sides a force of militia was enrolled, and the fronts became established. The Republicans occupied the whole of the sea coast and all the eastern and central part of the Alpujarra, while the Nationalists, who were more cautious, did not venture to advance beyond Lanjarón. Órgiva was evacuated, and lay between the lines, which remained fixed in these positions until the end of the war.

Meanwhile, behind the fronts what one may call the interior war was being organized on either side. In Granada, where the small garrison felt itself almost submerged by the hostile masses of the working classes, the plan from the first was to rule by terror. Day after day, therefore, executions were held on an impressive scale. At Almeria the shootings began more gradually, but, stimulated by what was happening next door, worked up to a climax. In a civil war there is enough hatred and suspicion in the air to make anything possible, so that in the stagnation of the fronts the competition as to who could kill most non-combatants became the order of the day. But as a rule these things only happened spontaneously in the large towns. Village solidarity forbade the harming of people who belonged to their own community, and in the Alpujarra, where there had never been hatred between the classes, where all the richer families had fled, this was more than ever the case. Yet assassinations did occur. In the Nationalist territory in the west lorries manned by members of the Falangist and Catholic Youth Movement of Granada collected villagers whose names they had on their lists, drove them to the ravine of Tablate, where an image of the Virgin of Agonies looked down on the road, and machine-gunned them. In the Republican territory to the east lorries manned by members of the Anarcho-Syndicalist Youth Movement of Almeria, painted all over with letters and slogans and bristling with arms, drove into the villages and ordered the *alcaldes* or mayors to hand over their fascists to them. When these simple men, peasants or artisans, who did not know what the word fascist meant, told them that they had all fled, the youths in the lorries, who did not mean to be baulked of their sport, returned at nightfall and, seizing certain people whose names had meanwhile been secretly given them by informers, drove them out of the village to the edge of a convenient ravine and shot them there. In almost every case these men were peasant farmers who had been denounced by people who owed them money or who felt some private spite against them.

And now the militia, recruited in Almeria, began to arrive and were quartered in the houses of the people who had fled. The churches of Berja, Cádiar, Válor, and no doubt of other places too, were burned by parties of incendiaries, while that at Ugíjar, which was used as a powder magazine, blew up accidentally. None of these things, however, happened at Yegen. Either it was too humble to attract the attention of the visiting lorries, or no informer could be found to make secret denunciations. The village therefore escaped and, apart from the brief imprisonment of its *alcalde*, the carpenter Facundo, was spared the reprisals that followed the Nationalist victory. One may say that there were very few villages south or east of Madrid that got off so lightly.

The Civil War was followed by a period of famine which, prolonged by a severe drought, lasted till 1949. This, however, brought wealth and prosperity to the villages of the Sierra Nevada. On these high mountains there can never be any serious lack of water, so that the crops came up as usual while the price of foodstuffs soared to meet the demands of the black market. For the first time in their history, therefore, the peasants of these remote regions obtained a fair reward for their labour. Some saved money and emigrated with their families to the Argentine, others bought land and increased the size of their holdings, and all but the very poorest found themselves in a better position than before.

Such, at least, was the account I got when I returned to Spain in the last year of the drought. Maria and Rosario had been back to see their families, and from time to time people from Yegen visited Malaga and came to our house. But I could not repress a wish to see the village again for myself. One day, therefore, in May 1955 my wife and I set out.

The bus took us to Almeria. The place was the same, yet how its appearance had changed since I had seen it last! The dead little town, so charming in its animated immobility, like the reflection of a pasteboard city in rippled water, had put on a purpose and bustle that seemed quite foreign to its nature. Where now were those clean, bright barbers' shops in which one could spend an hour being shaved and shampooed and turned into a walking garden of heliotrope and jasmine? All gone. Where was that club or casino through whose windows one could watch, as through the plate-glass of an aquarium, a collection of glorified beings, motionless all day like gods in their leather armchairs, absorbed in the deep satisfaction of being themselves? The building was still there, but now its inmates either talked or read or had expressions on their faces. It seemed clear that the city had grown tired of its role of Narcissus and, with the help of some development schemes concocted in Madrid, had thrown itself into active life.

We took the train from Almeria to Guadix, and from there hired a car over the Sierra Nevada along a very rough road, built during the Civil War, that crossed it by the Puerto de la Ragua, a pass that lies a few miles to the east of the Puerto del Lobo. The *venta* on the northern face, which in spring and autumn, when blizzards are to be expected, used to give a certain reassurance to travellers, was now a hut for shepherds: in the past it had a sinister reputation for the murders and

robberies committed at it. We came out on the summit. Patches
of snow like long white shadows, patches of turf studded with
saxifrages and gentians, a solitary shepherd standing among
his sheep. Then down 5,000 feet to Ugíjar, which in its nest of
feathery grey olive trees boxed in by smooth red cliffs seemed
to have changed little. The proprietress of the parador, a
bulky woman of gipsy aspect who had been here since the days
of horse diligences, recognized me at once. 'So you're back
again,' she said. 'Well, let me tell you, here we've been
through bad times. I've been in prison, my husband died of the
treatment they gave him, my brother too. Who wouldn't be a
Frenchman or an Englishman!' But which side had she been
on? She did not tell me, and I felt so much resentment under
her off-hand manner that I did not care to put even the usual
cautious question, 'Was that in the early days or was it later?'
For apart from the fiction, now maintained nowhere but in the
Press, that only the other side did nasty things, it seems that an
attitude of calculated vagueness has been growing up on this
subject. The phrase one often hears today is that So-and-so
'suffered for his ideas', as though ideas were a thing like small-
pox that marked one for life or killed one, but what those ideas
were, whether they were of the sort held by the Reds or of the
sort held by the Falangists, no one any longer cares, though in
general conversation there is still a certain reluctance about
defining them. This little hypocrisy – a typical piece of scar tis-
sue – shows that, in spite of the efforts of the Falange to keep
the memory of the Civil War alive, the wounds it caused are
healing fast. The official propaganda, by insisting too much
and so boring everyone, has defeated its own objects.

After lunch we hired a muleteer and a mule to take us up to
Yegen. Naturally we did not choose the road which winds in
curves up the mountain-side, but the direct track. As we
climbed the long gravelly spurs, which before the phylloxera
plague had been planted with vines and after it had not been
planted at all, I was surprised to see the fine crops of wheat, a
couple of feet high, that were growing without irrigation. This

showed that the good land had ceased, as it had done for so long, to put the poor land out of use. By this time we had risen almost to the level of the breast-shaped hills, and it was becoming cooler. A small breeze began to blow, there was a smell of thyme and lavender, and the chink-chink of the mule's hooves on the loose stones made little points of sound in the silence.

We passed the *puente*, or natural bridge, which connects the rolling downlands of quaternary times with the ancient mountain flank, and began to climb more steeply. Olive trees closed in round the path, the wheat grew tall and thick on the terraces, water ran everywhere. There was a smell of wet earth and of crushed mint. Then the path flattened out to run alongside an irrigation channel, and we arrived at the first grey, unmortared walls of the village. A number of old women had fetched out their chairs and were sitting there – white hair, parchment faces, bleary eyes, dresses of worn and pumice-tinted black, threadbare from wear and washing. As we came up, they stopped speaking. I could see them stare, hesitate, stare again, then they came forward one by one with outstretched hands. 'Why, it's Don Geraldo!' The poor in these countries of sunshine age quickly, and I found it hard to recognize in them the young married women and girls who had come to my first dances.

A short way farther on we stopped at the house of Enrique, Maria's younger brother, who was to put us up. His wife Dolores was expecting us, and with her was her only child, an unusually pretty little girl of ten. Her name was Mariquilla. In her demurely joyful look she had the air of knowing that she was the future heroine of a fairy tale, for since her parents spent all the money they could save on her clothes, in that grubby peasant world she looked like a princess. Yet all the children, I noticed, were better dressed than they used to be. Many of the houses had been whitewashed, there was a church clock that struck the hours, and Don José Venegas, the shopkeeper and senior member of the community, had – this we were told almost immediately – installed a water-closet. We went to call on him. His once black mat of hair was now a silky white, but in spite of this, he said, he would still be young if he had not had the misfortune to be raided a few years back by the Reds of the sierra, who had beaten him severely to make him tell them where his money was hidden. After that he had spent several weeks in hospital. To make up for this, however, his wife, Doña Cándida, did not seem to have changed at all in thirty years. Spanish women's hair, unless they belong to the working classes, is mysteriously exempt from the usual fate of chevelures and retains its pitch blackness and lustre to the end. Nor was her face lined. Plump and soft and kind and smiling, with eyes as sweet as fondants and as glistening as jujubes, she took us into her tiny garden and showed us her collection of flowers.

'Yes,' said Don José, as he poured us out a glass of cognac in his office, 'one may say that in many ways things are better than when you were here last. The bus from Granada stops daily, the children all go to school, the old-age pension, which has just been increased, has done a great deal for the poorer classes. Even the trees in the plaza, which in the old days would never grow because they were not irrigated, have shot up and give their shade. The next thing will have to be modern sanitation – perhaps you have heard already that I have made a modest start in this direction. But in one way we are worse off than we used to be, for we hardly ever see fresh fish. Before the war, as you may remember, men used to bring it up every night on mules from the coast, but today, with plenty of work going at good wages, no one is going to go to all that trouble to earn a few pesetas. So, as there's no meat except when the goats are kidding, we have to make do with chick-peas and lentils and salt cod, which in the end become a little monotonous.'

'Still,' said his wife, 'we mustn't complain.'

'No, indeed,' answered Don José. 'Of course not. Lite may be simple here, but anyhow it is a good deal healthier and saner than it is in the towns.'

From the village shop we went on to look at my old house. The big door into the patio was open, and a very ancient lady, dressed simply in black, was sitting in the entrance. Behind her chair stood her servant, a young woman with a solemnly bored but deferential air, and in front of her – this was the reason for her sitting here – a mason was doing some light repairs to the plaster. A spray of grape-vine dangled against the grey wall above their heads, and in the old lady's air of rustic refinement and in her maid's ceremonious stance I felt that I was looking at a daguerreotype of the previous century. In fact, this was Don Fadrique's sister, who more than fifty years before had married and gone to live at Murtas. From that time till Doña Lucía's death, when she had inherited the house, she had never once returned to Yegen because, since her brother and sister were not on speaking terms but ruled the village as rival *caciques*, she would have been unable to stay with the one without offending the other.

I introduced myself, and a look of recognition came into her eyes. She invited my wife and myself into the house. But I knew that the refugees who had occupied it during the war had done it some damage, and that the outer wall of the granary, which I had made into my sitting-room, had collapsed and never been rebuilt. I thanked her, therefore, but refused, as I did not care to see it in such a state.

That night after supper a number of my old friends, who had heard of my arrival in the village, turned up at Enrique's house. Chairs were borrowed from the neighbours, and a circle formed in the upper room. Juan el Mudo, still handsome and tall, Federico the sybarite philosopher, Cecilio and his sisters, José Pocas Chichas, now married and father of a grown-up family, the daughters of Uncle Maximiliano and of Uncle Miguel Medina, the two young Rats, Isabel and Ana, and others whose names have not appeared in this book. Many more had been scattered over Spain by the war, many had died, among them my particular friend Paco, who after emigrating with his family to the Argentine had suddenly dropped dead in a field. But where were the young faces that I remembered? All those who sat in the room around me had white or silver-greying hair, their cheeks were lined and furrowed, and they came stiffly up the stairs. The people to whom I instinctively turned for recognition, the men and women in their twenties and early thirties, stared back at me with blank faces. I had to make myself understand that, though the village as a whole had not changed, every leaf on every one of its trees was different.

We talked of the past, Juan leading the conversation with reminiscences of the sierra, its cattle, its robbers, and even its wolves, and the others recalling things that had happened in the village. And then some name would come up, the name of a person who had died, and, while the women let out heavy sighs, the men nodded their heads gravely. *La vida es un soplo*, 'Life is a puff of air', one of them would say; and another would answer, *La muerte no para*, 'Death stops for no one'; or *Venimos emprestados*, 'Our lives are only loaned to us.' Till, after a pause and another volley of sighs, the conversation would start up again on a different subject.

The night was silent. No circle of barking dogs or crowing cocks. No loud, harsh voices interlocked under the window. Then dawn came, and with a clicking of hooves on cobbles and a patter of goats and cows, the village emptied itself into the fields. We drank some coffee and went out. And there in front of us, at the first break in the street, stretched the great plains of air with beyond them an inextricable tangle of coloured mountains. The sound of water was all round us and there was a sense of greenery and freshness. No, I said to myself, the picture I formed of this place was not an illusion.